Transformed by Design

Our Willingness God's Work

Kathryn Alverson

Transformed
by Design

Our Willingness God's Work

take heart books

Transformed by Design Our Willingness God's Work
Copyright © 2025 by Kathryn Alverson
All rights reserved. No part of this book may be reproduced or used in any manner without written permission of the copyright owner except for the use of quotations in a book review. For more information email: kathryn.alverson@yahoo.com

ISBN: 978-1-958818-12-1 (paperback)

Published by
Take Heart Books LLC
Toledo, OH

take heart books

Cover Concept by Kathryn Alverson
artwork from Canva®

Scripture quotations taken from the Holy Bible, New Living Translation, copyright ©1996, 2004, 2015 by Tyndale House Foundation. Used by permission of Tyndale House Publishers, Carol Stream, Illinois 60188. All rights reserved.

Scripture quotations marked (NIV) are taken from the Holy Bible, New International Version®, NIV®. Copyright © 1973, 1978, 1984, 2011 by Biblica, Inc.™ Used by permission of Zondervan. All rights reserved worldwide. www.zondervan.com The "NIV" and "New International Version" are trademarks registered in the United States Patent and Trademark Office by Biblica, Inc.™

Scripture taken from the New King James Version® marked (NKJV). Copyright © 1982 by Thomas Nelson. Used by permission. All rights reserved.

Transformed by Design
   Our Willingness God's Work

a gift for: _____

from: _____

date: _____

With gratitude:
To every reader with an open heart to all that God desires to do in, and through, your life.
To my beautiful family whom I deeply love.

Special love and adoration to my earthly and my Heavenly Father, who have loved me unconditionally through the good, the bad and the beautiful.

Introduction

I AM FILLED WITH HUMBLE GRATITUDE AS I INVITE YOU to explore the thoughts, ideas, and truths God has laid on my heart over the past year. This book was birthed in my heart last year, and God promised that, if I was obedient to write every day, He would provide the manna (which, in this case, was a reflection for that day). Before I closed my eyes at night, I would pray for God to place a song in my head and a thought in my heart the next morning. Day-in and day-out, He showed up and amazed me, opening my ears, eyes, and heart. He even challenged some of my expectations. I had planned to do all my writing in the mornings, but He moved me to marinate on the truth He gave me throughout the day and to make room for Him to fully impress it on my heart. He illuminated His Word in unique ways, reminding me of its depth and power. He provided perfect help through my faithful sister and two special friends gifted in all things administrative, which I am not. My amazing children encouraged me to write, and my loyal husband provided the space for me to do what God created me to do. But more than anything, God held me step-by-step, showing up in the most fascinating ways.

The significance of the butterfly represents beauty and divine transformation. Making the choice to move towards God invites Divine change. Walking on a trail near my house one day, God provided a unique opportunity to observe a beautiful blue butterfly at such a close proximity. The photograph I made appeared zoomed. I marveled at God's creation, thanking Him for such an intimate moment and reflecting on the opportunities He gives me to see his power and action through ministry, others and my own personal relationship with Him. This brilliant butterfly

had landed on the rock path and it brought to mind how God himself provides all we need to be who He created us to be while remaining the solid rock of stability and security where we land.

Choosing to move towards God in an up close and personal way each and everyday invites all we need for divine significance, purpose, and change. This book, like Christ's love, is for anyone at any place in their spiritual journey. You may be a seasoned believer, new to your faith, or not even sure what you believe. But you are reading this book by design, so I pray you will be open to what God has in store specifically for you. My prayer is for you to be encouraged, challenged, and expectant. There are some spiritual, emotional, and even physical challenges sprinkled throughout this book, providing different ideas for self care that may appeal to you, but my prayer is that you would enjoy this journey, open your heart, and experience God in a unique way.

January 1

THE TIME HAS COME FOR FRESH STARTS AND NEW CHALLENGES. We all ask ourselves: *What can I do differently this year to move toward spiritual, emotional, and physical health?* The answer to that question awaits you in the quiet place that you must cultivate to hear from God.

All too often we will set our sights in a direction that seems wise, but we have failed to seek God first. One of the many benefits of prayer is the aligning of our will to God's. He is your Creator and He alone holds the answers to all your wanderings. **Matthew 6:33** leads us to "seek the Kingdom of God above all else," and all else will be given to you.

Pray and ask God today to breathe His breath of life into your spirit and give you a renewed desire to be all He has created you to be and a fresh fire to chase after Him, believing He and He alone holds the answers you seek.

> Seek the Kingdom of God above all else, and live righteously, and he will give you everything you need. —Matthew 6:33

> I will give you a new heart and put a new spirit in you; I will remove from you your heart of stone and give you a heart of flesh. —Ezekiel 36:26 (NIV)

January 2

Learning to accept and appreciate God's timing is central to our spiritual, emotional, and physical well-being. The best medicine for anxiety, worry, and stress is trusting God completely. Stop and ask yourself what areas of your life you struggle to trust Him with.

Pray and ask the Holy Spirit to help you lean into Christ's arms with all the fear that surrounds those sensitive places. Diving deeper into our relationship with God, strengthens *Holy Spirit confidence* in that we become more aware of His presence and wisdom there is an art to learning to be held by God and as with anything—it takes practice.

Psalm 46:10 tells us to "be still, and know that I am God." That is when we can live in that sweet spot of total surrender.

> Be still, and know that I am God. — Psalm 46:10

> Trust in the Lord with all your heart;
> do not depend on your own understanding. — Proverbs 3:5

> Let me hear of your unfailing love each morning,
> for I am trusting you. Show me where to walk,
> for I give myself to you. — Psalm 143:8

January 3

CONSIDER THE CLOSEST RELATIONSHIPS IN YOUR LIFE. The ones you cherish and can hardly wait to share special news with. That is the type of relationship our heavenly Father longs to have with us.

From the beginning of time, that has been the longing of His heart. How can we cultivate that kind of nearness to Jesus? It has to begin with the Holy Spirit stirring in your soul, which is happening since you are reading this book. Then must come an intentionality on our part to *respond to His invitation.* There is no better investment of your time and energy than getting to know your Creator on a deeper level and letting Him open your heart and eyes to how He knows you. We all long to be fully known and fully loved. Our Heavenly Father is the only One capable of satisfying this legitimate desire.

> *For we are God's masterpiece. He has created us anew in Christ Jesus, so we can do the good things he planned for us long ago.* —Ephesians 2:10

> *"She gave this name to the Lord who spoke to her: 'You are the God who sees me,' for she said, 'I have now seen the One who sees me.'"* —Genesis 16:13 (NIV)

January 4

WE ARE NEVER MORE STRESS FREE THAN WHEN we take comfort in resting in the arms of our Heavenly Father. So often in Scripture we are instructed to not fear, but to "be strong and courageous." **Deuteronomy 31:6, Joshua 1:9,** and **Isaiah 41:10** are just a few examples of this. God knows how fragile we really are and how we are prone to worry, but He also knows the solution to this angst is being fully reliant on Him, resting in the truth that He is sovereign and just waiting to be invited into our burdens. Where in your life do you hold back with God, thinking your circumstances are too unimportant for His attention? If something is troubling you, *tell Him.* It may be that you just need a fresh perspective on a daunting issue, or there may be a peace you receive simply because you asked. He cares about it all and not only is He capable of easing our anxiety but He has already won every battle we face.

> *So be strong and courageous! Do not be afraid and do not panic before them. For the Lord your God will personally go ahead of you. He will neither fail you nor abandon you.* — Deuteronomy 31:6

> *This is my command—be strong and courageous! Do not be afraid or discouraged. For the Lord your God is with you wherever you go.* — Joshua 1:9

> *Don't be afraid, for I am with you. Don't be discouraged, for I am your God. I will strengthen you and help you. I will hold you up with my victorious right hand.* — Isaiah 41:10

January 5

LOVE, AFFIRMATION, SECURITY, AND GUIDANCE ARE ALL ATTRIBUTES WE DESIRE. We are all created with those legitimate needs and look to have them met through our human relationships or alternative spiritual paths, but all of this falls short. Some of us are blessed with great earthly relationships, but they cannot be our source, and no counterfeit religion can fill the God-sized void. We must give the Lord the opportunity to do what only He can do and be what only He can be in our lives. He reaches for us and extends the most important invitation we ever receive. He offers Himself, giving everlasting, unconditional love, eternal security, and divine leadership for our lives.

How are we responding to be with the lover of our souls, who also happens to be the Savior of the world? He says *He sees you* and He desires intimacy with you. **Draw near to God, and He will draw near to you. (James 4:8 ESV)**

> *Come close to God, and God will come close to you.*
> *— James 4:8*

January 6

EVERY DAY IS A SPECIAL OCCASION BECAUSE IT'S A NEW opportunity to worship God by the way we live and love. **Lamentations 3:22–23 tells us that "his mercies begin afresh every morning."** What a gift it is that He never tires of meeting us where we are and giving us another chance to become more of who He made us to be.

There is so much in this life that we have no control over, but what we do have is the power to choose everyday if we will be led by the Spirit or our flesh. Following our flesh is stifling, self-centered, and boring. *Following the Spirit is vibrant* and life-giving, and brings new opportunities to experience God. Following Jesus is a lifestyle that, once you get a taste of it, you don't want to turn back. What does it look like today for you to be devoted to Jesus and to be open to his leading, direction, and love? You will not be disappointed.

> *The faithful love of the Lord never ends! His mercies never cease. Great is his faithfulness; his mercies begin afresh each morning.* — Lamentations 3:22-23

> *Now all glory to God, who is able, through his mighty power at work within us, to accomplish infinitely more than we might ask or think.* — Ephesians 3:20

> *"That is what the Scriptures mean when they say, 'No eye has seen, no ear has heard, and no mind has imagined what God has prepared for those who love him.'"* — 1 Corinthians 2:9

January 7

SUNDAYS ALWAYS HAVE THE POTENTIAL TO BE SPECIAL. It's a great day to be expectant and reflective at the same time. When I used to be a personal trainer, I would encourage women to meal prep on Sundays. I even met with a friend today who shared that picking out her outfits stresses her out during the week, and I encouraged her to "outfit prep."

When we are prepped, we feel more confident and less anxious. Sunday is also a great day to set a spiritual, emotional, and physical challenge for the week.

For example:
» Spiritual: Pray first thing in the morning, "Father, help me to be led by the Spirit and not my flesh today."
» Emotional: Meditate this week on a new Scripture that speaks to you, repeating it out loud to yourself.
» And maybe for your Physical: Drink more water.

Pray and ask the Lord to lead you in what would be beneficial for you this week and follow through. Share with a friend for accountability.

As iron sharpens iron, so a friend sharpens a friend. — Proverbs 27:17

Physical training is good, but training for godliness is much better, promising benefits in this life and in the life to come. — 1 Timothy 4:8

January 8

THERE IS AN ART TO ALLOWING GOD TO MEET YOUR DEEPEST NEEDS. I say it is an art because it can be very unique for each person and be expressed in different ways depending on that person.

As you grow in your faith, your intimacy with God will become the sweet spot of life. For instance, with me, intimacy has a lot to do with security and being held. It brings me great security believing and knowing God is always with me and I face nothing alone **(Isaiah 41:10)**. I also love snuggling up on my prayer rug with a blanket wrapped around me, talking to Jesus or just sitting with an expectant heart, listening for that still, quiet voice. Sometimes I just imagine my Heavenly Father's arms wrapped around me, letting me know all is well, because *with God, it always is.*

> *Don't be afraid, for I am with you. Don't be discouraged, for I am your God. I will strengthen you and help you. I will hold you up with my victorious right hand. — Isaiah 41:10*

> *And we know that God causes everything to work together for the good of those who love God and are called according to his purpose for them. — Romans 8:28*

January 9

Trust is one of the foundational ingredients of deep, life-giving relationships. In fact, it's really impossible to have true intimacy with someone without it. We have been taught that trust is not a feeling but a decision. We need to ask, then, what goes into the decision-making process. The answer would be facts.

I personally have made the decision to trust Jesus in all areas, and I made that decision based on absolute truth, such as **John 3:16** and **Zephaniah 3:17**.

I know Jesus gave His life for me, that He is always with me. He rescued me from myself and actually delights in me. That gives me great freedom and security. I also know *He knows way better* than I do what is best for me, and as long as I stay dependent on Him, He will show me the way to go (**Psalm 32:8**). He is bigger than my mistakes, and that frees me up to be human. I can rest in the sovereignty of His arms and know He will never let me go.

> "For this is how God loved the world: He gave his one and only Son, so that everyone who believes in him will not perish but have eternal life." — John 3:16

> "For the Lord your God is living among you. He is a mighty savior. He will take delight in you with gladness. With his love, he will calm all your fears. He will rejoice over you with joyful songs." — Zephaniah 3:17

> "The Lord says, 'I will guide you along the best pathway for your life. I will advise you and watch over you.'" — Psalm 32:8

January 10

THE WORLD AND CULTURE ARE CONSTANTLY SENDING THE message that being busy is equal to being important. It is literally the first response people give to the question, "How are you?" Women especially can fall prey to the lie that, the more things you can juggle, the better and more productive you are. This type of mindset creates an atmosphere of constant striving. So often the striving mindset is one of the first places God will point out that needs to change in order to make space for Him.

A great prayer to pray is, "Father, help me to get done what you desire for me to get done today. Nothing more, nothing less." Think of all the things Jesus accomplished, yet He was never in an anxiety-ridden panic. **Philippians 4:6–7** teaches us to not be anxious but to *pray and invite God* into what we are doing or need and learn to be comfortable relying on Him and not ourselves.

> Don't worry about anything; instead, pray about everything. Tell God what you need, and thank him for all he has done. Then you will experience God's peace, which exceeds anything we can understand. His peace will guard your hearts and minds as you live in Christ Jesus. — Philippians 4:6-7

January 11

WHILE THERE ARE DEFINITELY MANY UNCERTAINTIES IN THIS LIFE, there are also quite a few things we can be certain of. God created us and desires to have intimate fellowship with us. If we respond to His invitation, our relationship with God has the potential to be our most valuable gift.

We can also be certain of good and evil and how there is constantly a spiritual war going on around us, whether we realize it or not. **1 Peter 5:10** tells us that when we have suffered hardship (not if), it is the Holy Spirit who will strengthen us to get through it. We can know that, no matter what we face in this lifetime, we will never do it alone. Leaning into our relationship with God helps us navigate the most difficult waters. What a blessed assurance that we can *walk in Holy Spirit confidence* through the hardest things with a hedge of protection around our heart. His name is Jesus!

> *In his kindness God called you to share in his eternal glory by means of Christ Jesus. So after you have suffered a little while, he will restore, support, and strengthen you, and he will place you on a firm foundation.*
> *— 1 Peter 5:10*

> *Teach these new disciples to obey all the commands I have given you. And be sure of this: I am with you always, even to the end of the age.*
> *— Matthew 28:20*

January 12

So often there is a tendency to treat our faith as an accessory to our life, like an add-on that is easy to compartmentalize, but that is a great recipe for a mediocre Christian life. God's desire is to be our life. **John 14:6** teaches us that Jesus is "the way, the truth, and the life." He provides everything we need to connect with God, and that is what makes life rich and satisfying.

When you are connecting with God, things as mundane as walking to the mailbox can bring joy. Take time to appreciate the beautiful sky, the cool air, pretty flowers, maybe even a neighbor walking by who needs to be encouraged. *Make the choice in the morning to surrender* that day to God and ask Him to reveal Himself to you. He will not disappoint and will also give you opportunities to reflect His love and kindness to others. Ask God to breathe His fresh breath of life into you daily and enjoy His goodness.

> "Jesus told him, 'I am the way, the truth, and the life. No one can come to the Father except through me.'" — John 14:6

> Taste and see that the Lord is good. Oh the joys of those who take refuge in Him! — Psalm 34:8

January 13

Have you ever thought about what the cross really means to you? Ask yourself the question, "When I see the cross or think about it, does it bring an emotional response?" Some people may say it brings a feeling of reverence or holiness, which is certainly understandable. But I would ask, does it bring a sense of awe and sacrifice? If not, there is a great opportunity for growth there.

When we are in awe of the cross, there is a sense of gratitude for Jesus because of the sacrifice He made. He chose to create a path to eternity for you and me. It was His sacrificial love that will one day usher us to our heavenly home. The cross should move us into action for Kingdom work. We should learn to worship God with the way we love and live. When we think about all He has done for us, it should motivate us to be openhanded with our lives here *allowing Him to lead*, guide, and direct us.

> And so, dear brothers and sisters, I plead with you to give your bodies to God because of all he has done for you. Let them be a living and holy sacrifice—the kind he will find acceptable. This is truly the way to worship him.
> — Romans 12:1

January 14

One beautiful characteristic about living the Christian life is our continual transformation. If we will cooperate with the Holy Spirit's work in our hearts, we will never remain the same. God created us in His image, and everything He allows into our lives—good or bad—He will use.

Honestly, one of the most intriguing things about God for me, as a baby Christ follower, was that He knew way better than I did what was good for me, and He created me with a purpose in mind. I knew I needed to attach myself to Him if I was to live out that purpose and experience the abundant life He had in store.

What can you do this week to move closer to God in spirit, mind, and body? Meditate on **Psalm 86:11** and open your heart to *allow God to teach you* His way. Listen to a worship song first thing in the morning to set the tone for your day. Move your body if you are able a little more every day, being thankful you can, and praise Him for all He created you to be.

> *Teach me your ways, O Lord, that I may live according to your truth! Grant me purity of heart, so that I may honor you.* — Psalm 86:11

> *For God is working in you, giving you the desire and power to do what pleases him.* — Philippians 2:13

January 15

SOME OF THE MOST HURTFUL, FRAGILE EMOTIONS WE DEAL WITH are those brought on by the feeling of being rejected. I have learned that the root of rejection is a lack of meaningful love in our lives. Obviously we are all raised by broken people, maybe some more than others, but this side of heaven, we all, including those who raise us, have some degree of brokenness. For this reason, so often the love we are raised on can be fragmented and not feel truly secure. This is why the sooner we can accept and receive the love of our heavenly Father, the more confident we can become in allowing that perfect love—His love—to protect our hearts from counterfeit forms of love in the world. **1 John 4:16–21** gives a beautiful invitation to the perfect love *He is waiting to lavish* on all who will invite Him in.

> *We know how much God loves us, and we have put our trust in his love. God is love, and all who live in love live in God, and God lives in them. And as we live in God, our love grows more perfect. So we will not be afraid on the day of judgment, but we can face him with confidence because we live like Jesus here in this world. Such love has no fear, because perfect love expels all fear. If we are afraid, it is for fear of punishment, and this shows that we have not fully experienced his perfect love. We love each other because he loved us first. If someone says, "I love God," but hates a fellow believer, that person is a liar; for if we don't love people we can see, how can we love God, whom we cannot see? And he has given us this command: Those who love God must also love their fellow believers.* — 1 John 4:16-21

January 16

How comforting would it be to know you were always at the right place at the right time? It would bring great peace and alleviate a lot of anxiety, and it could also cure FOMO disease (Fear of Missing Out). *When we seek God early in our day* and invite Him into our plans, we can feel confident that where we are and when we are there is exactly as it should be. So often we say to ourselves the toxic "what if." **Proverbs 16:9** tells us "a man's heart may plan his way, but the Lord directs his steps." Oftentimes we think we have more power than we actually do.

As you invite God into your day, ask Him to direct your steps and your conversations. The Lord goes before us and He has divine appointments set up for us we don't even know about. This is just one of the reasons life with God is so exciting. We never know what He has in store.

> We can make our plans, but the Lord determines our steps. — Proverbs 16:9

> For just as the heavens are higher than the earth, so my ways are higher than your ways and my thoughts higher than your thoughts. — Isaiah 55:9

> You can make many plans, but the Lord's purpose will prevail. — Proverbs 19:21

How often do we hear people say, "I talk to myself all the time"? That statement is very true, and not only do we talk to ourselves, but we also listen to ourselves. We really need to ask ourselves, "What kind of messages am I constantly sending to myself?" Are the words you're speaking giving life or death?

In order to speak life, we have to allow the Lord's thoughts and words to be in the forefront of our minds and hearts. Two of the most valuable things we can do in this life is get to know God and know ourselves through the loving eyes of our Father in heaven. He says we are His "masterpiece" (**Ephesians 2:10**), and we are "chosen" (**1 Peter 2:9**). God loves and values us exactly where we are right now, and *we should learn from Him*. Who better to build us up and teach us our value than the very One who created us? He is more than worthy of our trust.

> *For we are God's masterpiece. He has created us anew in Christ Jesus, so we can do the good things he planned for us long ago.* — Ephesians 2:10

> *But you are not like that, for you are a chosen people. You are royal priests, a holy nation, God's very own possession. As a result, you can show others the goodness of God, for he called you out of the darkness into his wonderful light.*
> — 1 Peter 2:9

January 18

EPHESIANS 6 TEACHES US ALL ABOUT THE ARMOR OF GOD: the helmet of salvation, the breastplate of righteousness, the shield of faith, the sword of the Spirit, the belt of truth, and the shoes of peace. As followers of Christ, we are encouraged to put on our armor every day.

Equally important to this armor is walking in our identity in Christ. I would challenge you that your most important accessory is your cloak of identity, living out the truth that you are first and foremost God's child. You are who He says you are. We all have other relationships and responsibilities in our lives, but the core of who you are is His: His to hold, His to love, His to guide, and, most importantly, His to define. That's where *Holy Spirit confidence* grows and takes root. The more you walk in that victory, the more natural it becomes.

> But to all who believed him and accepted him, he gave the right to become children of God. — John 1:12

> For we are God's masterpiece. He has created us anew in Christ Jesus so we can do the good things he planned for us long ago. — Ephesians 2:10

How many times have you heard people say the endearing comment about someone they love and confide in, "He/she is my person?" We would conclude that is the first person they run to with a victory or a defeat. Believe me, I value the gift of our human relationships with all their highs and lows, knowing that God teaches us mightily through them. But what if Jesus was truly your person, the first place you ran to with celebrations or sadness? How might that change the posture of your heart to sit at His feet first?

Psalm 73:23 tells us God is always with us and holds us by our hand. What a beautiful truth to rest in, knowing that *He never leaves us* or forsakes us. He is our forever friend: we never have to wonder whether He has our best interests in mind, and we can be confident we will be heard and understood.

> Yet I still belong to you; you hold my right hand.— Psalm 73:23

> There are friends who destroy each other, but a real friend sticks closer than a brother. — Proverbs 18:24

January 20

Psalm 145:3 reminds us that the Lord is great beyond our understanding and worthy of our praise. As we get to know our Heavenly Father and grow closer to Him, the truth of His worthiness in different areas becomes clearer and clearer. He is worthy of our affection and trust as well as our praise.

Our love for Jesus is what changes us, not the rules we attempt to follow. We have to cultivate a love for Jesus that is greater than our love of anything that hinders our faith. Relationships take time to grow. So *every day is a new opportunity* to experience Him in a different way. As we grow in love we also grow in trust, discovering all the ways He has been working in our circumstances and hearts when we didn't realize it, and looking forward with expectation for what's to come.

> Great is the Lord! He is most worthy of praise! No one can measure his greatness. — Psalm 145:3

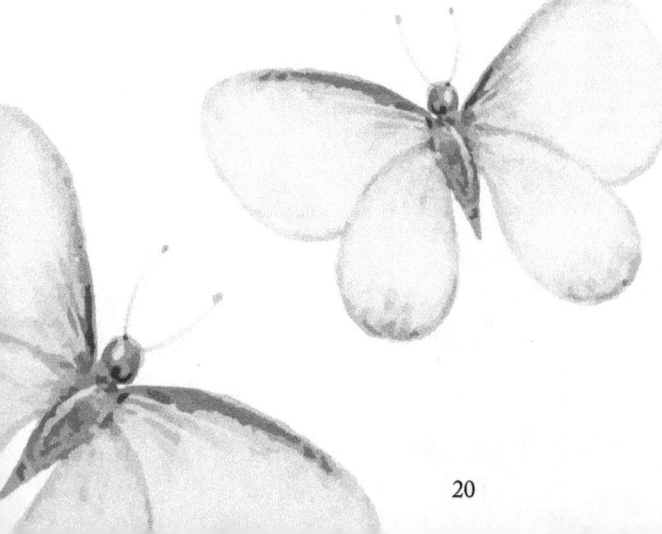

January 21

THERE ARE TWO POWERFUL LINES in a popular worship song that say, "I'm a child of God" and "I am who You say I am." This is one of the most precious truths we learn when we dip our toes in the water of a relationship with Christ. For a lot of us who have been through some difficult things, our sense of worth and identity gets fragmented and warped. However, thankfully, we have a heavenly Father who meets us where we are and gently re-frames our ideas about ourselves and even the purpose of our lives.

Romans 12:2 reminds us not to conform to this world, but to be renewed in our mind. This week, challenge yourself to practice God's presence by talking to Him multiple times a day. Say out loud to yourself in the morning, *I am who You say I am.* Limit your sugar intake and replace it with an extra fruit or vegetable, worshiping God by taking care of the body He gave you.

> Don't copy the behavior and customs of this world, but let God transform you into a new person by changing the way you think. Then you will learn to know God's will for you, which is good and pleasing and perfect. — Romans 12:2

> So whether you eat or drink, or whatever you do, do it all for the glory of God.
> —1 Corinthians 10:31

January 22

WORDS ARE SO POWERFUL AND WE ALL NEED LIFE-GIVING WORDS of encouragement daily, but so often we seek the affirmation we so desperately crave in the wrong places. We will either seek it in the broken people we are in relationship with, or we pay too much attention to the opinions of the culture and believe lies that somehow we aren't measuring up to some standard that's not even real. We need to bring ourselves to a place of believing, receiving, and relying on the words of truth that come straight from the heart of God.

1 John 4:16 teaches us to *lean into the love God has* for us and that, when we abide in Him, we abide in love. He never tires or grows weary of lavishing His truth and words of life over you. He is the well that never runs dry, and His is the voice we need to listen to for affirmation and love.

> *We know how much God loves us, and we have put our trust in his love. God is love, and all who live in love live in God, and God lives in them.* —1 John 4:16

> *Give thanks to the God of heaven. His faithful love endures forever.*
> — Psalm 136:26

January 23

I<small>N ORDER FOR US TO CONTINUE ON OUR JOURNEY</small> of who God created us to be, there is healing in certain areas that needs to take place. I once heard the beautiful words that whatever is hidden cannot be healed. With all grace and mercy, the Holy Spirit will allow events to resurface in God's perfect timing when we are capable, with God's help, to revisit that memory. It takes a certain measure of desire and maturity to deep-dive into pain and hurt, but we can rest in knowing we never do it alone.

In **Exodus 33:14** the Lord says to Moses, "My Presence will go with you and I will give you rest" (ESV). We can be confident in the promise that, if the Spirit brings it up, *He will walk us through* it with rest and guidance along the way, leading us into healing and peace.

> "The Lord replied, 'I will personally go with you, Moses, and I will give you rest—everything will be fine for you.'" — Exodus 33:14

> Teach these new disciples to obey all the commands I have given you. And be sure of this: I am with you always, even to the end of the age.
> — Matthew 28:20

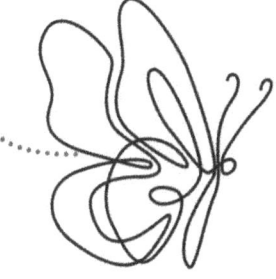

January 24

THE FEELING OF DISCONTENTMENT IS LIKE A POISON to our soul. I have often said it is one of Satan's favorite strategies to make Christ followers ineffective in Kingdom work and fall prey to a mediocre faith at best. The opposite of discontentment is satisfaction in Jesus.

What does that actually look like? By definition, satisfaction means fulfillment of one's expectations and needs and also pleasure derived from something or someone in this case.

Psalm 37:4 encourages us, "Take delight in the Lord, and he will give you your heart's desires." We can find peace knowing that God knows better than we do what will truly make us happy. Moving toward Jesus and learning how *He can be your constant* companion will bring such a sweet joy to your life that nothing can replace.

> *Take delight in the Lord, and he will give you your heart's desires.*
> *— Psalm 37:4*

> *You make known to me the path of life; you will fill me with joy in Your presence, with eternal pleasures at your right hand. — Psalm 16:11 (NIV)*

January 25

We were created to live our lives completely relying on God. That means being open-handed with the time, talents, and gifts He has given us. We need to be willing to be interrupted, being sensitive to the Holy Spirit. **1 Corinthians 16:13** reminds us to stay alert and be full of courage.

Our day-to-day lives are sprinkled with divine appointments in which we have opportunities to experience blessings and be a blessing to others. One of the most beautiful attributes of walking in step with God is being a vessel of His love, hope, and comfort to others.

We should *ask God daily* to give us spiritual eyes to see and open hearts to receive all He may have in store for us. **1 Corinthians 2:10** teaches that God reveals opportunities through the Holy Spirit, so we should not only stay alert, but also be expectant.

> *Be on guard. Stand firm in the faith. Be courageous. Be strong.*
> — 1 Corinthians 16:13

> *But it was to us that God revealed these things by his Spirit. For his Spirit searches out everything and shows us God's deep secrets.*
> — 1 Corinthians 2:10

January 26

We would all benefit from starting our day with the anticipation that God is going to move and we will get to see it. **Isaiah 30:18** says God is longing to be good to you. He is going to be good to the people who are looking for His goodness and expecting His favor. There is great truth in the saying, "You will find what you're looking for." When we are looking for God's activity in circumstances and in the lives of those around us, not only does it encourage an expectant heart posture, it also helps us to experience childlike faith. Our heavenly Father is more than able to do the most amazing things in and around a heart that is open and looking for His activity.

Where in your life or in the lives of those you love are you longing to see movement? *We can rest knowing He is always* steps ahead of us working for our good and His glory.

> So the Lord must wait for you to come to him so he can show you his love and compassion. For the Lord is a faithful God. Blessed are those who wait for his help.
> — Isaiah 30:18

> Now all glory to God, who is able, through his mighty power at work within us, to accomplish infinitely more than we might ask or think.
> — Ephesians 3:20

January 27

How amazing is it that there is no place too deep or dark for the Lord to rescue us from? I love the imagery of Jesus meeting us where we are and then extending His hand to lead, guide, and direct us where to go next. The truth is, God will place people around you for community and leaders before you to shepherd you, but ultimately it comes down to the decision to walk hand-in-hand with Jesus to the next step.

Ephesians 5:8 explains once we were in the dark, but now we have *the very light of Christ shining* through because of our union with Him. What a glorious privilege to have the light of the world directing our next step. So often in our lives the next step is more important than the big picture. The surrender involved to stay in step with Jesus and resist moving ahead on our own is faith-building and worth it.

> *For once you were full of darkness, but now you have light from the Lord. So live as people of light!* — Ephesians 5:8

> *He lets me rest in green meadows; he leads me beside peaceful streams.* — Psalm 23:2

January 28

WHEN I WAS VERY NEW TO LEARNING what it looked like to really follow Jesus, I loved to meet older women who were wise and living close to God and ask them questions. Once I asked a friend, "If you could tell me one thing as a young Christian woman, what would you say?" She smiled as if that was an easy question and replied, "I would tell you to guard your heart." **Proverbs 4:23** teaches you to "guard your heart above all else, for it determines the course of your life."

So what does it look like to guard our hearts? Maybe for some of us it's being more selective about whom we spend time with or what music we listen to. We are all sensitive in different areas. Focus on heart health this week. Begin your days asking God to lead you towards relationships that are good for you. Meditate on **Proverbs 4:23** and *invite the Holy Spirit* to show you new ways to guard your heart. Focus on physical heart health by doing a little extra cardio this week.

> *Guard your heart above all else, for it determines the course of your life.*
> *— Proverbs 4:23*

January 29

ONE OF THE BIGGEST HURDLES IN THE CHRISTIAN LIFE is learning what it looks like to surrender our ways and trust God's ways instead. First of all, we have to believe His ways are better than our own, and that does not happen overnight. As we are learning to trust, we have to take small steps of faith and give God the opportunity to show up (**Psalm 37:5**). God knows our hearts, so He honors the effort of seeking Him. We are human and will make mistakes, but He is bigger than our blunders and is more than able to get us back on track to accomplish His will in spite of human error. Some of us long for things to be black and white or right and wrong when *God often teaches us* so much in the gray and uncertain. We often give ourselves too much credit and think we are way more in control than we are, but, thankfully, our role is to stay close to the One who is sovereign over all.

> *Commit everything you do to the Lord.*
> *Trust him, and he will help you.*
> — Psalm 37:5

January 30

God never ceases to amaze me with the creative ways He touches our hearts with divine appointments in an ordinary day. Today I had the pleasure of meeting an older gentleman who happened to be a veteran at a local thrift store. As his personal ministry to others, he was graciously giving out wooden cross necklaces onto which he had beautifully soldered a nail. He would not take money in exchange, claiming they were a gift. I was already struck with emotion by such a beautiful gesture, and then he offered one to me. I replied, "Absolutely! This makes me cry." He said, "It should make us all cry with thankful emotion by what Jesus did for us on the cross."

And I couldn't agree more. The cross should touch us in a powerful way. If it doesn't, that is a great opportunity to grow and *learn more about Jesus' sacrifice* and the impact His one decision has on all of humanity. This is where redemption, sacrifice, and eternal life come together in the ultimate expression of true love.

> There is no greater love than to lay down one's life for one's friends.
> — John 15:13

Much too often our culture glorifies the idea of being independent and self-sufficient. People allow pride to get in the way of reaching out and expressing their need for help or connection. Independent mindsets often lead to isolation, which is one of our spiritual enemy's tactics. The opposite of isolation is community, and we all need it. **1 Peter 4:8–11** emphasizes loving each other deeply and offering hospitality, along with using our gifts to serve one another.

Pray and ask God for creative ideas to serve and love the people around you. The act of simply being interested in others can make them feel valued and respected. God designed us for dependence on Him, which means we should seek His will daily. It is only by Christ's strength that we can navigate loving others well. **2 Corinthians 3:5** tells us we cannot do anything in our own strength, but our true competence and strength comes from spending time in God's empowering presence.

> *Most important of all, continue to show deep love for each other, for love covers a multitude of sins. Cheerfully share your home with those who need a meal or a place to stay. God has given each of you a gift from his great variety of spiritual gifts. Use them well to serve one another. Do you have the gift of speaking? Then speak as though God himself were speaking through you. Do you have the gift of helping others? Do it with all the strength and energy that God supplies. Then everything you do will bring glory to God through Jesus Christ. All glory and power to him forever and ever! Amen.* — 1 Peter 4:8-11

> *It is not that we think we are qualified to do anything on our own. Our qualification comes from God.* — 2 Corinthians 3:5

February 1

WE WILL ALL RECEIVE A MULTITUDE OF STIMULI ABOUT LOVE THIS MONTH. In fact, many people who seem to be content in their singleness at other times may grow discontent over the Valentine season. I would love to challenge you, single or not, to focus on the One who should be and longs to be your first love. **Deuteronomy 6:4–5** commands us, "Love the Lord your God with all your heart, all your soul, and all your strength."

So what are some practical ways we can live that out? Loving with all your heart may look like being raw and vulnerable in your prayer time. Instead of feeling shame about your heart posture towards something or someone, ask God to help you change it. Explore your soul, *inviting the Holy Spirit* to illuminate places that need a fresh touch from God, and humbly address changes you need to make. Realize you can do none of this in your own strength, and when God reveals an area that needs work, leaning into His strength will supply all the help you need.

> Listen, O Israel! The Lord is our God, the Lord alone. And you must love the Lord your God with all your heart, all your soul, and all your strength.
> — Deuteronomy 6:4-5

> And this same God who takes care of me will supply all your needs from his glorious riches, which have been given to us in Christ Jesus.
> — Philippians 4:19

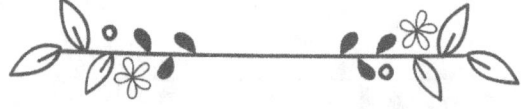

February 2

THERE ARE MANY INSTANCES IN LIFE THAT REQUIRE US TO MOVE PAST our feelings into action. It could be responsibilities dealing with family or work, but oftentimes it's in our relationships. We were created for interaction with others and fellowship with God, but all too often we neglect this need because it takes time and effort. There are a multitude of rewards and blessings that come with learning the art of moving past feelings and living based on truth. Truth tells us to "draw near to God and he will draw near to you" **(James 4:8 ESV)**. We may not feel His nearness immediately, but we can rest on the promise He is present. *As we draw near in faith*, His living water runs in and through us in ways too amazing for us to know **(Hebrews 10:22)**. God honors our desire to draw near to Him, and the intimacy created in those moments is certainly worth the effort.

> Come close to God, and God will come close to you. — James 4:8

> Let us go right into the presence of God with sincere hearts fully trusting him. For our guilty consciences have been sprinkled with Christ's blood to make us clean, and our bodies have been washed with pure water. — Hebrews 10:22

February 3

ONE OF MY MOST REPEATED PRAYERS FOR PEOPLE is for them to fall in love with Jesus and share life with Him. God longs to be invited into our hearts and deeply desires to share His heart with us. How is it that the Almighty God of the universe would feel so strongly that He would allow us to be familiar with His ways? **Psalm 25:4–5** says, "Show me your ways, Lord, teach me your paths. Guide me in your truth and teach me."

God wishes to guide and teach us because He always wants what is best for His children. We were designed to be imitators of God, so as we learn more about His heart, He simultaneously changes ours. *Pray and ask God* to reveal His heart to you in a new way, and invite Him to examine yours, trusting that both of these prayers will result in greater intimacy with Him. This intimacy is the Abundant Life Jesus came for us to experience.

> *Show me the right path, O Lord; point out the road for me to follow. Lead me by your truth and teach me, for you are the God who saves me. All day long I put my hope in you.* — Psalm 25:4-5

> *You satisfy me more than the richest feast. I will praise you with songs of joy.* — Psalm 63:5

February 4

TAKE A MOMENT AND THINK OF THOSE PEOPLE IN YOUR LIFE who you feel safe with—those who you know love you and have your best interests in mind—and the peace that comes with knowing you can trust them with anything. Ask yourself: is that how I communicate with God? When we are raw and vulnerable with Him, we give Him an opportunity to invade our messiness and feel His power. **Isaiah 40:29** tells us that "He gives power to the weak and strength to the powerless." When I was single, I began a habit of writing love letters to God. I would share my heart with Him, and I came to believe He was holding onto me. Even though He knew it all anyway, it increased my awareness of His presence (**Exodus 33:14**).

Pray and thank God that He cares for your heart like only He can, and write Him a letter everyday, sharing your highs and lows. He is the best listener you know.

> He gives power to the weak and strength to the powerless. — Isaiah 40:29

> "The Lord replied, 'My Presence will go with you, and I will give you rest.'"
> —Exodus 33:14 (NIV)

> I love the Lord because he hears my voice and my prayer for mercy. Because he bends down to listen, I will pray as long as I have breath! — Psalm 116:1-2

February 5

TRUSTING GOD'S TIMING IS A SOUGHT-AFTER VIRTUE. The secret to trusting His timing is actually believing He is all-knowing, all-powerful, everywhere, and always for our good. The Message translation of Scripture says that "He knows us far better than we know ourselves, knows our [longing] condition, and keeps us present with Him. That's why we can be sure that every detail in our lives can be turned into something good" **(Romans 8:27–28)**.

We need to tell ourselves there is a reason for the "no," "not now," or "wait" answers we receive from God. There is nothing good for us that He wants to hold back **(Psalm 84:11)**. He is always more interested in our needs than in our wants, and He will meet those needs in the right way at the right time. As we *grow in relationship with God*, our wants will also grow to mirror what He wants to do in and through our lives. Once we learn to rest in His arms allowing Him to carry us where we need to go, there will be a peace accompanying that kind of trust is that is truly indescribable.

> *And the Father who knows all hearts knows what the Spirit is saying, for the Spirit pleads for us believers in harmony with God's own will. And we know that God causes everything to work together for the good of those who love God and are called according to his purpose for them.* — Romans 8:27-28

> *For the Lord God is our sun and our shield. He gives us grace and glory. The Lord will withhold no good thing from those who do what is right.*
> — Psalm 84:11

> *God's way is perfect. All the Lord's promises prove true. He is a shield for all who look to him for protection.* — 2 Samuel 22:31

February 6

THERE ARE TWO OPPOSING HEART POSTURES FROM WHICH WE NAVIGATE life, circumstances, and relationships: love rooted in belief in God's truth and sovereignty or fear rooted in unbelief and the false reality that we are in control. **Proverbs 21:21** reminds us to love freely without fear, this is how we can experience the joy of being a blessing to others as we trust Gods work in their lives. Living from this posture of love is a sign of freedom and confidence realizing that outcomes in situations or how a loved one's heart is responding to God is out of our control. Surrendering people and circumstances to God frees us up to love well and do what God has actually called us to do, which never involves playing the role of the Holy Spirit. **John 15:12** commands us to *love each other deeply* as Christ has loved us. Pray and ask the Holy Spirit to lead, guide, and direct you to love well those God has placed along your path today.

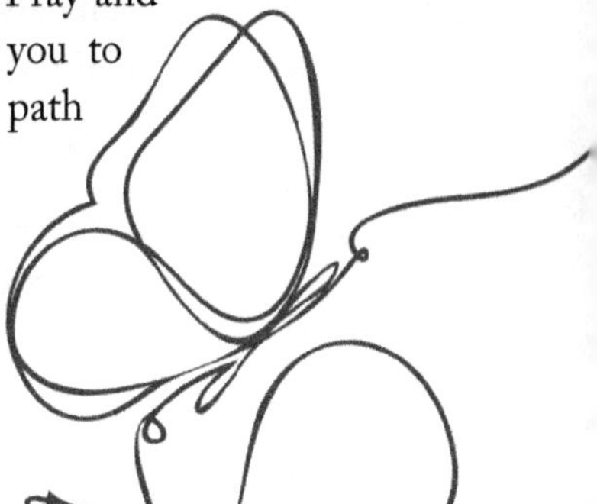

> *Whoever pursues righteousness and unfailing love will find life, righteousness, and honor.*
> — Proverbs 21:21

> *This is my commandment: Love each other in the same way I have loved you.*
> — John 15:12

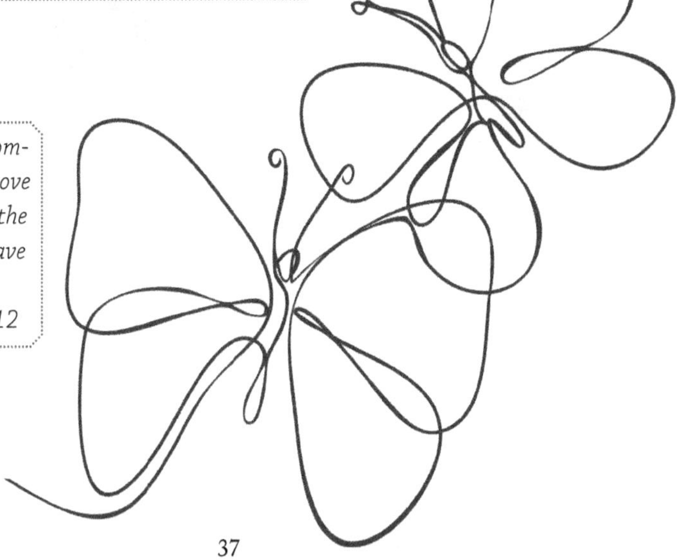

IN THE ARENA OF HEALTHY RELATIONSHIPS, THERE IS OFTEN CHATTER ABOUT LOVE languages, whether discussing family dynamics, workplace appreciation, or romance. If there is discord in marriage, one may say what his or her love language is, as a reminder for when strategizing something to make amends.

How beautifully amazing is it that God speaks all our love languages perfectly. God's perfect love for us was personified in Jesus Christ, and we can learn to love others through Christ regardless of their specific love language. When the love of Christ shines through our actions, there is an undeniable undercurrent of warmth and compassion. "What would Jesus do?" is a well known question, but asking ourselves how Jesus would love in any given scenario is equally important. *Ask God to help you* love sacrificially, as He has done for you (**1 John 4:9**).

> *This is how God showed his love among us: He sent his one and only Son into the world that we might live through him.* — 1 John 4:9(NIV)

> *"Love your enemies! Do good to them. Lend to them without expecting to be repaid. Then your reward from heaven will be very great, and you will truly be acting as children of the Most High, for he is kind to those who are unthankful and wicked. You must be compassionate, just as your Father is compassionate."*
> — Luke 6:35-36

February 8

OUR STUDENTS AT CHURCH ARE HAVING AN IN-HOUSE RETREAT this weekend and my prayer for them this morning was: "Heavenly Father, I pray they leave different than they came." I often find myself praying this for myself and others before a church service or meeting. How can we create space spiritually and mentally to invite change? Our Advocate, the Holy Spirit, was sent to us by God to teach us, to remind us of the truth we know, and to inspire us towards change (**John 14:26–27**). As we go to services, read the Word of God, and even during our communion with God in prayer, we should come with an expectant heart that is willing to receive direction, revelation, and encouragement. God desires to breathe fresh breath into our lives. His love and provision is always life-giving, and we should *seek and pray for opportunities* to experience His goodness (**Lamentations 3:25**).

> But the Advocate, the Holy Spirit, whom the Father will send in my name, will teach you all things and will remind you of everything I have said to you. Peace I leave with you; my peace I give you. I do not give to you as the world gives. Do not let your hearts be troubled and do not be afraid. — John 14:26-27 (NIV)

> The Lord is good to those whose hope is in him, to the one who seeks him.
> — Lamentations 3:25 (NIV)

February 9

OUR SPIRITUAL, EMOTIONAL, AND PHYSICAL HEALTH ARE BIRTHED out of our thought life. **Colossians 3:2** urges us to fill our thoughts with heavenly realities and not be too distracted by the world. We have been brought into new life in Christ when we invite Him in to be Lord of our lives. We may not always have control over what comes into our thoughts, but we can decide whether we will entertain those thoughts or bring them under Christ authority for examination. Focusing on the Spirit over the flesh demands intentionality and an awareness of how quickly we can backslide into negative thought patterns. God desires to be brought into every area of our lives, but so often we want to compartmentalize certain areas and keep Him at a distance.

Pray and thank God that He wants all of you. He will help you focus on what brings life, not death and destruction (**Romans 8:6**). Intentionally moving towards Christ daily will eventually shift the trajectory of our thoughts as the result of a transformed heart.

> Set your minds on things above, not on earthly things. — Colossians 3:2 (NIV)

> The mind governed by the flesh is death, but the mind governed by the Spirit is life and peace. — Romans 8:6 (NIV)

GOD IS LOVE. The foundation of the Christian faith is that God took human form in the body of Christ and that Christ was fully God, fully human at the same time, offering His human body as a sacrifice that we may live and have eternal life despite our sin and brokenness. 1 Corinthians 13:1–3 reminds us that we can acquire or be born with many gifts and talents, but if we don't have love, we have nothing.

It is impossible for us to love God, love others, or love ourselves without the guidance and leadership of the Holy Spirit. Loving God is rooted in remaining in awe of all He is and all He helps us to be (**Matthew 19:26**). Loving others is rooted in sacrifice (**1 Corinthians 13:4–8**). Loving ourselves is rooted in embracing our identity in Christ (**Psalm 139**). These are three areas that are always worth our effort to lean into God, to foster continuous growth and change. *Pray and thank God* that we are not called to do anything on our own.

> "Jesus looked at them intently and said, 'Humanly speaking, it is impossible. But with God everything is possible.'" — Matthew 19:26

> If I could speak all the languages of earth and of angels, but didn't love others, I would only be a noisy gong or a clanging cymbal. If I had the gift of prophecy, and if I understood all of God's secret plans and possessed all knowledge, and if I had such faith that I could move mountains, but didn't love others, I would be nothing. If I gave everything I have to the poor and even sacrificed my body, I could boast about it; but if I didn't love others, I would have gained nothing.
> — 1 Corinthians 13:1-3

Embracing the reality that God created you on purpose for a purpose is the beginning of fulfillment this side of heaven. Every part of you, including spiritual gifts, personality, abilities, experiences, and passions are all woven together for you to make a difference in the world around you. **Jeremiah 1:5** explains that, before God shaped us in the womb, He knew the plans He had for us.

Our human nature and the culture urge us to do our own thing and be self-made, which so often leads to striving, emptiness, and discontentment. Ask yourself the question: Are you surrendering to God and inviting Him to shape you? Meditate on Jeremiah **18:1–6** and *invite God* to soften your heart and open your eyes to new ways to serve and grow. Go to bed a few minutes earlier this week and use that time to thank God for the unique way He created you.

> *I knew you before I formed you in your mother's womb. Before you were born I set you apart and appointed you as my prophet to the nations.* — Jeremiah 1:5

> *"The Lord gave another message to Jeremiah. He said, 'Go down to the potter's shop, and I will speak to you there.' So I did as he told me and found the potter working at his wheel. But the jar he was making did not turn out as he had hoped, so he crushed it into a lump of clay again and started over. Then the Lord gave me this message: 'O Israel, can I not do to you as this potter has done to his clay? As the clay is in the potter's hand, so are you in my hand.'"* — Jeremiah 18:1-6

> *In him we were also chosen, having been predestined according to the plan of him who works out everything in conformity with the purpose of his will.*
> — *Ephesians 1:11 (NIV)*

February 12

I RECENTLY LEARNED HOW A CONVERSATION I HAD WITH AN ACQUAINTANCE several months ago put a whole new season in motion in her life. To be clear, it wasn't me putting anything in motion. It was the Holy Spirit's guidance working in both of us that made for a divine exchange. **Colossians 4:6** leads us to speak with grace, clarity, and truth, being prepared to give a respectful answer when asked about our faith. We should all be willing to be interrupted, open to opportunities to either seek or give God honoring encouragement.

One of Satan's strategies is to keep us busy and always in a hurry while not taking time to notice what God is doing in and around us. God uses ordinary people to give encouragement, compassion, and sometimes guidance. *Pray and ask God* for sensitivity to His activity around you and never allow yourself to be in so much of a hurry that you block a blessing God is ready to reveal.

Let your conversation be gracious and attractive so that you will have the right response for everyone. — Colossians 4:6

For it will not be you speaking, but the Spirit of your Father speaking through you. — Matthew 10:20

February 13

HAVE YOU EVER BEEN STANDING IN THE MIDDLE OF A LARGE GROUP OF PEOPLE, yet you felt completely alone? This feeling can cause a sense of emptiness and insignificance. The reality is that isolation can take place whether alone or in a room full of people. **Proverbs 27:17** directs us to allow others in our lives to sharpen our character, but this sharpening can only occur with authenticity and transparency. There are a plethora of reasons we lean into isolation, shame, pride, depression, and even a lack of trust in others. While all of the above may be valid, we have to acknowledge the reality God is bigger (**Philippians 4:13**). It does take effort on our part to insert ourselves into a healthy community, but the benefits are powerful. Our need to be completely understood and known can only be perfectly filled in Christ; however, God gives us the gift of human relationships to encourage, love, share burdens, and, most importantly, continue *pointing each other towards Christ.*

> As iron sharpens iron, so a friend sharpens a friend.— Proverbs 27:17

> For I can do everything through Christ, who gives me strength.
> — Philippians 4:13

> Not giving up meeting together, as some are in the habit of doing, but encouraging one another—and all the more as you see the Day approaching.
> — Hebrews 10:25

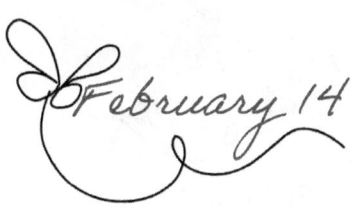

Today is Valentine's Day, and even though it's one of those cheesy overdone holidays, it is in fact a fun opportunity to celebrate love. For birthdays and holidays at my house, I have a tradition of creating a celebratory atmosphere by decorating our kitchen table. My daughter texted me today thanking me for always making everyone feel special, and I immediately thought of how the Lord invites us every day to the table of life. Providing food and water to satisfy our souls and the security offered by resting in His presence of love and mercy (**Psalm 23:6**). We are special to the Almighty God of the universe, and His desire is that we would turn to His presence for affirming love, recharging and equipping us for daily life.

Have you ever felt a tug in your Spirit or just a prompting that you should go sit with God and be near to Him? *That is the Holy Spirit inviting you into the presence of God.* May we be people that sit with Him, talk to Him, and believe He hears us and is already in the process of filling our cups with His goodness and grace.

> *Surely your goodness and unfailing love will pursue me all the days of my life, and I will live in the house of the Lord forever.* — Psalm 23:6

> *Seek the Lord while he may be found; call on him while he is near.* — Isaiah 55:6 (NIV)

February 15

Have you ever thought about how you "bookend" your days? In other words, what is the last thing you think about before closing your eyes and the first thing you go to when rising in the morning? These are two critical times that can greatly affect our sleep or the success of the day. **Psalm 19:14** tells us to let the words of our mouth and the meditations of our heart be acceptable in the Lord's sight as He is our redeemer and our rock. It is heart-transforming to *speak the Word of God out loud* to ourselves morning and night. I have often encouraged women to read **Psalm 139** out loud to themselves when they are struggling to connect with their identity in Christ or to read **Psalm 91** when having trouble with sleep or unwanted thoughts at night. There is power in the living Word of God, and what a privilege it is to find peace for our minds, encouragement for our faith, and rest for our weariness in the grand infallible collection of God's promises and love.

> *May the words of my mouth and the meditation of my heart be pleasing to you, O Lord, my rock and my redeemer.* — Psalm 19:14

> *All Scripture is God-breathed and is useful for teaching, rebuking, correcting and training in righteousness, so that the servant of God may be thoroughly equipped for every good work.* — 2 Timothy 3:16-17

Have you ever noticed how all too often conversations are centered around grumbling and complaining? Whether we are gathered at the gym or unfortunately even at church, there are always discussions swirling about how this or that could be executed more efficiently or why a process is taking so long. We have really become a very demanding, critical, and impatient society. **James 5:9** and **Philippians 2:14** are just a couple of places in the Scriptures where we are urged to stop this heart posture of entitlement.

Years ago I worked at a gym with an older gentleman who was a very strong believer and follower of Jesus. He shared with me that at one time in his life he turned his entire prayer life into praises. He knew that the Lord was always a step ahead of him, so he would just thank God for already being at work in his petitions. He said this radically changed his negativity, giving him an attitude of gratitude he still carries today. *Focusing more on praise* will nourish your soul and be an encouragement to those around you.

> Don't grumble about each other, brothers and sisters, or you will be judged. For look—the Judge is standing at the door! — James 5:9

> Do everything without complaining and arguing. — Philippians 2:14

> Let everything that has breath praise the Lord. Praise the Lord. — Psalm 150:6 (NIV)

February 17

WE DON'T ALWAYS HAVE THE POWER TO CHOOSE what thoughts are in our minds upon awakening, but we do have the power to choose what we do with those thoughts. Those first few moments are deciding factors of our heart posture and direction for the day. Oftentimes before my feet hit the floor I have already invited God to fill my cup with His living water and invade my mind with what is good and fruitful for the day (**Psalm 19:14**). So no matter what is happening with our emotions or circumstances, we always have the power to choose to follow God in that moment with the assurance that He is more than able to help us navigate any given situation. It takes discipline and intentionality for our Spirit to be louder than our flesh, but the more we yield to our Spirit and follow Jesus, the less power our flesh will hold. *Thank God* that we have the privilege to choose Him and rejoice in knowing "His mercies are new every morning" (**Lamentations 3:23**).

May the words of my mouth and the meditation of my heart be pleasing to you, O Lord, my Rock and my Redeemer. — Psalm 19:14

Great is his faithfulness; his mercies begin afresh each morning. — Lamentations 3:23

This is the day the Lord has made. Let us rejoice and be glad in it.— Psalm 118:24

February 18

WOULDN'T IT BE AMAZING TO WAKE UP EVERY MORNING and be able to say, "I am enough, right here, right now; exactly who I am is enough"? The truth is, we can, because our competence and identity are found in Him, once we have invited Jesus to be Lord of our lives (**2 Corinthians 3:5**). Everything we need to take care of ourselves spiritually, emotionally, and physically is available to us. We do, however, need to invite the Holy Spirit into every part of who we are for wisdom, creativity, and direction. Seek out new physical activities for exercise or try a new healthy recipe or restaurant. Begin your days this week by reminding yourself that you are enough because God says you are, and *go to the Scriptures* for the affirmation you seek (**Psalm 139:13–16**). Realize that negative self-talk, self pity, and grumbling grieve the very heart of God and His desire is for you to walk in victory, confident in your God-given identity and the price He paid for us to be called His children.

> It is not that we think we are qualified to do anything on our own. Our qualification comes from God.— 2 Corinthians 3:5

> You made all the delicate, inner parts of my body and knit me together in my mother's womb. Thank you for making me so wonderfully complex! Your workmanship is marvelous—how well I know it. You watched me as I was being formed in utter seclusion, as I was woven together in the dark of the womb. You saw me before I was born. Every day of my life was recorded in your book. Every moment was laid out before a single day had passed. — Psalm 139:13-16

> So in Christ Jesus you are all children of God through faith.
> —Galatians 3:26 (NIV)

February 19

CULTIVATING A HEART POSTURE OF CONTENTMENT CREATES AN ATMOSPHERE of peace, joy, and expectation of what is to come. Discontentment, on the other hand, produces discouragement, comparison, and a sense of anxiety about the future. God's desire is that we would trust Him enough to rest securely in His arms, knowing He is more than able to lead us where we need to be and that His timing for everything in our lives is intentional (**Psalm 32:8**).

The world encourages striving, urgency, and a restlessness that will steal joy and peace. If God has you in a holding pattern or a state of limbo, it is always for our good and according to His plan. **Psalm 31:15** reminds us that, at the right time, God will provide all we need. We live in a world of immediate satisfaction, and so often that kind of bliss leaves as fast as it comes. *Spend some time with God* seeking to deepen your trust in His ways and His timing, being content to stay in step with the One who knows best.

> "The Lord says, 'I will guide you along the best pathway for your life. I will advise you and watch over you.'" — Psalm 32:8

> My future is in your hands. Rescue me from those who hunt me down relentlessly. — Psalm 31:15

> Commit to the Lord whatever you do and he will establish your plans. The Lord works out everything to its proper end-even the wicked for a day of disaster. — Proverbs 16:3-4 (NIV)

February 20

THE REALITY THAT OUR MOST DIFFICULT TRIALS AND STRUGGLES BRING to the surface God's most amazing grace and redemptive work in our hearts is such an encouraging truth. **James 1:2–4** tells us we should consider these adversities joy in that they give us the opportunity to persevere and grow in spiritual maturity. The thought on my heart upon waking this morning was, "Father, thank you that You are my rock," and what a firm foundation He is. This certainty is a hedge of protection for my heart and creates the assurance that, no matter what may happen, *my tight grip on God will help me* navigate through (**Joshua 23:8**). Our unhindered devotion to God can easily slip through our fingers without intentionality. We have to keep our reliance alive with God much like a romantic relationship. He really is the knight in shining armor who picks us up over and over. This steadfast faithfulness is perfect love.

Dear brothers and sisters, when troubles of any kind come your way, consider it an opportunity for great joy. For you know that when your faith is tested, your endurance has a chance to grow. So let it grow, for when your endurance is fully developed, you will be perfect and complete, needing nothing.— James 1:2-4

Rather, cling tightly to the Lord your God as you have done until now. — Joshua 23:8

Know therefore that the Lord your God is God; he is the faithful God, keeping his covenant of love to a thousand generations of those who love him and keep his commandments. — Deuteronomy 7:9 (NIV)

February 21

WALKING ON THE TRAIL NEAR MY HOUSE ONE DAY I was overwhelmed with the idea that Jesus is the lover of my soul. As soon as that truth crossed my mind, I looked down and there was a heart-shaped leaf that felt like such a God wink, and it warmed my soul with how intentional He can be when we keep the channel of communication open with Him. **Romans 8:38–39** reminds us that absolutely nothing can separate us from God's perfect love; yet, so often we fail to realize the tenderness of His heart for us. **Jeremiah 31:3** speaks of God's everlasting love and that He has drawn you with unfailing kindness. The beautiful reality that we have the privilege of being in this intimate relationship with Him is because He first pursues us and desires personal connection, not only as our Savior, but Father and friend. He wants us to *prayerfully be sensitive* as the Holy Spirit reveals acts of kindness and love directly from Him, the perfect lover of our souls.

> *And I am convinced that nothing can ever separate us from God's love. Neither death nor life, neither angels nor demons, neither our fears for today nor our worries about tomorrow-not even the powers of hell can separate us from God's love. No power in the sky above or in the earth below-indeed, nothing in all creation will ever be able to separate us from the love of God that is revealed in Christ Jesus our Lord. — Romans 8:38-39*

> *"Long ago the Lord said to Israel: 'I have loved you, my people, with an everlasting love. With unfailing love I have drawn you to myself.'" — Jeremiah 31:3*

> *You see, at just the right time, when we were still powerless, Christ died for the ungodly. — Romans 5:6 (NIV)*

February 22

TIME AND AGAIN WE HEAR THE ADVICE, "Don't try doing things in your own strength, lean into God's strength to accomplish your goals." How is this played out in our daily lives? First, ask yourself, "Is this my plan or God's?" (**Psalm 55:22**). Very often at the beginning of my day, I will ask God to help me get done what He wants me to get done, nothing more, nothing less. It's my way of inviting Him in to direct my steps and also to interrupt me if He so chooses. This makes me more open-handed with my time and more welcoming of divine opportunities. When we are operating in a mode of self-sufficiency, we tend to be more controlling of our schedule and may sometimes miss opportunities for divine interruptions or connection. When there is no margin during your day it's likely you are over committed. It is worth it to dedicate your days to God early in the morning. It helps us to be in step with Him and His activity. When we *lean into His strength and direction,* our spirits are sensitive to His invitation to join in His work in and around us.

> *Give your burdens to the Lord, and he will take care of you. He will not permit the godly to slip and fall.* — Psalm 55:22

> *Making the most of every opportunity, because the days are evil.* — Ephesians 5:16 (NIV)

A GREAT INDICATION OF WHETHER OUR HOPE AND FAITH LIES WITH ourselves or with God is how we respond to the curve balls life throws. We can have our eyes fixated on one destination or direction and all of a sudden that plan comes to a screeching halt. The words of **Isaiah 55:8** tell us our thoughts are not His thoughts and His ways are often different than ours. In light of this truth, we need to look at any redirection through the lens of the sovereignty of God. One of the most beautiful gifts of maturing in our faith is the reality and comfort in believing God's plans for us are better than our own. We also tend to get distracted by our circumstantial plan, while God's ultimate plan is our love for, relationship with and dependence on Him. The ultimate goal for us is nearness to Christ, and there is a supernatural confidence that is only found under His wings (**Psalm 91:4**). For these reasons, we can rejoice in the curve balls, believing there are no surprises to God and that *His rerouting is always for our good.*

> "'My thoughts are nothing like your thoughts,' says the Lord. 'And my ways are far beyond anything you could imagine.'" — Isaiah 55:8

> He will cover you with his feathers. He will shelter you with his wings. His faithful promises are your armor and protection. — Psalm 91:4

> Give thanks in all circumstances, for this is God's will for you in Christ Jesus. — 1 Thessalonians 5:18 (NIV)

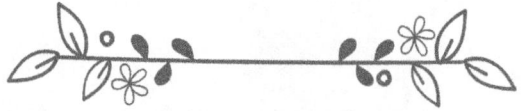

February 24

THERE IS A RADICAL DIVIDE BETWEEN HEAD KNOWLEDGE AND HEART knowledge of Jesus. Some say it's "the 18 inches that can keep people out of heaven." Our perfect heavenly Father doesn't want us to settle for merely knowing Bible stories and being able to give the right answers or checking spiritual boxes. He wants us to dive deep into pursuing that love relationship that makes you glow from the inside out and makes people wonder what's different about your reactions to circumstances. There is joy that you seem to have even carrying out the mundane tasks of life. **John 8:12** describes how Jesus is "the light of the world" and how *when we follow Him*, His light shines in and through us. A mediocre head knowledge of Christ doesn't contain the vibrancy of an on-fire heart for God. **Jeremiah 29:13** says we will seek Him and find Him when we seek Him with all of our heart. This is what a heart that has been captivated by Jesus does. It's not holding back. It's fully engaged, fully present, and receiving the all-consuming, unconditional love He has for you.

> "Jesus spoke to the people once more and said, 'I am the light of the world. If you follow me, you won't have to walk in darkness, because you will have the light that leads to life.'" — John 8:12

> If you look for me wholeheartedly, you will find me. — Jeremiah 29:13

> Either way, Christ's love controls us. Since we believe that Christ died for all, we also believe that we have all died to our old life. He died for everyone so that those who receive his new life will no longer live for themselves. Instead, they will live for Christ, who died and was raised for them. — 2 Corinthians 5:14-15

February 25

WE LIVE IN A TIME WHEN DISTRACTIONS ARE EVERYWHERE. Consider being in a waiting room at the doctor's office or in the sauna at the gym where people used to actually have organic conversations and smile at one another, inviting interaction. These days our faces are in our phones, and lots of times our minds are captivated by things that have nothing to do with us. More than ever we need to learn to reset and refocus our minds and hearts to what is life-giving and eternal (**Philippians 4:8**).

Ask yourself, "What do I spend the majority of time thinking about?" Consider if you need to shift the meditations of your heart to something deeper than meaningless curiosity or temporal entertainment (**Ephesians 5:11**). Take some time this week to be intentional about training your mind. We can control what we think about and learn to focus more on ways to join with God in His activity in and around us. **John 5:19–20** reminds us God is always working. *Pray daily* this week that God would give you spiritual eyes to see divine happenings and let the meditations of your heart lead you back to Him.

> *And now, dear brothers and sisters, one final thing. Fix your thoughts on what is true, and honorable, and right, and pure, and lovely, and admirable. Think about things that are excellent and worthy of praise.* — Philippians 4:8

> *Take no part in the worthless deeds of evil and darkness; instead, expose them.*
> *— Ephesians 5:11*

> *"So Jesus explained, 'I tell you the truth, the Son can do nothing by himself. He does only what he sees the Father doing. Whatever the Father does, the Son also does. For the Father loves the Son and shows him everything he is doing. In fact, the Father will show him how to do even greater works than healing this man. Then you will truly be astonished.'"* — John 5:19-20

> *Therefore, holy brothers and sisters, who share in the heavenly calling, fix your thoughts on Jesus, whom we acknowledge as our apostle and high priest.*
> *— Hebrews 3:1 (NIV)*

February 26

ONE OF THE MOST CONSISTENT PRAYERS I PRAY FOR MY CHILDREN is that they would choose wisely when it comes to their time and the people with whom they surround themselves. The reality is that our choices, good or bad, have a ripple effect and are always about more than us or what seems to be the matter at hand. We live in a spiritual atmosphere where all we see is the tip of the iceberg; meanwhile, God is perpetually up to more.

Proverbs 18:15 says "the heart of the discerning acquires knowledge, for the ears of the wise seek it out." We have the privilege to continually petition God for discernment and wisdom in all of our choices. There is no area of our lives that is not under His provision and protection. God desires to be invited into all we are doing now and certainly into the future plans we dream . Our ultimate goal for the choices and plans we make is that they are in alignment with His timing and direction for our lives. *The One who created us should be the One that leads the way.*

> Intelligent people are always ready to learn. Their ears are open for knowledge.
> — Proverbs 18:15

> For those who are led by the Spirit of God are the children of God.
> — Romans 8:14

How powerful is it that merely seeking to be in the presence of God can reorient our minds. The truth is that our minds and hearts both can be battlefields where war is waged daily. We can actually become desensitized to the internal conflict and accept it as normal. God's desire is that our hearts and minds remain stable, calm, and secure in the midst of uncertainties and trials. **Psalm 46:1** encourages us that God is our refuge, an ever-present help in trouble. It should give us great assurance to know we can come to Jesus anytime, anywhere, with anything, and His ears are open to our circumstances. Our hope does not lie in the changing of our situation but in knowing He will help us navigate through (**John 16:33**). Some seasons of our lives feel like emotional roller coasters, but we can *have Holy Spirit confidence* during the instability. What a miraculous gift that we never face anything alone.

> God is our refuge and strength, always ready to help in times of trouble.
> — Psalm 46:1

> I have told you all this so that you may have peace in me. Here on earth you will have many trials and sorrows. But take heart, because I have overcome the world. — John 16:33

> The Sovereign Lord is my strength; he makes my feet like the feet of a deer, he enables me to tread on the heights. — Habakkuk 3:19 (NIV)

THE ALMIGHTY GOD OF THE UNIVERSE IS A GOD OF RESTORATION. He undeniably longs for all of creation to be restored to fellowship with Him. **2 Corinthians 5:18–20** encourages us that, through Christ, God made a way for that restoration to take place. While we still have breath in our lungs, it is never too late to turn back to God. Our salvation is the ultimate goal. Although there is brokenness and pain this side of heaven, God desires to heal you now for your good and the good of those who may be touched by your story. **Psalm 34:18** says the Lord is close to the brokenhearted and heals their wounds. Very often something will surface that God wants to navigate us through and we will once again run from it, stuffing it down only for it to resurface later. We do have to make the decision to do the heart work to heal those wounds. God is patient and kind, but He is persistent and does not want us weighed down by our past. *Pray and ask God* to reveal the pockets of your heart that need His healing and let Him bring joy to your journey.

> "And all of this is a gift from God, who brought us back to himself through Christ. And God has given us this task of reconciling people to him. For God was in Christ, reconciling the world to himself, no longer counting people's sins against them. And he gave us this wonderful message of reconciliation. So we are Christ's ambassadors; God is making his appeal through us. We speak for Christ when we plead, 'Come back to God!'" — 2 Corinthians 5:18-20

> The Lord is close to the brokenhearted; he rescues those whose spirits are crushed. —Psalm 34:18

> Restore to me the joy or your salvation and grant me a willing spirit, to sustain me.— Psalm 51:12 (NIV)

February 29

How do you tend to respond when someone says God laid something on their heart, or when a friend tells you they feel the Holy Spirit is leading them in a certain direction? The way our hearts respond to these statements reveals a lot about if we believe God is speaking to His children. Some believe God only speaks to "super spiritual" people, but the reality about Jesus is He always meets us where we are, and sometimes He pursues and speaks to us before we have even cultivated a love relationship with Him.

The writer of **Psalm 143:10** prays, "Teach me to do your will, for you are my God; your Spirit is good. Lead me in the land of uprightness." One of the most repeated questions is, "What is God's will for my life?" The answer is that you'd be in an intimate, dependent, thriving relationship with Him. **Ephesians 1:11** declares we have "an inheritance [and are] predestined according to the purpose of Him who works all things according to the counsel of His will." We can *stand firm on the promise that* as we abide in Him, He will delight in communicating with us thus revealing how to step by step live out His will for our lives.

> *Teach me to do your will, for you are my God. May your gracious Spirit lead me forward on a firm footing.* — Psalm 143:10

> *Furthermore, because we are united with Christ, we have received an inheritance from God, for he chose us in advance, and he makes everything work out according to his plan.*
> — Ephesians 1:11

> *Your kingdom come, your will be done, on earth as it is in heaven.*
> — Matthew 6:10 (NIV)

March 1

Our thought life is such a determining factor in our actions, feelings, and (possibly most importantly) our perspective. Think how your perspective on a situation can turn it from devastating to manageable in a matter of minutes even when nothing circumstantial has changed. We may ask ourselves: In the grand scheme of things, does this matter (**2 Corinthians 4:17**)?

Our thought life is not something to be managed as much as it is something to cultivate. The more we run towards Jesus and godly pursuits, the healthier our thought life will be as a result of a healthy heart. Our thoughts reveal areas in our hearts that are in need of a fresh touch from God. This should not bring shame or dread, but rather hope and expectation for God to move and pour His living water on a dry spot. Our thought life fuels our perspective, and our thoughts flow from our hearts. Thank goodness *we serve a God* who continually transforms all of the above.

> *For our present troubles are small and won't last very long. Yet they produce for us a glory that vastly outweighs them and will last forever!*
> — 2 Corinthians 4:17

> *Being confident of this, that he who began a good work in you will carry it on to completion until the day of Christ Jesus.* — Philippians 1:6 (NIV)

March 2

Many times people long to experience an intimate relationship with God, but it seems as if there is a wall that is impossible to break through. The Lord welcomes us coming to Him in these moments, being honest and vulnerable with him about this sense of disconnect. The Scriptures urge us to get rid of hindrances and obstacles that keep us from being totally surrendered to the Lord (**Hebrews 12:13**).

A good question to bring to God is: What might be blocking my sense of nearness to You, or what area am I not bringing under Your authority? We can know these heartfelt pleas delight the Lord because He wants us to experience the overflowing fullness of God (**Ephesians 3:19**). It should warm our hearts to know our loving heavenly Father wants no wedge between us. Whatever He may bring to our attention that might be hindering us is only for *our good and His glory*. When God desires to remove anything, He always replaces that void with something so much better.

> *Mark out a straight path for your feet so that those who are weak and lame will not fall but become strong.* — Hebrews 12:13

> *May you experience the love of Christ, though it is too great to understand fully. Then you will be made complete with all the fullness of life and power that comes from God.* — Ephesians 3:19

> *And my God will meet all your needs according to the riches of His glory in Christ Jesus.* — Philippians 4:19 (NIV)

 *March 3*

One of the most sought after characteristics of a Christ follower is joy. People are drawn to it. They are curious about it. And whether they realize it or not, they want it. When someone has the light of Christ and joy in the midst of the mundane or suffering, it is truly beautiful and captivating to others. Scriptures remind us that when we long for and pursue righteousness, we will be satisfied (**Matthew 5:6**). We can know this is true not only because it is written in the Word of God, but when righteousness is your focus, you find eternal joy that never runs dry (**Isaiah 58:11**).

Be intentional this week in shining your light of joy from the inside out. Try some new colorful fruits or vegetables to fuel you, and enjoy God's creation outdoors. Seek out a new serving opportunity, or cut something out of your schedule if you are over-committed and have no margin for down time. *Try and seek God* on what you need. He will show you.

> *God blesses those who hunger and thirst for justice, for they will be satisfied.*
> *— Matthew 5:6*

> *The Lord will guide you continually, giving you water when you are dry and restoring your strength. You will be like a well-watered garden, like an ever-flowing spring. — Isaiah 58:11*

March 4

THERE IS AN OLD SAYING THAT THE BEST WAY TO HELP YOURSELF IS to help someone else. While there can be a couple of drawbacks to this school of thought, there is also a lot of truth. We don't want serving to be an excuse to not do heart work on ourselves, but the reality is that, as we minister to others, the Holy Spirit teaches us truths we need as well (**2 Corinthians 1:4–6**).

We can love, encourage, and support others the same way God himself has worked in our lives. When we are serving others, we are actively seeking to be on mission with God, which helps us not fall into the trap of a self-focused faith and keeps our focus on eternal things. Every so often we should *step out in roles of serving* that are out of our comfort zone. It's a great way to learn more about ourselves and others while helping us not get stagnant, not to mention keeping us humble. **John 15:16** encourages us to bear fruit, and being fruitful is medicine for our soul.

> He comforts us in all our troubles so that we can comfort others. When they are troubled, we will be able to give them the same comfort God has given us. For the more we suffer for Christ, the more God will shower us with his comfort through Christ. Even when we are weighed down with troubles, it is for your comfort and salvation! For when we ourselves are comforted, we will certainly comfort you. Then you can patiently endure the same things we suffer. — 2 Corinthians 1:4-6

> You didn't choose me. I chose you. I appointed you to go and produce lasting fruit, so that the Father will give you whatever you ask for, using my name. — John 15:16

March 5

THERE IS A POPULAR WORSHIP SONG THAT USES THE PHRASE, "Crucify my flesh with yours that my new life will be secure." The beautiful reality communicated through these lyrics is that allowing Jesus to be Lord of our life is continually denying our flesh and following the leadership of the Holy Spirit. **Galatians 2:20** reminds us our new life in Christ is not about us but Christ in us. Our human nature is so resistant to the idea of not getting our own way that we spend seasons running from God and chasing dreams that haven't included seeking His divine guidance. We seek security from circumstances and people instead of embracing the reality that freedom and security are under the umbrella of God's will for us, which is both where joy is found and for our good. *When we welcome Jesus* in our hearts, we receive new birth and new hope, satisfaction guaranteed.

> *My old self has been crucified with Christ. It is no longer I who live, but Christ lives in me. So I live in this earthly body by trusting in the Son of God, who loved me and gave himself for me.* — Galatians 2:20

> *Praise be to the God and Father of our Lord Jesus Christ! In his great mercy he has given us new birth into a living hope through the resurrection of Jesus Christ from the dead.* — 1 Peter 1:3 (NIV)

March 6

LISTENING TO A FRIEND'S PERSONAL TESTIMONY AND GOD'S STORY through her life brought spiritual markers to mind. Spiritual markers are reminders of how God has worked in and through our unique stories and help us recall His faithfulness (**Psalm 36:5**). Reflecting on these seasons can motivate us to continue stepping out in faith, confident that the Lord has our back and is working behind the scenes for our best interest. **John 5:1** encourages us that He is always at work, giving us inspiration towards His will and equipping His people in Kingdom work. Another beautiful reason to recognize moves of God that we experience is it gives fresh energy to share our excitement with others. I've heard people say the world needs less sermons and more stories to draw others to Christ. While I love a good sermon or teaching moment, there is no denying the Holy Spirit's power *when a person shares how God has transformed their heart.*

> Your unfailing love, O Lord, is as vast as the heavens; your faithfulness reaches beyond the clouds. — Psalm 36:5

> The Lord your God will circumcise your hearts and the hearts of your descendants, so that you may love him with all your heart and with all your soul, and live.
> — Deuteronomy 30:6 (NIV)

March 7

ENGAGING IN INTIMATE, VULNERABLE DIALOGUE WITH GOD is the lifeline of our faith. Learning to hear from our heavenly Father and recognizing the Spirit's promptings in our lives comes with maturity and experiences of sharing life with Jesus. Hearing God's voice must begin with belief that He speaks. God urges His followers to *seek His voice* (Matthew 7:7–8). There are many reasons He longs for this two-way communication with us. Some include relationship building, direction, divine intervention, and teaching us to grow in discernment (**Hebrews 5:14**). Living and walking by faith comes by seeking and following the Lord step by step, welcoming His guidance daily. Oftentimes we may feel stagnant or stuck spiritually because we have neglected to act on the last instruction God asked of us. Step-by-step obedience is necessary for our continued growth and living out the purpose and plans God will bring to fruition in our lives.

> *Keep on asking, and you will receive what you ask for. Keep on seeking, and you will find. Keep on knocking, and the door will be opened to you. For everyone who asks, receives. Everyone who seeks, finds. And to everyone who knocks, the door will be opened.* — Matthew 7:7-8

> *Solid food is for those who are mature, who through training have the skill to recognize the difference between right and wrong.* — Hebrews 5:14

> *And without faith it is impossible to please God, because anyone who comes to him must believe that he exists and that he rewards those who earnestly seek him.* — Hebrews 11:6 (NIV)

March 8

HAVE YOU EVER DECIDED ON A NEW CAR OR A NEW haircut and then suddenly that's all you see? The truth is, once we get something we desire on our brain, our eyes are drawn to it. The same thing happens in our yearning to witness evidence of God's creation and activity (**Proverbs 8:17**). Simply *meditating on the goodness of God* can remind us that we worship a personal God who longs to reveal Himself to us if we would seek to notice Him. Since the Lord understands us so perfectly, He knows exactly what or who to place in our path to reveal Himself (**1 Corinthians 2:10**).

Many times I will pray, "Lord, please reveal yourself to me." Yesterday I prayed this prayer and, on an evening walk, I looked down on two small sticks that made a cross. They even resembled nails. My heart smiled at the gracious love poured out in that moment, and in eternity.

> *I love all who love me. Those who search will surely find me.*
> *— Proverbs 8:17*

> *But it was to us that God revealed these things by his Spirit. For his Spirit searches out everything and shows us God's deep secrets. — 1 Corinthians 2:10*

> *And walk in the way of love, just as Christ loved us and gave himself up for us as a fragrant offering and sacrifice to God.*
> *— Ephesians 5:2 (NIV)*

March 9

ONE OF SATAN'S MOST COMMON STRATEGIES TO DERAIL SPIRITUAL GROWTH is isolation. There are several reasons people give to avoid community: being introverted, being ashamed of a past or present circumstance, feeling like it's pointless, fearing vulnerability, or not wanting to be involved in the mess of others' lives. We are instructed by Scripture to share one another's burdens; be encouraging, loving, and strengthening each other's faith. Stepping out of our comfort zone and pushing past our "natural bents" to be part of community is necessary (**Galatians 6:2**). We increase one another's zeal toward Christ and Kingdom work as we lean on our brothers and sisters of faith and on God (**Proverbs 27:17**). We have mastered the art of procrastination, making excuses for why it's not a good time to commit. It is true that some communities may not be a good fit, but as *we seek God and respond,* He will lead us to the right people.

> *Share each other's burdens, and in this way obey the law of Christ.*
> *— Galatians 6:2*

> *As iron sharpens iron, so a friend sharpens a friend. — Proverbs 27:17*

March 10

A RICH, VIBRANT RELATIONSHIP WITH JESUS IS the result of someone who has fallen in love with our Lord and Savior, as opposed to someone who has learned to follow a set of guidelines. The Christian life is so much more about becoming than doing. When we are captivated by the person of Christ, pleasing Him with our lives will follow (**1 John 5:3**). If we find ourselves struggling to be obedient, we may need to nurture our end of the love relationship. If there is a desire to go deeper with God, we may need to build a new discipline into our spiritual habits. This may look like asking God daily to help you be a fruit-bearing disciple and servant, but praising Him that, first and foremost, you are His child (**Psalm 139:13–14**). Saying these truths out loud can strengthen your bond with Him and remind you of our spiritual inheritance as His children. Creatively combine physical and spiritual training this week by setting aside extra time daily to stretch your body. *Use these quiet moments to reflect* on how completely and perfectly your heavenly father loves you.

> *Loving God means keeping his commandments, and his commandments are not burdensome.* — 1 John 5:3

> *You made all the delicate, inner parts of my body and knit me together in my mother's womb. Thank you for making me so wonderfully complex! Your workmanship is marvelous-how well I know it.* — Psalm 139:13–14

> *See what great love the Father has lavished on us, that we should be called children of God! And that is what we are! The reason the world does not know us is that it did not know him.* — 1 John 3:1 (NIV)

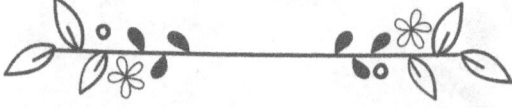

March 11

THE IDEA OF CONFESSION IS NOT USUALLY SOMETHING any of us get excited about, but the freedom that follows is undeniable (**1 John 1:9**). There is nothing we can do or mess we can get into that is too much for God, and confession to Him is the first step towards vulnerability and repentance. God is already fully aware of our bad choices, but, more importantly, He is more aware than we are of the deeper issues in our hearts that motivate those choices. As we acknowledge our predicaments to God and others, change and healing can begin (**Jeremiah 15:19**). We can rejoice in the truth that our God is a God of restoration, and that it's the Holy Spirit who works in and through us towards repentance. *We are never on our own.* The most beautiful thing about confession is that it follows conviction, which is an indication of the Spirit working in our hearts, giving us the desire to please God with our lives and becoming more of who God has called us to be.

> *But if we confess our sins to him, he is faithful and just to forgive us our sins and to cleanse us from all wickedness.* — 1 John 1:9

> *"This is how the Lord responds: 'If you return to me, I will restore you so you can continue to serve me. If you speak good words rather than worthless ones, you will be my spokesman. You must influence them do not let them influence you!'"* — Jeremiah 15:19

> *For it is God who works in you to will and to act in order to fulfill his good purpose.* — Philippians 2:13 (NIV)

March 12

WE ARE NEVER MORE OF A BLESSING TO OTHERS THAN WHEN we are steadfast in our own faith, abiding in Jesus. Oftentimes the strength and stability of a Christ-centered life is what draws others in and makes them feel safe. Allowing the love of our heavenly Father to flow in and through us is an honor, and we should look out for divine opportunities to do so (**1 John 4:16**).

As we ourselves are abiding in God's love, we receive supernatural sensitivities to those around us. Praying prior to entering a large gathering—asking God to intentionally lead you towards people and conversations—can help us have meaningful interactions with others. There is both a mystery and awe connected with the reality of being conduits of God's tender awareness of His children and what they are facing. We should *embrace the existence of the spiritual realm* around us and the stories God is writing in our midst.

> We know how much God loves us, and we have put our trust in his love. God is love, and all who live in love live in God, and God lives in them. — 1 John 4:16

> "In his defense Jesus said to them, 'My Father is always at his work to this very day, and I too am working.'" — John 5:17 (NIV)

> "Jesus replied, 'You do not realize now what I am doing, but later you will understand.'" — John 13:7 (NIV)

> For our light and momentary troubles are achieving for us an eternal glory that far outweighs them all. So we fix our eyes not on what is seen, but on what is unseen, since what is seen is temporary, but what is unseen is eternal.
> — 2 Corinthians 4:17-18 (NIV)

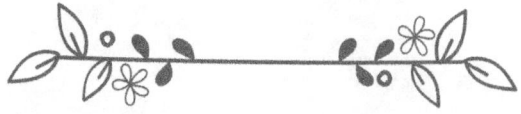

March 13

So often in prayer I have said, "Thank you, Jesus, for rescuing me from myself." When I think back to seasons of uncertainty (void the direction of God) I remember the instability I experienced. I feel blessed to recall the exact time and place the Spirit of God whispered to my heart, "I have something different for you" (**Psalm 30:1–3**). I remain in awe of how God is pursuing our hearts before we even realize we need a Savior. Embracing the idea that our heavenly Father chases us down and uniquely draws us to Himself in His perfect timing is never less than miraculous. His power to save, transform, and engage in a lifelong personal relationship with us should be enough to make us celebrate every day (**2 Corinthians 5:18–20**). I love the idea that God meets us where we are but loves us too much to leave us there. When *we are walking with God*, we are growing and being refined day by day. Any uncertainty can be met with hope and the confidence that God knows what He is doing and that our lives are safe in His hands.

> *I will exalt you, Lord, for you rescued me. You refused to let my enemies triumph over me. O Lord my God, I cried to you for help, and you restored my health. You brought me up from the grave, O Lord. You kept me from falling into the pit of death. — Psalm 30:1-3*

> *And all of this is a gift from God, who brought us back to himself through Christ. And God has given us this task of reconciling people to him. For God was in Christ, reconciling the world to himself, no longer counting people's sins against them. And he gave us this wonderful message of reconciliation. So we are Christ's ambassadors; God is making his appeal through us. We speak for Christ when we plead, 'Come back to God!' — 2 Corinthians 5:18-20*

> *I cling to you; your right hand upholds me. — Psalm 63:8 (NIV)*

March 14

Our God is the ultimate healer. He is a God of restoration, regeneration, and renewal. These attributes allow us to live with hope, joy, and freedom, as well as strength from the Holy Spirit to navigate life (**1 Peter 5:10**). We know there will be trouble and suffering this side of heaven, but we can rest in the truth that nothing is too hard for God and that he creates beauty from ashes (**Isaiah 61:3**). We should marvel at the reality that no hardship we experience will be wasted. The pockets of pain we experience make the light of Christ shine brighter as he heals and brings back to life places that were desolate. There is joy in the process of regeneration as new energy is found in weariness. There is great security and freedom in knowing we face nothing alone. We can live fully *un-abandoned*, *answering the call to serve Christ* and others all because of the cross and the redeeming love of God.

> *In his kindness God called you to share in his eternal glory by means of Christ Jesus. So after you have suffered a little while, he will restore, support, and strengthen you, and he will place you on a firm foundation.* — 1 Peter 5:10

> *To all who mourn in Israel, he will give a crown of beauty for ashes, a joyous blessing instead of mourning, festive praise instead of despair. In their righteousness, they will be like great oaks that the Lord has planted for his own glory.*
> *— Isaiah 61:3*

> *Israel, put your hope in the Lord, for with the Lord is unfailing love and with him is full redemption.* — Psalm 130:7

March 15

No matter where we are in our personal relationship with God, how we are trusting Him is always an area to examine. How often do people say, "You just need to trust God"? What does that really look like and how do we get to that level of security and reliance on Him? While there is no one-size-fits-all answer, there are absolute truths about the character of God that deem Him trustworthy (**Psalm 145:13**). God is all-knowing, all-powerful, and the only person in this world that is all good all the time (**Job 12:13**). As we grow in our realization of God's character, we can dismantle the unrealistic expectations we put on anything else. God desires to give us light for our path daily. *Seeking His guidance* encourages us towards the lifestyle of dependence we all need but seldom experience due to our tendency towards self sufficiency. Every day is a new opportunity to build a lifestyle of trust. Take some time and examine areas where you are not trusting God. May we intentionally choose to surrender these issues daily, and allow His peace to fill our hearts as we learn to rest in His presence and provision.

> *For your kingdom is an everlasting kingdom. You rule throughout all generations. The Lord always keeps his promises; he is gracious in all he does.*
> *— Psalm 145:13*

> *But true wisdom and power are found in God; counsel and understanding are his.*
> *— Job 12:13*

> *Let the morning bring me word of your unfailing love, for I have put my trust in you. Show me the way I should go, for to you I entrust my life.*
> *— Psalm 143:8 (NIV)*

March 16

OPPORTUNITIES TO SHARE HOW GOD HAS MOVED IN YOUR LIFE with others is a double blessing. God's stories always are an encouragement for the hearer, and each time we share is a chance to notice something we may have overlooked in the past, much like seeing a movie multiple times. Proclaiming the goodness of God in our lives is also a great way to stay spiritually motivated and expectant (**Luke 8:39**). Giving God glory helps us have the attitude of gratitude we need to be joyful and allow the light of Christ to shine in and through us (**Matthew 5:16**). Recalling the ways God has helped us navigate through difficult seasons serves as a hope to others that He will be present with them the same way. The Lord always goes before us, and there are people *the Holy Spirit will prompt you* to engage and share how God has moved in your life. Your God story could serve as an encouragement towards perseverance and hope for another.

> "'No, go back to your family, and tell them everything God has done for you.' So he went all through the town proclaiming the great things Jesus had done for him." — Luke 8:39

> In the same way, let your good deeds shine out for all to see so that everyone will praise your heavenly Father. — Matthew 5:16

> But in your hearts revere Christ as Lord. Always be prepared to give an answer to everyone who asks you to give the reason for the hope that you have. But do this with gentleness and respect. — 1 Peter 3:15 (NIV)

March 17

Exploring and becoming captivated by the Word of God is essential to our spiritual health. Embracing the truth that Scripture is God-breathed—that the pages are alive with God's love, wisdom, truth, and direction—is necessary and a place for us to marinate (**Matthew 4:4**). The Bible is our secret weapon we can hold in our hearts to stand against the cultural lies, shame, temptation, or even our own emotions. We need to develop the habit of clinging to the scriptures during all seasons of suffering and joy. We even begin to crave the stability and life-giving messages we receive as the Holy Spirit illuminates the words. Determine to read through a new book of the Bible this week. It may take a while, but as the sun shines longer in the spring you can add an evening walk and listen, meditating on the words being spoken. *Allow the scriptures to do* what they were intended for, breathing life and whispering God's truth to your heart.

> "But Jesus told him, 'No! The Scriptures say, "People do not live by bread alone, but by every word that comes from the mouth of God."'" — Matthew 4:4

> I have hidden your word in my heart that I might not sin against you.
> — Psalm 119:11

> Keep this Book of the Law always on your lips; meditate on it day and night, so that you may be careful to do everything written in it. Then you will be prosperous and successful. — Joshua 1:8

March 18

REMAINING IN AWE AND ADORATION OF THE SACRIFICIAL LOVE Jesus demonstrated at the cross can greatly impact our hearts. The crucifixion and resurrection of Christ is the backbone of our faith and our source of never-ending hope (**John 11:25–26**). Jesus overcoming the grave is the most spectacular picture of what a powerful God we serve and is a fact that sets Christianity apart from other beliefs (**Romans 1:16**). As we choose to walk in the victory and resurrection power available through Christ, we can rise above circumstances and situations that normally would wreak havoc on our lives. Oftentimes I will say out loud, "Father, I can do this in Your power, not my own."

Because of the cross, we can also experience authentic peace, joy, and restoration even while parts of our hearts remain under construction this on side of heaven (**Psalm 29:11**). The love, power, and hope of the cross should cushion our hearts and stay in the forefront of our minds. What great proof of God's amazing love.

> *"Jesus told her, 'I am the resurrection and the life. Anyone who believes in me will live, even after dying. Everyone who lives in me and believes in me will never ever die. Do you believe this, Martha?'" — John 11:25-26*

> *For I am not ashamed of this Good News about Christ. It is the power of God at work, saving everyone who believes-the Jew first and also the Gentile.*
> *— Romans 1:16*

> *The Lord gives his people strength. The Lord blesses them with peace. — Psalm 29:11*

> *For if, while we were God's enemies, we were reconciled to him through the death of his Son, how much more, having been reconciled, shall we be saved through his life!— Romans 5:10 (NIV)*

March 19

Our love relationship with the Lord is the most vital part of our spiritual health. In addition, our human connections are essential (**Ecclesiastes 4:9–10**). As we examine our friendships, we should consider the dynamics of those relationships and make sure there is some variety. For example, are there people in your life you feel confident you can turn to for a wise perspective? Are there people you are prayerfully attempting to influence towards Christ? Do you have mutual friendships where you are like-minded and can *love, encourage, and support each other* in positive ways (**Proverbs 17:17**)? Sometimes we can get comfortable in certain types of camaraderie at the expense of not engaging in other kinds of life-giving relationships. God lovingly gave us the gift of others in our lives, and He uses the body of Christ to inspire, admonish, and authentically share life. He will surround you with people who will be the hands and feet of Jesus as well as providing the opportunity for you to be the same for them.

> *Two people are better off than one, for they can help each other succeed. If one person falls, the other can reach out and help. But someone who falls alone is in real trouble.*
> — Ecclesiastes 4:9-10

> *A friend is always loyal, and a brother is born to help in time of need.*
> — Proverbs 17:17

> *Now you are the body of Christ, and each one of you is a part of it.*
> — 1 Corinthians 12:27 (NIV)

March 20

People often ask the question, "If God already knows, why do I need to tell Him?" The truth is, He does already know, but as we share our situation out loud, we are inviting His presence into our heart and thought processes regarding the issues we face. I often say one of the most beautiful characteristics of God is that He knows our hearts better than we do, and not only can He show us areas of concern, but He graciously shows us the way out (**Psalm 139:23–24**). As we reach out to Him with our pain, He is simultaneously at work in us, opening our eyes and softening our hearts to His perspective and direction (**Ephesians 1:16–18**). Much like our sharing with a friend, the more vulnerable we are, the deeper and more transparent the relationship becomes. *The more we share,* the more comfortable it becomes as this continual communication with our heavenly Father actually turns into a lifestyle. Jesus is the most trustworthy and wise companion you will ever have, and He's always listening.

> *Search me, O God, and know my heart; test me and know my anxious thoughts. Point out anything in me that offends you, and lead me along the path of everlasting life.* — Psalm 139:23–24

> *I pray for you constantly, asking God, the glorious Father of our Lord Jesus Christ, to give you spiritual wisdom and insight so that you might grow in your knowledge of God. I pray that your hearts will be flooded with light so that you can understand the confident hope he has given to those he called—his holy people who are his rich and glorious inheritance.* — Ephesians 1:16–18 (NIV)

> *Before they call I will answer; while they are still speaking I will hear.* — Isaiah 65:24

March 21

THIS MORNING AS I BEGAN TO GET READY, I went to turn on the TV for background noise and felt the prompting of the Holy Spirit to embrace the silence. The quietness brought revelation and encouragement for the conversations God knew were coming my way in the hours ahead (**Hebrews 13:21**). We all love listening to music, audio books, or podcasts in the car, but so often the drive time can be the perfect opportunity to focus on the presence of Jesus and hear that still, quiet voice we so desire. The world persistently clamors for our attention and promotes busyness as being productive. Oftentimes the most productive choice would be taking time to seek, listen, and wait on God for direction (**Psalm 37:7**). Learning to live this type of dependent lifestyle will not feel natural at first, but receiving the peace it can bring will leave you desiring more (**Philippians 4:6–7**). There is nothing better than the pure tranquility of a heart *being sensitive and attentive* to the Holy Spirit's fellowship.

> May he equip you with all you need for doing his will. May he produce in you, through the power of Jesus Christ, every good thing that is pleasing to him. All glory to him forever and ever! Amen. — Hebrews 13:21

> Be still in the presence of the Lord, and wait patiently for him to act. Don't worry about evil people who prosper or fret about their wicked schemes. — Psalm 37:7

> Don't worry about anything; instead, pray about everything. Tell God what you need, and thank him for all he has done. Then you will experience God's peace, which exceeds anything we can understand. His peace will guard your hearts and minds as you live in Christ Jesus. — Philippians 4:6–7

> Submit to God and be at peace with him; in this way prosperity will come to you. — Job 22:21 (NIV)

March 22

How many times have you heard somebody say, "I didn't mean for it to go this far"? These words probably resonate with all of us at one time or another and usually on the tail end of some sort of compromise on our part. We all have areas in our lives that call for more self-control, areas of sin patterns and struggles. The good news is when we accept the Lordship of Christ in our hearts, there is the indwelling of the Holy Spirit that creates caution before danger **(1 Thessalonians 4:8)**. We will oftentimes sense hesitancy when areas of compromise attempt to capture our imagination **(2 Corinthians 10:5)**. Praying to be sensitive to the Holy Spirit's caution light makes it more difficult to ignore in the heat of the moment. Every time we heed these warnings in obedience, we build spiritual muscle. *Nurturing our love relationship* with Christ is the most powerful way to stand against temptation and compromise. Allowing Christ to shine brightly in your soul crowds out the darkness.

> Therefore, anyone who refuses to live by these rules is not disobeying human teaching but is rejecting God, who gives his Holy Spirit to you.
> — 1 Thessalonians 4:8

> We destroy every proud obstacle that keeps people from knowing God. We capture their rebellious thoughts and teach them to obey Christ. — 2 Corinthians 10:5

> You, dear children, are from God and have overcome them, because the one who is in us is greater than the one who is in the world. — 1 John 4:4 (NIV)

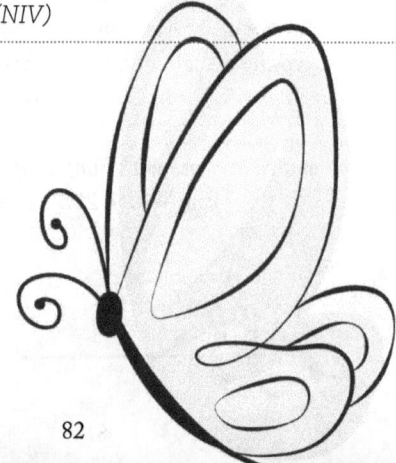

March 23

ALL TOO OFTEN, EMOTIONAL DISTRESS ARISES FROM our past or future. We can experience shame from our past as well as anxiety about the future. However, living a lifestyle of dependence on God means being fully present and attentive to what is happening right now. While wrestling through past struggles (i.e., harms by us or harms to us) is part of the equation, the more important reality is that God is able to heal all that pain, bringing victory and restoration (**Isaiah 43:18–19**). As we move forward in repentance and recovery, the healing power of Christ is on full display. Anxiety over the future can keep us paralyzed with fear to the point of not moving forward in any direction. *Meditating on the promises* in Scripture regarding our future can rewire our thought life away from fear and toward holy expectation (**Philippians 1:6, Proverbs 19:21-22, 2 Corinthians 4:17**). Another way to look at being present with God is arguably one of the most sought after characteristics of a Christian, which is to abide in Him. Cultivating a rhythm of abiding in Christ is foundational to experiencing joy and peace.

> *But forget all that—it is nothing compared to what I am going to do. For I am about to do something new. See, I have already begun! Do you not see it? I will make a pathway through the wilderness. I will create rivers in the dry wasteland.* — Isaiah 43:18-19

> *And I am certain that God, who began the good work within you, will continue his work until it is finally finished on the day when Christ Jesus returns.* — Philippians 1:6

> *You can make many plans, but the Lord's purpose will prevail. Loyalty makes a person attractive. It is better to be poor than dishonest.* — Proverbs 19:21-22

> *For our present troubles are small and won't last very long. Yet they produce for us a glory that vastly outweighs them and will last forever!* — 2 Corinthians 4:17

> *"To the Jews who had believed him, Jesus said, 'If you hold to my teaching, you are really my disciples. Then you will know the truth, and the truth will set you free.'"* — John 8:31-32 (NIV)

March 24

THE BEGINNING OF HOLY WEEK IS REFERRED TO AS PALM SUNDAY. The significance being the King of the Universe making His way to Jerusalem on a donkey is an example of humility and one of many illustrations of Jesus doing the opposite of what the religious leaders expected of the Messiah (**Matthew 23:5–7**). Jesus was not motivated by attention and fanfare. He didn't need to be because He had the power of our heavenly Father working in and through Him to attract people to Himself, not to be served but to serve (**Matthew 20:28**).

What would it look like to be intentional this week to align our hearts to Jesus in humility and loving others sacrificially? Prayerfully ask God to keep the cross with all its significance on the forefront of your mind, reflecting each day on the person of Jesus and the hope of eternity we have only because of Him. *Seek an opportunity to share the Gospel with someone, to tell them how a relationship with Jesus changes everything.* Prepare your heart to celebrate Him this week and worship Him with how you love.

> Everything they do is for show. On their arms they wear extra wide prayer boxes with Scripture verses inside, and they wear robes with extra long tassels. And they love to sit at the head table at banquets and in the seats of honor in the synagogues. They love to receive respectful greetings as they walk in the marketplaces, and to be called 'Rabbi.' — Matthew 23:5–7

> For even the Son of Man came not to be served but to serve others and to give his life as a ransom for many. — Matthew 20:28

> A new command I give you: Love one another. As I have loved you, so you must love one another. — John 13:34 (NIV)

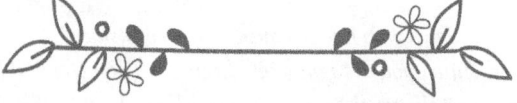

March 25

I ASKED A GROUP OF WOMEN TODAY, "What does Jesus being willing to go to the cross mean to you personally?" Our faith will only thrive when our relationship with Jesus is personal and something we cherish above all else (**Mark 12:30–31**). If your connection to God lacks the vibrancy you desire, there are always small adjustments you can try that make intimacy deeper as well as more satisfying. Embracing God's tender mercy to meet us where we are and knowing His willingness to be there for us as we move towards Him is a reality of His love (**Revelation 3:20**). *Contemplating what Christ endured* and the price He paid at Calvary lays the foundation for our gratitude and eagerness to live sacrificially for Him. So often I think to myself, "Look what He did for me!" It is an honor and privilege to live for Him (**Philippians 1:29**). God has prepared work for every one of us to accomplish from Him, by Him, and for Him. His strength and love will equip us along the way as His face continues to shine upon us.

> 'And you must love the Lord your God with all your heart, all your soul, all your mind, and all your strength.' The second is equally important: 'Love your neighbor as yourself.' No other commandment is greater than these.
> — Mark 12:30–31

> Look! I stand at the door and knock. If you hear my voice and open the door, I will come in, and we will share a meal together as friends. — Revelation 3:20

> For you have been given not only the privilege of trusting in Christ but also the privilege of suffering for him. — Philippians 1:29

> The Lord bless you and keep you; the Lord make his face shine on you and be gracious to you; the Lord turn his face toward you and give you peace.
> — Numbers 6:24-26 (NIV)

# March 26

As I woke up this morning, I had the song on my heart "You Reign Above it All," and that powerful phrase will not leave my mind. Several people I care about were going through some very difficult, dark waters yesterday. So I am welcoming the assurance in my heart that He is indeed reigning over everything (**Psalm 103:19**). God has ultimate power over our universe and eternity forever, and that absolute truth should bring us great peace and security. As someone who has sought security in all the wrong places, knowing I am safe in my Savior's arms is especially delightful to me. The media and sometimes people do not hesitate to remind us of everything evil in our midst. So it is that much more important for us to remember the true narrative that our God reigns supreme. We have to cultivate that sweet spot in our spirits so that when negativity and doom seem so loud, the mighty roar of our King, the one and only God is louder. *Thank Him out loud* for the eternal hope as well as victory that sends darkness running in fear and defeat every time.

> *The Lord has made the heavens his throne; from there he rules over everything. — Psalm 103:19*

> *The Lord is my light and my salvation; whom shall I fear? The Lord is the stronghold of my life; of whom shall I be afraid? — Psalm 27:1 (NIV)*

March 27

A FRIEND WHO HAS STRUGGLED WITH LONELINESS IN THE PAST said the most beautiful words today over coffee: "I've come so far in my battle with loneliness that sometimes I want everyone to go away so I can just be with Jesus." Pursuing and nurturing that deep level of intimacy with the Lord can be the most fulfilling time we spend this side of heaven (**Mark 1:35**). Reflecting on how Jesus Himself went away to seek God, how much more do we in our frail human nature need to do the same? Time spent with the Lord refuels and equips us in every way. When we are spiritually energized, that energy overflows into our physical bodies and mental stamina (**1 Timothy 4:8**). Even in the midst of activities during the day, we can fellowship with God by *meditating on His Word* in our heart (**Psalm 1:1–2**). This is actually one of the best ways to feel connected to Him and stay in step with your Spirit instead of catering to the flesh. His presence with us is a gift we should embrace.

> *Before daybreak the next morning, Jesus got up and went out to an isolated place to pray.* — Mark 1:35

> *Physical training is good, but training for godliness is much better, promising benefits in this life and in the life to come.* — 1 Timothy 4:8

> *Oh, the joys of those who do not follow the advice of the wicked, or stand around with sinners, or join in with mockers. But they delight in the law of the Lord, meditating on it day and night.* — Psalm 1:1-2

> *Teach these new disciples to obey all the commands I have given you. And be sure of this: I am with you always, even to the end of the age.* — Matthew 28:20

March 28

IMAGINE WHAT IT WOULD HAVE BEEN LIKE TO HAVE A SEAT AT THE LAST SUPPER WITH JESUS. His heart was to prepare His disciples for the season ahead revealing critical areas where they should invest their energy. (**John 13:34–35, John 14:15–16**). He looked to His Father for continued direction and strength (**Ephesians 3:16–19**). The disciples were given the opportunity, much like we are today, to trust the God who sees ahead. I spent some time today with a young lady struggling with God's timetable in her life. This can be a challenge for all of us at one time or another but we can cling to the truth that He knows what's coming in the season ahead and He will give us all the direction we need at the right time, whether we understand it or not (**Proverbs 3:4–6**). Learning to *walk by faith* and not by sight may be one of the most challenging tasks this side of heaven, but how beautiful it is that we serve a God who sees ahead.

> "So now I am giving you a new commandment: Love each other. Just as I have loved you, you should love each other. Your love for one another will prove to the world that you are my disciples." — John 13:34–35

> If you love me, obey my commandments. And I will ask the Father, and he will give you another Advocate, who will never leave you. — John 14:15–16

> I pray that from his glorious, unlimited resources he will empower you with inner strength through his Spirit. Then Christ will make his home in your hearts as you trust in him. Your roots will grow down into God's love and keep you strong. And may you have the power to understand, as all God's people should, how wide, how long, how high, and how deep his love is. May you experience the love of Christ, though it is too great to understand fully. Then you will be made complete with all the fullness of life and power that comes from God.
> — Ephesians 3:16–19

> Then you will find favor with both God and people, and you will earn a good reputation. Trust in the Lord with all your heart; do not depend on your own understanding. Seek his will in all you do, and he will show you which path to take. — Proverbs 3:4–6

> "Let the morning bring me word of your unfailing love, for I have put my trust in you. Show me the way I should go, for to you I entrust my life." — Psalm 143:8 (NIV)

March 29

JESUS DID NOT ENDURE THE CROSS FOR US TO MANAGE SIN AND SHAME. The cross sets us free to live life abundantly and be confident that, when we accept Jesus as our Lord and Savior, we have a new life in Him (**Colossians 1:19–20**). Walking in resurrection power isn't trying to live better. It is being renewed day by day through the Scriptures and being obedient to the Holy Spirit's leading in our life. We no longer have to be in bondage, giving into the desires of our flesh (**Galatians 5:17**). Our flesh searches for cheap substitutes for true fulfillment that are temporary at best. Jesus chose to make the ultimate sacrifice for us to live out the purposes and plans God had in mind for us even before He shaped us in our mothers womb (**Jeremiah 1:5**). I love the imagery of Jesus seated at the right hand of the Father, illustrating resurrection power and life. I long for the day I get to *thank Him* face to face for all He has done and continues to do for all of humanity. We should never lose our wonder of the cross.

> "For God in all his fullness was pleased to live in Christ, and through him God reconciled everything to himself. He made peace with everything in heaven and on earth by means of Christ's blood on the cross." — Colossians 1:19-20

> The sinful nature wants to do evil, which is just the opposite of what the Spirit wants. And the Spirit gives us desires that are the opposite of what the sinful nature desires. These two forces are constantly fighting each other, so you are not free to carry out your good intentions. — Galatians 5:17

> I knew you before I formed you in your mother's womb. Before you were born I set you apart and appointed you as my prophet to the nations. — Jeremiah 1:5

> We do this by keeping our eyes on Jesus, the champion who initiates and perfects our faith. Because of the joy awaiting him, he endured the cross, disregarding its shame. Now he is seated in the place of honor beside God's throne. — Hebrews 12:2

March 30

HEART POSTURES, ATTITUDES, AND EVEN REACTIONS TO WORDS or circumstances have everything to do with perspective. The cross serves as the ultimate perspective shifter. So often we wonder why people have to endure hardships in this life, but meditating on what Jesus suffered can quickly reorient the way we navigate tragedy (**Isaiah 25:8**). We do have free will this side of heaven; therefore, we make choices that result in sin. In Christ we are forgiven, and the hope of eternity is our future. Embracing this precious gift of forgiveness and extending it to others enables us to live this new life in Christ marked by grace, love, and power (**Ephesians 1:7–8**). Christ followers should be vessels of inspiration for anyone we have the privilege to encounter. Our minds are training grounds, and the more we *intentionally fill our thought life* with the promises of our Father, the more our perspectives will be hopeful, confident, and come from a place of love, not fear—not because of who we are but only because of Christ in us.

> *He will swallow up death forever! The Sovereign Lord will wipe away all tears. He will remove forever all insults and mockery against his land and people. The Lord has spoken!* — Isaiah 25:8

> *He is so rich in kindness and grace that he purchased our freedom with the blood of his Son and forgave our sins. He has showered his kindness on us, along with all wisdom and understanding.*
> — Ephesians 1:7–8

> *"For God, who said, 'Let light shine out of darkness,' made his light shine in our hearts to give us the light of the knowledge of God's glory displayed in the face of Christ. But we have this treasure in jars of clay to show that this all-surpassing power is from God and not from us."* — 2 Corinthians 4:6-7 (NIV)

March 31

THE CELEBRATION OF EASTER SO OFTEN BRINGS THE RESURRECTION to life in our hearts. People will communicate "He is risen" with a spring in their step and joy on their face. The reality that Jesus overcame the grave brings with it a supernatural power that cannot be denied (**Romans 1:16**). Christ's restoration to life should fuel our zeal to rise up and challenge ourselves personally this season. What are some opportunities to grow spiritually, mentally, and physically you may have been putting on the back burner? Spring is a great, energetic time for new beginnings. Our spirits are renewed by the Word of God. Read and journal through a book of the Bible you have never studied before (**Philippians 4:8**). Are there habits or relationships in your life that the Lord has pressed in on? Commit to surrender and be obedient this season; nothing provides new energy like obedience. *Nurture a friendship* by taking a hike and enjoying God's artwork in creation. These are all worthy investments of your time moving toward spiritual, mental, and physical wholeness.

> *For I am not ashamed of this Good News about Christ. It is the power of God at work, saving everyone who believes—the Jew first and also the Gentile.*
> *— Romans 1:16*

> *And now, dear brothers and sisters, one final thing. Fix your thoughts on what is true, and honorable, and right, and pure, and lovely, and admirable. Think about things that are excellent and worthy of praise. — Philippians 4:8*

> *May God himself, the God of peace, sanctify you through and through. May your whole spirit, soul and body be kept blameless at the coming of our Lord Jesus Christ.*
> *— 1 Thessalonians 5:23 (NIV)*

April 1

WOMEN ARE INNATELY PREDISPOSED TO BEING GOVERNED BY EMOTIONS. We naturally feel things deeply and, in our own ways, have a desire to care for and nurture others. These are all beautiful feminine characteristics, and although we have different personalities and temperaments, we value love and relationships. How can we steward this feminine energy in ways that are beneficial to ourselves and others?

We have to be rooted in absolute truth when it comes to our connection with God, ourselves, and others (**Colossians 2:7**). Growing in knowledge of God's faithfulness and how He sees us builds our confidence in Him and encourages us to see ourselves as He sees us (**Psalm 111:7, 1 Samuel 16:7**). Meditating on these truths is a powerful investment of time. The Lord will lead us as to how we can display His love and tenderness, navigating our care for others as well as for ourselves. *We need to pray daily* that our emotions and feelings are supported by truth. The steadiness of God's Word brings stability where we need it, and He already knows exactly what we need.

> *Let your roots grow down into him, and let your lives be built on him. Then your faith will grow strong in the truth you were taught, and you will overflow with thankfulness.* — Colossians 2:7

> *All he does is just and good, and all his commandments are trustworthy.* — Psalm 111:7

> *The Lord doesn't see things the way you see them. People judge by outward appearance, but the Lord looks at the heart.* — 1 Samuel 16:7

> *God would surely have known it, for he knows the secrets of every heart.* — Psalm 44:21

April 2

YOU COULD ASK A WIDE VARIETY OF PEOPLE, men and women, where they struggle, and a common answer would be in their thought life. A healthy thought life influences our spiritual, emotional, and physical well-being. We are all created differently; therefore, seeking God's guidance as to what is best for us is wise (**Isaiah 58:11**). We are inundated by numerous plans and programs to make us healthy, wealthy, and wise, but the overload of information itself can wreak havoc on our state of mind. So often our tendency is to complicate things when a simple approach would be a better option . The Scriptures encourage us to do things like take thoughts captive and guard our hearts (**2 Corinthians 10:5, Proverbs 4:23**). Immediately identifying fiery darts sent by our spiritual enemy is critical to getting rid of them as fast as they come. *Pray with confidence* for sensitivity to caution signs. God always listens and responds with love and provision. Our heavenly Father will lovingly help us purify our thoughts and hearts. He longs to be invited into it all.

> *The Lord will guide you continually, giving you water when you are dry and restoring your strength. You will be like a well-watered garden, like an ever-flowing spring. — Isaiah 58:11*

> *We destroy every proud obstacle that keeps people from knowing God. We capture their rebellious thoughts and teach them to obey Christ.*
> *— 2 Corinthians 10:5*

> *Guard your heart above all else, for it determines the course of your life.*
> *— Proverbs 4:23*

> *Come close to God, and God will come close to you. Wash your hands, you sinners; purify your hearts, for your loyalty is divided between God and the world. — James 4:8*

April 3

TODAY IS MY SWEET MAMA AND DADDY'S ANNIVERSARY. As soon as my eyes opened this morning, I was overcome with gratitude knowing they are both celebrating every day in heaven with Jesus. Glancing at the clock, it was 6:13am, which are both significant and special numbers in my life, there was my first God wink of the day (**Psalm 139:3**). Being the baby of my family and extremely emotionally attached to my imperfect, amazing parents, I am continually in awe of how my perfect heavenly Father has stood in the gap, filling my heart with His sweet love and presence in their absence (**Lamentations 3:22–23**). The hope of heaven provides a hedge of protection around our hearts that absolutely nothing in this chaotic world has the power to penetrate. As *we set our sights on the eternal*, the temporal takes second place and is less likely to be un-stabilizing. The reality of the cross and promise of eternal life provides the gift of not having to say goodbye to those we love who are in Christ. We get to live with the joyful expectancy of a sweet reunion with our loved ones and most importantly, Jesus.

> You see me when I travel and when I rest at home. You know everything I do. — Psalm 139:3

> The faithful love of the Lord never ends! His mercies never cease. Great is his faithfulness; his mercies begin afresh each morning.
> — Lamentations 3:22–23

> I consider that our present sufferings are not worth comparing with the glory that will be revealed to us. — Romans 8:18 (NIV)

April 4

THERE IS A STILL, QUIET VOICE I OFTEN HEAR IN MY SPIRIT THAT WHISPERS, "Stay in your lane." Although this phrase may not sound super spiritual, it is directly related to me operating out of the fruits of the Spirit, such as self-control, humility, peace, and joy (**Galatians 5:22–23**). Staying in your lane looks like nurturing your own spiritual health, prayerfully responding when the Holy Spirit invites you into situations, and trusting God with outcomes and His timing in people's lives and circumstances (**2 Peter 3:8–9**). Surrender is a key element to spiritual maturity and also a natural medicine for anxiety. Seeking God's guidance in helping us differentiate between responsibility and concern is time well spent. So often we give ourselves too much power and think God needs our help when He does not (**Ephesians 3:20**). *Humbly staying in step with the Spirit* helps guard our hearts from the tendency to control and move ahead of God. We are wise to remind ourselves: He sees the whole picture and we do not.

> *But the Holy Spirit produces this kind of fruit in our lives: love, joy, peace, patience, kindness, goodness, faithfulness, gentleness, and self-control.*
> *— Galatians 5:22–23*

> *But you must not forget this one thing, dear friends: A day is like a thousand years to the Lord, and a thousand years is like a day. The Lord isn't really being slow about his promise, as some people think. No, he is being patient for your sake. He does not want anyone to be destroyed, but wants everyone to repent.— 2 Peter 3:8–9*

> *Now all glory to God, who is able, through his mighty power at work within us, to accomplish infinitely more than we might ask or think. — Ephesians 3:20*

> *Now our knowledge is partial and incomplete, and even the gift of prophecy reveals only part of the whole picture! — 2 Corinthians 13:9*

April 5

ONE OF THE MOST COMPELLING BENEFITS OF READING SCRIPTURE is the reminder of what a powerful God we serve. Today is my very special, oldest daughter's birthday and my heartfelt prayer for her has always been that she would fall head over heels in love with Jesus. As we become aware of how mightily He moved in the lives of people years ago, we can come to realize He is the same God today (**Hebrews 13:8**). He is consistent, loving, good, and merciful, full of wisdom, desiring us to seek His direction. Since He is a personal God, we need to *invite Him into personal matters*. So often we compartmentalize our communication with God under the impression we shouldn't bother Him with small things. The truth is that, if it matters to us, it matters to Him. Notice how our biblical ancestors, such as Moses, David, and Paul, sought God, and how Esther and Daniel were so brave in following the direction they were given. Obviously culture changes and times are different, but the same God who was intimate with these heroes of the faith is available for you and me right now, forever and always. Amen.

> *Jesus Christ is the same yesterday, today, and forever.*
> *— Hebrews 13:8*

> *For the Lord is good. His unfailing love continues forever, and his faithfulness continues to each generation.*
> *— Psalm 100:5*

April 6

ONE OF THE MOST PREVALENT ENEMIES OF A JOY-FILLED LIFE is discontentment. Our culture encourages many forms of this poisonous heart posture, such as comparison, complaining, and the never-ending need for more. The powerful antidote for this unhealthy state of mind is cultivating an atmosphere of praise that will literally crowd out discontentment, much like darkness vanishes with light (**John 1:5**). Focusing on joy, hope, and love in today's world may seem like a challenge, but it's actually a part of working out our salvation and, as believers, what we are called to do (**Romans 15:13**). As we learn to find satisfaction and comfort in simply enjoying the presence of Jesus, He truly can be our refuge anytime, anywhere (**Psalm 18:2**). When a sense of discontentment settles in, instead of seeking something new or different, tap into what you already have inside: Christ, who lives in your heart and desires to fill you with satisfaction by simply being in His presence. *Give Him a chance* before turning to lesser things.

> The light shines in the darkness, and the darkness can never extinguish it.
> —John 1:5

> I pray that God, the source of hope, will fill you completely with joy and peace because you trust in him. Then you will overflow with confident hope through the power of the Holy Spirit. — Romans 15:13

> The Lord is my rock, my fortress, and my savior; my God is my rock, in whom I find protection. He is my shield, the power that saves me, and my place of safety. — Psalm 18:2

> Yes, everything else is worthless when compared with the infinite value of knowing Christ Jesus, my Lord. For his sake I have discarded everything else, counting it all as garbage, so that I could gain Christ... — Philippians 3:8

April 7

OUR LIFE THIS SIDE OF HEAVEN IS TRULY A JOURNEY. The way our heavenly Father is continually at work in our lives, weaving together His masterpiece in and through our stories, is brilliantly fascinating (**Psalm 139:16**). Along with accepting Jesus as Lord and Savior, there is another critical choice to make which is cooperating with the Holy Spirit's work of transforming us more into His image (**2 Corinthians 3:18**). God's desire is that our burdens would be light, making space for His love and joy to freely flow in and through our hearts and actions. We are not meant to be stagnant, so prayerfully ask, "In what small ways could I move this week?" Get out of your comfort zone and invite someone to church or a Bible study. Study the fruits of the Spirit and select one you struggle with to intentionally work on. *Pause and take time* for some deep breaths, topping it off with three things you are thankful for each day. A willingness to make small efforts can reap eternal rewards.

> *You saw me before I was born. Every day of my life was recorded in your book. Every moment was laid out before a single day had passed.* — Psalm 139:16

> *So all of us who have had that veil removed can see and reflect the glory of the Lord. And the Lord—who is the Spirit—makes us more and more like him as we are changed into his glorious image.* — 2 Corinthians 3:18

> *So let's not get tired of doing what is good. At just the right time we will reap a harvest of blessing if we don't give up.* — Galatians 6:9

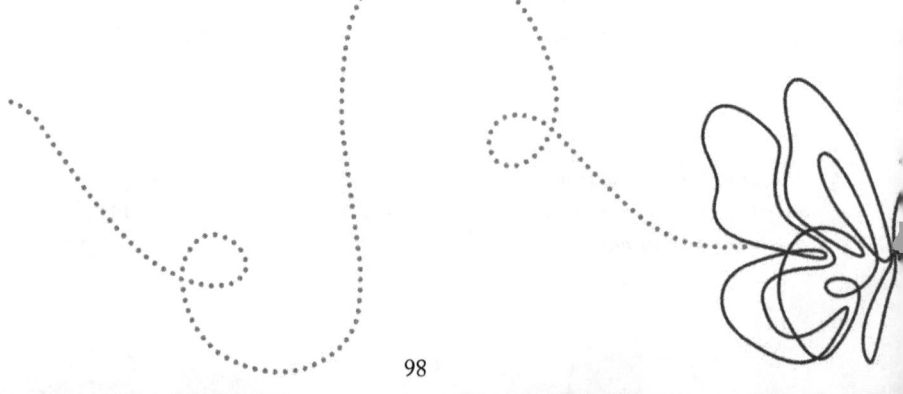

April 8

SEEKING TO FOLLOW CHRIST IS DEVELOPING A LIFESTYLE of utter dependence. Our human nature has a tendency towards independence, often exercising self-protection or self-promotion. Relying on ourselves leads to striving, disappointment, and anxiety, all of which can be poison to our soul. God's desire is for us to live in freedom and to rest in the truth that reliance on Him will keep us in the right place at the right time (**Proverbs 3:5–6**). Cultivating a heart that is willing to surrender and walking in humility is essential to complete dependence (**1 Peter 5:6–7**). Most of us will say God is all-knowing, all-powerful, and always has our best interests in mind, yet our actions, anxiety, and fear say otherwise (**James 1:8**). Our words are powerful and we need to *preach to ourselves the absolute truth* from the Scriptures of God's divine love and wisdom and our own fragility. He knows how much we need Him and so should we.

> *Trust in the Lord with all your heart; do not depend on your own understanding. Seek his will in all you do, and he will show you which path to take.*
> — *Proverbs 3:5–6*

> *1 Peter 5:6–7 So humble yourselves under the mighty power of God, and at the right time he will lift you up in honor. Give all your worries and cares to God, for he cares about you.* — *1 Peter 5:6–7*

> *Their loyalty is divided between God and the world, and they are unstable in everything they do.* — *James 1:8*

April 9

OFTENTIMES THE POWERFUL LYRICS OF WORSHIP SONGS will be in my heart as I wake up. This morning it was, "All praise to the Lord Most High, all praise to the One who saved my life, all praise to Jesus Christ, High King of Heaven, my King forever." These words are a powerful description of the supernatural magnificence of our God and all He is capable of (**Psalm 147:5**). Recognizing God in this way urges me to place myself under His authority, being confident of all that He is and keenly aware that any good in me is only because of Him and the redemptive work on the cross He has graciously provided (**Ephesians 2:8**).

As we *embrace our gift of salvation* and His Lordship in our lives, it strengthens us from the inside out, equipping us to accomplish what He has called us from and to (**James 1:2–3**). It is so encouraging to realize no trials or situations we experience are wasted but used as opportunities to mature in our faith and lean into God. He is our source, strength, and hope. He is King of kings and Lord of lords.

> *How great is our Lord! His power is absolute! His understanding is beyond comprehension! — Psalm 147:5*

> *God saved you by his grace when you believed. And you can't take credit for this; it is a gift from God. — Ephesians 2:8*

> *Dear brothers and sisters, when troubles of any kind come your way, consider it an opportunity for great joy. For you know that when your faith is tested, your endurance has a chance to grow. — James 1:2–3*

> *Together they will go to war against the Lamb, but the Lamb will defeat them because he is Lord of all lords and King of all kings. And his called and chosen and faithful ones will be with him. — Revelations 17:14*

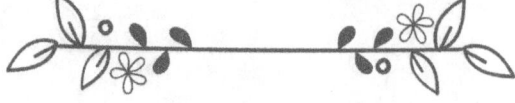

April 10

As believers, we are called to live counter-culturally in many ways (**Romans 12:2**). For example, instead of being the center of our own existence, we invite God to reside on the throne of our hearts and actions. Our desire and ability to make our lives reflect His holiness and purity are only possible because of Christ and a willingness to move toward Him daily (**1 Corinthians 1:30**). The world around us encourages gratifying our flesh at all costs. The more we allow Jesus to fill us with His life-giving peace, love, and security, the less vulnerable we are to destructive patterns of sin and idolatry. This mindset is similar to satisfying our appetites with nutritious food so as not to be starving or grabbing whatever is in front of us (**Romans 13:14**). *Choosing to fertilize our spirit over our flesh* requires wisdom and commitment. Basking in the light of Christ and seeking His presence is the abundant life that truly satisfies.

> Don't copy the behavior and customs of this world, but let God transform you into a new person by changing the way you think. Then you will learn to know God's will for you, which is good and pleasing and perfect. — Romans 12:2

> God has united you with Christ Jesus. For our benefit God made him to be wisdom itself. Christ made us right with God; he made us pure and holy, and he freed us from sin. — 1 Corinthians 1:30

> Instead, clothe yourself with the presence of the Lord Jesus Christ. And don't let yourself think about ways to indulge your evil desires. — Romans 13:14

> Let them praise the Lord for his great love and for the wonderful things he has done for them. For he satisfies the thirsty and fills the hungry with good things. — Psalm 107:8-9

April 11

RELATIONSHIPS ARE SO VERY IMPORTANT TO THE HEART OF GOD. The intimate fellowship we have with Him is what breathes life into all our other connections. Encouraging a group of ladies this morning, I was comparing keeping our love relationship alive with God to keeping the spark alive in a romance (**Romans 12:11–12**). Oftentimes we want this vibrant relationship with God to develop overnight, but as with any authentic, deep connection, it will take time. The beautiful reality is that He has time and there is nothing more important to Him than your head knowledge of who He is transferring to heart knowledge of who He is to you personally (**Ephesians 3:17–19**). *Our intimate connection with our creator* is the key element in finding fulfillment and purpose in this life. No other person, substance, or endeavor can satisfy like being tightly held in the arms of our heavenly Father.

Never be lazy, but work hard and serve the Lord enthusiastically. Rejoice in our confident hope. Be patient in trouble, and keep on praying.
— Romans 12:11-12

Then Christ will make his home in your hearts as you trust in him. Your roots will grow down into God's love and keep you strong. And may you have the power to understand, as all God's people should, how wide, how long, how high, and how deep his love is. May you experience the love of Christ, though it is too great to understand fully. Then you will be made complete with all the fullness of life and power that comes from God. — Ephesians 3:17-19

You will show me the way of life, granting me the joy of your presence and the pleasures of living with you forever. — Psalm 16:11

April 12

OUR GENUINE ADORATION OF GOD GREATLY DETERMINES OUR HEART POSTURE and perspective on life. So often we adore Him based on what we have seen Him do in and around us instead of simply who He is. When we fix our eyes on the attributes, nature, and mere character of our Creator, we cannot help but be in awe (**Deuteronomy 7:9**). Just like a human relationship, becoming well acquainted with His ways takes commitment and intentionality. Developing this reverence and affection is our best investment of time this side of eternity (**Jeremiah 29:13**). One of the most beautiful realities of God is that He does not change. So once our hearts are truly captivated by Him, there is no turning back. Even if we fall away, the emptiness will eventually drive us back into His everlasting arms (**Isaiah 40:28–29**). As long as we have breath in our lungs, we can *turn to Him*. He never gives up on us, and He is always there, now and forever.

> Understand, therefore, that the Lord your God is indeed God. He is the faithful God who keeps his covenant for a thousand generations and lavishes his unfailing love on those who love him and obey his commands.
> — Deuteronomy 7:9

> If you look for me wholeheartedly, you will find me. — Jeremiah 29:13

> Have you never heard? Have you never understood? The Lord is the everlasting God, the Creator of all the earth. He never grows weak or weary. No one can measure the depths of his understanding. He gives power to the weak and strength to the powerless. — Isaiah 40:28–29

> No power in the sky above or in the earth below—indeed, nothing in all creation will ever be able to separate us from the love of God that is revealed in Christ Jesus our Lord. — Romans 8:39

April 13

THIS IS THE DAY MY EARTHLY FATHER ENTERED HEAVEN. I wrote a poem for him years ago that was read at his memorial service, which I later realized mirrors my heart for my heavenly Father.

Unconditional love is what fathers should give,
you've been an example by the way you live.
You've taught me how to dance the dance, and
be unafraid to take a chance.
Through the years, we've been through so much
you've calmed my spirit with just a touch.
When I've been lost, you helped me find my way
teaching me the value of every day.
We've fought many battles and come out on top
your faith, hope, and love have never stopped.
In your heart, please understand
I'm thankful that you held my hand.
In my heart, you'll always be,
an ever present part of me.

I'm forever thankful for my imperfect, earthly father and forever grateful for my perfect heavenly Father, who holds me close when I miss my daddy. To God be the glory for the cross, resurrected life, and eternal gift of living with Him forever.

> *The Lord is like a father to his children, tender and compassionate to those who fear him.* — Psalm 103:13

> *And you saw how the Lord your God cared for you all along the way as you traveled through the wilderness, just as a father cares for his child. Now he has brought you to this place.* — Deuteronomy 1:31

April 14

WE ARE ENCOURAGED AS FOLLOWERS OF CHRIST TO HAVE CHILDLIKE FAITH. This is the kind of faith that is marked by humility and a confidence in God that leans towards dependence and trust (**Matthew 18:4**). There is a natural innocence and purity in most children, whereas we, as adults, have to be intentional in keeping our hearts and minds pure with a clear conscience.

Seeking the Lord with a pure heart and clean hands welcomes His wisdom and guidance (**Psalm 24:4–5**). There is something valuable for us to consider in this childlike posture spiritually, emotionally, and physically. Challenge yourself this week by beginning your day with seeking God in holy expectation of what he may teach you. Tell Him, "Lord, I humble myself in your arms, trusting you to carry me today" (**1 Peter 5:6**). Remember an activity you did as a child—such as jump rope, hula hoop, or skipping—and incorporate that into your exercise over the next few days. Color, dance, be creative, and have fun. *Pray to be a good disciple*, servant, wife, mother—just remember first and foremost you are His child.

> *So anyone who becomes as humble as this little child is the greatest in the Kingdom of Heaven. — Matthew 18:4*

> *Only those whose hands and hearts are pure, who do not worship idols and never tell lies. They will receive the Lord's blessing and have a right relationship with God their savior. — Psalm 24:4–5*

> *So humble yourselves under the mighty power of God, and at the right time he will lift you up in honor. — 1 Peter 5:6*

> *For you are all children of God through faith in Christ Jesus. — Galatians 3:26*

April 15

As women, we can be easily deceived into measuring our value based on our performance, appearance, how clean we keep our house, or how good of a wife, mother, or friend we are perceived to be. While all these areas may matter, none of them determine our worth or value. God chose us and we are valuable to Him and adopted into His family through Jesus' sacrifice on the cross (**Ephesians 1:4–5**). The priceless reality is that our position with God never changes. So neither does our identity because of Him. Our faith in the One who created us pulls us away from the lies the culture attempts to make us believe. I often encourage women to say out loud, "I am chosen by God, who knows what He will accomplish in and through my life. My role is to attach myself to Him and let Him lead" (**1 Peter 2:9, Psalm 37:5**). The more we *fill our hearts and minds* with this beautiful, unchanging affirmation from our heavenly Father, the less we crave it from others.

> *Even before he made the world, God loved us and chose us in Christ to be holy and without fault in his eyes. God decided in advance to adopt us into his own family by bringing us to himself through Jesus Christ. This is what he wanted to do, and it gave him great pleasure.* — Ephesians 1:4–5

> *But you are not like that, for you are a chosen people. You are royal priests, a holy nation, God's very own possession. As a result, you can show others the goodness of God, for he called you out of the darkness into his wonderful light.* — 1 Peter 2:9

> *Commit everything you do to the Lord. Trust him, and he will help you.* — Psalm 37:5

> *Obviously, I'm not trying to win the approval of people, but of God. If pleasing people were my goal, I would not be Christ's servant.* — Galatians 1:10

April 16

REFLECTING ON THE TRUTH THAT I AM FULLY KNOWN AND TRULY LOVED BY GOD is a source of security in my heart that is almost indescribable (**Psalm 5:11–12**). Although the magnitude and depth of His love is hard for us to comprehend, the more we draw close to Him, the more confident we become in His presence as our spiritual muscles strengthen.(**Hebrew 4:16**). Our shield of faith is what protects us from being led astray and falling away from God's best for us. How can we respond well to being cared for in this supernatural way? We can *choose daily* to move towards God, whatever that may look like in our particular season, asking ourselves the question, "Am I fully devoted to the One who has done everything for me?" (**Ephesians 3:20**). In what area are you holding back and why? Since we are indeed fully known and deeply loved by God, He alone is the one who is willing and able to guide us in every area, not merely to what is good but to what is best.

> *But let all who take refuge in you rejoice; let them sing joyful praises forever. Spread your protection over them, that all who love your name may be filled with joy. For you bless the godly, O Lord; you surround them with your shield of love.*
> *— Psalm 5:11–12*

> *So let us come boldly to the throne of our gracious God. There we will receive his mercy, and we will find grace to help us when we need it most. — Hebrews 4:16*

> *Now all glory to God, who is able, through his mighty power at work within us, to accomplish infinitely more than we might ask or think. — Ephesians 3:20*

> *Your own ears will hear him. Right behind you a voice will say, 'This is the way you should go,' whether to the right or to the left. — Isaiah 30:21*

April 17

ONE OF THE MOST OBVIOUS DISTINCTIONS BETWEEN believers and nonbelievers is that, as believers, our hope is not in this world. Regardless of our circumstances, there is a hope inside that is victorious and final. Oftentimes, trials can be a great opportunity to explain to others our peace in suffering and hardships (**1 Peter 3:15**). The victory we possess as followers of Christ is truly one of our most desirable characteristics. We follow and worship the one who has already won the battle (**2 Chronicles 20:17**). If you are watching a game being played and you already know which team wins, you look at mistakes made by the winning team differently because you know they end up winning in the end. This same mindset is available for us in that the victory over evil is won. We get to *choose to walk in that assurance* (**1 Corinthians 15:57**). We get to stand firm in the truth that no enemy that comes against us will prosper, and we do not have to be a slave to sin or fear.

> *Instead, you must worship Christ as Lord of your life. And if someone asks about your hope as a believer, always be ready to explain it.* — 1 Peter 3:15

> *But you will not even need to fight. Take your positions; then stand still and watch the Lord's victory. He is with you, O people of Judah and Jerusalem. Do not be afraid or discouraged. Go out against them tomorrow, for the Lord is with you!* — 2 Chronicles 20:17

> *But thank God! He gives us victory over sin and death through our Lord Jesus Christ.* — 1 Corinthians 15:57

> *This is my command—be strong and courageous! Do not be afraid or discouraged. For the Lord your God is with you wherever you go.* — Joshua 1:9

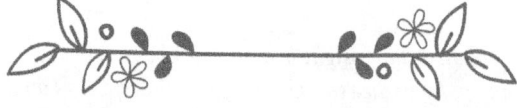

April 18

AT SOME POINT, MOST OF US HAVE HEARD THE PHRASE, "live life fully devoted to God." This is certainly not a lifestyle that just happens, that you automatically master when you have been a believer for a while. It is in fact a daily decision and requires commitment and action (**Luke 9:23**). Some of the action steps associated with full devotion are seeking Christlike perspectives on situations (**2 Corinthians 10:3–5**), trusting God in seasons of uncertainty (**Isaiah 41:10**), and confidently resting in the waiting for God to move or act (**Proverbs 3:5–6**). Although all of the above can be challenging, if we will *lean into Him moment by moment*, the Spirit of God will actually equip, encourage, and strengthen us to persevere (**1 Chronicles 16:11**). We have access to the healing, victory, and freedom we need to practice living in His presence. This is not a far-fetched, unattainable mindset; it is truly God's desire for all of His children.

> "Then he [Jesus] said to the crowd, 'If any of you wants to be my follower, you must give up your own way, take up your cross daily, and follow me.'"
> — Luke 9:23

> We are human, but we don't wage war as humans do. We use God's mighty weapons, not worldly weapons, to knock down the strongholds of human reasoning and to destroy false arguments. We destroy every proud obstacle that keeps people from knowing God. We capture their rebellious thoughts and teach them to obey Christ. — 2 Corinthians 10:3–5

> Trust in the Lord with all your heart; do not depend on your own understanding. Seek his will in all you do, and he will show you which path to take.
> — Proverbs 3:5–6

> Search for the Lord and for his strength; continually seek him.
> —1 Chronicles 16:11

> The Lord is close to all who call on him, yes, to all who call on him in truth.
> — Psalm 145:18

April 19

How we respond to God has everything to do with what we believe about Him. For instance, do we really believe God is good and always has our best interests in mind? The correct answers to these questions are yes and yes, but even mature followers of Christ struggle with unbelief at one time or another (**1 Timothy 6:12**). There will be seasons in which it will be a fight to *keep our eyes looking up to the capable hands of Jesus* instead of out at chaotic circumstances in a fallen world. These seasons will challenge us and grow our relationship with God in deep and powerful ways when we choose to cling to Him (**Romans 5:3–4**). We can rest in the security of knowing that no trial or curve ball in our life will surprise God or be too difficult for him to handle. He is always ready and more than capable of helping us navigate the worst of circumstances (**Psalm 9:9–10**). Absolutely nothing can tear down those whom God holds together.

> Fight the good fight for the true faith. Hold tightly to the eternal life to which God has called you, which you have declared so well before many witnesses.
> — 1 Timothy 6:12

> We can rejoice, too, when we run into problems and trials, for we know that they help us develop endurance. And endurance develops strength of character, and character strengthens our confident hope of salvation. — Romans 5:3–4

> The Lord is a shelter for the oppressed, a refuge in times of trouble. Those who know your name trust in you, for you, O Lord, do not abandon those who search for you. — Psalm 9:9–10

> He existed before anything else, and he holds all creation together. — Colossians 1:17

 *April 20*

Heading out to the gym this morning, I was blocked by my husband's truck, which was going to make me late for my cycle class. While my flesh was frustrated at first, my spirit whispered, "Maybe there is a reason for the delay," and immediately my perspective shifted. The situation made me ponder how we handle interruptions in our lives (**Proverbs 19:21**). Being inflexible is rooted in self-centered-*ness* and thinking we are more important than we are. The opposite is a posture of humility, with an awareness of God's sovereignty leading us to be more open-handed with our time and schedules. Maybe being held up is preventing us from an accident or will enable us to be at a certain place at the right time to help someone (**Colossians 3:2**). Jesus was never rushing around, too busy to slow down and see what was going on around Him. So often interruptions are opportunities to *join in God's work* or trust His timing. Either way, we should slow down, pay attention, and hold our time loosely.

> *You can make many plans, but the Lord's purpose will prevail.*
> — Proverbs 19:21

> *Think about the things of heaven, not the things of earth.*
> — Colossians 3:2

> *But let me say this, dear brothers and sisters: The time that remains is very short. So from now on, those with wives should not focus only on their marriage. Those who weep or who rejoice or who buy things should not be absorbed by their weeping or their joy or their possessions. Those who use the things of the world should not become attached to them. For this world as we know it will soon pass away.* — 1 Corinthians 7:29–31

> *Don't brag about tomorrow, since you don't know what the day will bring.*
> — Proverbs 27:1

April 21

I HAVE ALWAYS HELD THE FACTUAL NARRATIVE OF MARY AND MARTHA close to my heart (**Luke 10:38–42**). Living in our performance-based, busy culture, it's easy to spend more time doing church activities than actual time in the presence of Jesus, soaking Him in. We can admire Martha's hard work and servant's heart but acknowledge how distracted and resentful the tasks were making her. Mary, on the other hand, was focused on the most important thing any of us can do: basking in the radiance of Jesus, intent on hearing His every word. He is the well that never runs dry, but we need to posture ourselves like Mary and open our eyes, ears, and hearts, allowing Him to flow in and through us. This idea of sitting at His feet is what strengthens and equips us to be true disciples and respond well to God's calling on our lives (**Ephesians 4:1**).

This week, commit to exercising and eating well, taking care of the body God has given you, and set aside five minutes daily to just *sit at Jesus' feet*, focused on the amazing love He declared for us at the cross. He is worthy of our praise and attention.

> As Jesus and the disciples continued on their way to Jerusalem, they came to a certain village where a woman named Martha welcomed him into her home. Her sister, Mary, sat at the Lord's feet, listening to what he taught. But Martha was distracted by the big dinner she was preparing. She came to Jesus and said, "Lord, doesn't it seem unfair to you that my sister just sits here while I do all the work? Tell her to come and help me." But the Lord said to her, "My dear Martha, you are worried and upset over all these details! There is only one thing worth being concerned about. Mary has discovered it, and it will not be taken away from her." — Luke 10:38–42

> Therefore I, a prisoner for serving the Lord, beg you to lead a life worthy of your calling, for you have been called by God. — Ephesians 4:1

> The Lord will guide you continually, giving you water when you are dry and restoring your strength. You will be like a well-watered garden, like an ever-flowing spring. — Isaiah 58:11

> Come, let us worship and bow down. Let us kneel before the Lord our maker... — Psalm 95:6

April 22

LIVING OUR LIVES BEING FULLY RELIANT ON GOD IS A PROCESS. It requires abandoning self-sufficiency and having the courage to step out in faith. In order to learn to trust God, you have to start taking chances, even in the midst of uncertainty **(Psalm 37:3–7)**. This really begins with the realization that He alone knows what is best for us, and we are wise to seek Him on the front end of making plans. His divine direction and guidance are worth waiting for, but this kind of patience requires humility and self-control **(Psalm 27:14)**. I never lose my awe of the reality that God knows me better than I know myself and actually desires to walk me step-by-step down the right path. This looks like *being content and expectant* at the same time. God knows when our heart's desire is to embrace the purpose we were created for, and He delights in His children being surrendered and fully devoted to Him.

> Trust in the Lord and do good. Then you will live safely in the land and prosper. Take delight in the Lord, and he will give you your heart's desires. Commit everything you do to the Lord. Trust him, and he will help you. He will make your innocence radiate like the dawn, and the justice of your cause will shine like the noonday sun. Be still in the presence of the Lord, and wait patiently for him to act. Don't worry about evil people who prosper or fret about their wicked schemes. — Psalm 37:3–7

> Wait patiently for the Lord. Be brave and courageous. Yes, wait patiently for the Lord. — Psalm 27:14

> And may you be completely faithful to the Lord our God. May you always obey his decrees and commands, just as you are doing today. — 1 Kings 8:61

April 23

We all have relationships that are so comfortable that, even when sitting in silence with that person, we feel safe and refreshed. So often, when I choose silence over music or television, I sense the whisper of encouragement and guidance from the Spirit of God (**Psalm 46:10**). Silence is a powerful invitation for the Holy Spirit to speak, and *breaking away from noise* should be a discipline we practice. Even taking a few moments at the end of prayer to simply be in His presence can be life-changing. God desires us to feel His presence in such a tangible way it becomes the treasure we cannot live without (**Psalm 63:1**). This level of intimacy with God obviously needs to be cultivated and nurtured but is available to all believers. Since we are all different creations, we will experience Him in a multitude of ways, but the reality is our heavenly Father wants a relationship with you that is vibrant and captivating. The most beautiful part is that it's forever.

> Be still, and know that I am God! I will be honored by every nation. I will be honored throughout the world. — Psalm 46:10

> O God, you are my God; I earnestly search for you. My soul thirsts for you; my whole body longs for you in this parched and weary land where there is no water. — Psalm 63:1

> Now I am coming to you. I told them many things while I was with them in this world so they would be filled with my joy. — John 17:13

April 24

ON THE WAY TO SCHOOL THIS MORNING, MY SON WANTED TO PLAY A WORSHIP SONG entitled, "Made for More." The fact that my teenagers like worship music makes my heart smile in and of itself, but throughout the day I have reflected on the powerful message that we are made for more. So often when I pray, I will say, "Thank you, God, for all You are and all You enable me to be" (**Psalm 139:2–4**). Our unique gifts, talents, and passions all work together for God Himself to accomplish His purposes in and through us (**Psalm 119:73**). We should never settle for less than allowing God to continually grow and mold us during our journey on this earth. If you don't feel like you're living on purpose for a purpose, you are probably right and it's time to *get out of your comfort zone and seek new* opportunities (**Psalm 32:8**). One of the many benefits to living in community is knowing others well enough that they can speak into our lives and we can speak into theirs. Oftentimes we can help each other identify strengths we didn't know we had.

> You know when I sit down or stand up. You know my thoughts even when I'm far away. You see me when I travel and when I rest at home. You know everything I do. You know what I am going to say even before I say it, Lord.
> — Psalm 139:2–4

> You made me; you created me. Now give me the sense to follow your commands.
> — Psalm 119:73

> "The Lord says, 'I will guide you along the best pathway for your life. I will advise you and watch over you.'" — Psalm 32:8

> Let us think of ways to motivate one another to acts of love and good works. And let us not neglect our meeting together, as some people do, but encourage one another, especially now that the day of his return is drawing near.
> — Hebrews 10:24–25

April 25

I REALLY DO ENJOY AN IMPACTFUL WORSHIP EXPERIENCE of listening to a compelling preacher who is passionate about his message, but it's important that we don't rely on these external experiences to motivate our faith. Our devotion and passion for the Lord needs to be internal and displayed from the inside out (**Romans 8:23–25**). The hope and joy inside is the motivating factor in our journey as believers, and we have access to that internal bliss at any time, anywhere. Emotion-driven services are fun and can be spiritually meaningful, but they need to be followed up with discipleship and experiencing that level of delight simply by drawing near to Jesus and meditating in His presence (**Psalm 21:6**). If we find ourselves dissatisfied with a service and critical about the music or message, we may need to check our heart posture and *spend some quality time one-on-one at the feet of Jesus*, allowing our spirit to be replenished by the only One who can truly satisfy.

> *And we believers also groan, even though we have the Holy Spirit within us as a foretaste of future glory, for we long for our bodies to be released from sin and suffering. We, too, wait with eager hope for the day when God will give us our full rights as his adopted children, including the new bodies he has promised us. We were given this hope when we were saved. (If we already have something, we don't need to hope for it. But if we look forward to something we don't yet have, we must wait patiently and confidently.)* — Romans 8:23–25

> *You have endowed him with eternal blessings and given him the joy of your presence.* — Psalm 21:6

> *Before daybreak the next morning, Jesus got up and went out to an isolated place to pray.* — Mark 1:35

April 26

THE SOVEREIGNTY OF GOD IS ONE OF THE MOST MYSTERIOUS realities known to man. It is an amazing truth, so magnificent we can't even wrap our mind around it, yet also the absolute truth that we can rest in and count on (**Revelation 4:11**). The word sovereignty means power that cannot be matched, the supreme authority of all things, and a force to be reckoned with—meaning it cannot be ignored. Think about the sovereignty of God in light of your past, present, and future. No matter what kind of suffering we have experienced or landmines we have stepped on, there is absolutely nothing that can thwart God's plans for our lives. He will right any wrong and use it for our good and His glory (**James 1:2–4**). In the present, as we seek and depend on Him daily, He gives us manna and strengthens us for all He has called us to do this particular day (**Philippians 4:13**). We can *move forward with supernatural confidence* knowing our future is sealed, and the remaining time we have on this earth should be spent following His lead.

> You are worthy, O Lord our God, to receive glory and honor and power. For you created all things, and they exist because you created what you pleased.— Revelation 4:11

> Dear brothers and sisters, when troubles of any kind come your way, consider it an opportunity for great joy. For you know that when your faith is tested, your endurance has a chance to grow. So let it grow, for when your endurance is fully developed, you will be perfect and complete, needing nothing.
> — James 1:2-4

> For I can do everything through Christ, who gives me strength.
> — Philippians 4:13

> We can make our plans, but the Lord determines our steps.
> — Proverbs 16:9

April 27

THERE WAS A LOT OF HUSTLE AND BUSTLE AROUND OUR HOUSE this morning as my teenage daughter was hosting a surprise birthday party for a special friend. I was reflecting on their friendship and remembering my husband's prayers before they met and how God brought them together. God orchestrates connections with people for our benefit and His purposes (**Proverbs 27:17**). I had coffee with an amazing single friend today. We have been praying God would bring her the right husband but, more importantly, that she would walk closely with the Lord and that she would make good choices within potential relationships (**Proverbs 4:23**). Relationships are a vital part of who we are, and our heavenly Father, who knows us better than we know ourselves, is ready and waiting to lead us towards the right ones, as well as away from those who are not His best for us. We all need His wisdom and guidance in this critical area. A great question for us to *ask ourselves* is, "Does this person push me more towards Jesus or pull me away?" This answer will provide clarity and protection from settling for less than His best.

> As iron sharpens iron, so a friend sharpens a friend. — Proverbs 27:17

> Guard your heart above all else, for it determines the course of your life.
> — Proverbs 4:23

> Don't be fooled by those who say such things, for "bad company corrupts good character." — 1 Corinthians 15:33

> Don't team up with those who are unbelievers. How can righteousness be a partner with wickedness? How can light live with darkness?
> — 2 Corinthians 6:14

April 28

NAVIGATING RELATIONSHIPS WELL IS SOMETHING WE ALL NEED HELP WITH at one time or another. All of us are imperfect, broken people and we need the river of God's grace to love each other well (**1 John 4:7**). So often we struggle in our human connections because we try to get from those people things that they were not created to provide. We cannot determine our value and worth based on the way we are treated, nor can we rely on the opinions and affirmation of a fallen world. The truth of what God says about us frees us from the bondage of self-promotion and self-protection—both poison in regards to healthy interaction (**Colossians 3:12**). Reminding ourselves we are God's chosen creations allows the fruits of the Spirit to pour through us like healing rain on our relationships. Strengthen yourself this week by beginning your days with God's truth about your identity (**Deuteronomy 7:6**). *Reach out to someone* you need to reconnect with and invite them on a walk with the goal of being a vessel of God's lovingkindness. We are free to love sacrificially and authentically when we are rooted in Him.

Dear friends, let us continue to love one another, for love comes from God. Anyone who loves is a child of God and knows God. — 1 John 4:7

Since God chose you to be the holy people he loves, you must clothe yourselves with tenderhearted mercy, kindness, humility, gentleness, and patience. — Colossians 3:12

For you are a holy people, who belong to the Lord your God. Of all the people on earth, the Lord your God has chosen you to be his own special treasure. — Deuteronomy 7:6

We love each other because he loved us first. — 1 John 4:19

April 29

I HAD THE PRIVILEGE TODAY OF SPENDING SOME TIME WITH A BEAUTIFUL group of women whom, like myself, God in His rich mercy has delivered out of darkness into His love and light (**John 8:12**). While everyone in that room had experienced substance or sexual abuse, there are many other things the Lord rescued us from, including pride, control, and self-righteousness, not to mention simply trying to run our own lives. If we are in a personal, growing relationship with Jesus, we have been rescued and have something to celebrate. There are seasons when you may question the quality of your personal relationship with Jesus, or not feel as close to God as you long to be, but the reality is that you reading this—and desiring more—is evidence of God drawing you to Himself (**1 John 2:8**). His light is already shining, and we get to *join in that victory won for us on the cross.* We have no allegiance or reason to go back to anything God has rescued us from. Our past has been redeemed and we are new creations.

> "Jesus spoke to the people once more and said, 'I am the light of the world. If you follow me, you won't have to walk in darkness, because you will have the light that leads to life.'" — John 8:12

> Yet it is also new. Jesus lived the truth of this commandment, and you also are living it. For the darkness is disappearing, and the true light is already shining. — 1 John 2:8

> This means that anyone who belongs to Christ has become a new person. The old life is gone; a new life has begun! — 2 Corinthians 5:17

April 30

THERE IS NO QUESTION THAT FOLLOWING GOD'S WILL FOR OUR LIVES—surrendering to, abiding in, and trusting Him daily—does create an atmosphere of strength and peace (**Isaiah 40:29**). He is always at work around us and calls us to be involved in that work. We need to cultivate sensitivity to the Holy Spirit's promptings and respond with obedience. This could look like not being ashamed to be set apart by not engaging in certain activities. It could look like having a difficult conversation with a sister-in-Christ who is headed in a dangerous direction pulling her away from her faith (**Joshua 1:9**). We are called to be more concerned with what God is calling us to do than with our comfort. Sometimes this may look like caring more for someone's soul than the friendship or being left out of some situations because of your beliefs. Whatever the circumstance, we can *stand confidently on the truth* that the suffering is worth it because Jesus is worth it, and He doesn't want any of His children to settle for mediocre Christianity. He empowers us to do the hard things.

> *He gives power to the weak and strength to the powerless.* — Isaiah 40:29

> *This is my command—be strong and courageous! Do not be afraid or discouraged. For the Lord your God is with you wherever you go.* — Joshua 1:9

> *Be on guard. Stand firm in the faith. Be courageous. Be strong.*
> *— 1 Corinthians 16:13*

ONE OF THE MOST POWERFUL WEAPONS WE HAVE IS OUR TONGUE. Our words can be used to speak life or death into people and can greatly affect the way we perceive and experience circumstances (**Proverbs 15:4**). What we say should be helpful and encouraging even if it's a hard conversation, such as disciplining children or confronting sin in a fellow believer's life. These interactions should be seasoned with love, displaying the grace flowing through us in Christ (**Ephesians 4:29**). The beginning of the month is a great time to set goals spiritually, emotionally, and physically. Prayerfully consider what would be beneficial. Maybe commit your words to the Lord each morning, asking for wisdom and grace in your communication with others. Meditate on Scripture, and *ask the Holy Spirit* to display the fruits of the Spirit in your life (**Galatians 5:22–23**). As the weather gets warmer, get outside at least 30 minutes a day to walk, ride a bike, or do yard work. Think of how taking care of your body honors God as a "get to," not a "have to."

> Gentle words are a tree of life; a deceitful tongue crushes the spirit.
> — Proverbs 15:4

> Don't use foul or abusive language. Let everything you say be good and helpful, so that your words will be an encouragement to those who hear them.
> — Ephesians 4:29

> But the Holy Spirit produces this kind of fruit in our lives: love, joy, peace, patience, kindness, goodness, faithfulness, gentleness, and self-control. There is no law against these things! — Galatians 5:22–23

> Dear friend, I hope all is well with you and that you are as healthy in body as you are strong in spirit. — 3 John 1:2

TODAY IS THE NATIONAL DAY OF PRAYER FOR THIS YEAR and my prayer for this day is that stagnant prayer lives would be reignited and people who don't pray or don't understand its power would give it a chance (**Philippians 4:6–7**). Communicating with God begins with the desire for a relationship with Him. It is important for us to understand that the desire for something more and the yearning to go deeper with God is the Holy Spirit already at work in your soul, drawing you to Himself. God is inviting us to know Him intimately and wants our conversations with Him to be ongoing (**1 Thessalonians 5:17**). Praying is so much more than the formality it often gets reduced to. It is our ever-available connection to the King of the Universe, who wants us to talk with Him—not merely to Him—opening our hearts, ears, and eyes to receive what He says back. I encourage you to *meet with Him, write to Him*, turn off the noise, and listen for His voice. Fall in love with the Lover of your soul and enjoy the peace of His presence, allowing it to flow through every part of who He created you to be.

> Don't worry about anything; instead, pray about everything. Tell God what you need, and thank him for all he has done. Then you will experience God's peace, which exceeds anything we can understand. His peace will guard your hearts and minds as you live in Christ Jesus.
> — Philippians 4:6–7

> Never stop praying.
> — 1 Thessalonians 5:17

> You will show me the way of life, granting me the joy of your presence and the pleasures of living with you forever.
> — Psalm 16:11

May 3

ONE OF MY CONTINUAL REQUESTS TO GOD IS THAT HE WOULD help me navigate my relationships and help me love people well. We can stand on the promise that as we humble ourselves and seek His guidance He shows up and helps us care for others in a way we could never do apart from Him (**Psalm 17:6**). A critical piece of how well we love others is speaking truth in love, using wisdom and discretion or being silent as we listen, keeping our flesh quiet and prayerful (**Philippians 2:3**). The other piece of this puzzle is realizing in our frail human condition we will not always say the right thing, but we can feel confident that God in His sovereignty can cover our indiscretions. There is no question God gives us the privilege of being His earthly vessels, but we need to seek Him first in all we say and do (**Colossians 3:17**). It never ceases to amaze me that the sovereign God of the universe orchestrates relationships and divine appointments for us. May we all *be people who are sober and alert*, expectant of how we can reflect God's love today.

> *I am praying to you because I know you will answer, O God. Bend down and listen as I pray.* — Psalm 17:6

> *Don't be selfish; don't try to impress others. Be humble, thinking of others as better than yourselves.* — Philippians 2:3

> *And whatever you do or say, do it as a representative of the Lord Jesus, giving thanks through him to God the Father.* — Colossians 3:17

> *So now I am giving you a new commandment: Love each other. Just as I have loved you, you should love each other.* — John 13:34

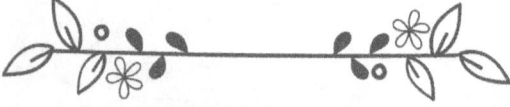

I WAS ON MY WAY TO TAKE AN EARLY MORNING CLASS at the gym and at the last minute decided on another one that had me arriving 30 minutes later. Upon walking in the lobby, I saw a friend who doesn't even go to our gym who needed to talk to me (**Proverbs 20:24**). We simultaneously celebrated God orchestrating the connection, and she was able to share some frustrating news that needed a fresh perspective. The news was of an unfortunate string of circumstances, but I couldn't help but notice the glow on her face and the reality that she had landed in a good spot with new employment, a great place to live, and surrounded by sisters-in-Christ (**Isaiah 55:8–9**). We were able to discuss how God so often uses unlikely means to accomplish His purposes, and how there will be situations and people's actions we don't understand (**Romans 11:33**). What we can *believe and understand* is there is no one more eager for us to be healed, restored, and exactly where we need to be than our loving heavenly Father, and He is ready and willing to make a way.

> The Lord directs our steps, so why try to understand everything along the way?
> — Proverbs 20:24

> "'My thoughts are nothing like your thoughts,' says the Lord.
> 'And my ways are far beyond anything you could imagine.
> For just as the heavens are higher than the earth,
> so my ways are higher than your ways
> and my thoughts higher than your thoughts.'" — Isaiah 55:8–9

> Oh, how great are God's riches and wisdom and knowledge! How impossible it is for us to understand his decisions and his ways! — Romans 11:33

> Then if my people who are called by my name will humble themselves and pray and seek my face and turn from their wicked ways, I will hear from heaven and will forgive their sins and restore their land. — 2 Chronicles 7:14

The ultimate gift from our union with Christ is certainly our salvation, but on top of a gift so lavish, there is even more. There is the daily opportunity to walk with Him, talk with Him, and lay our burdens at the foot of the cross, having the confidence that in His hands all is well (**Psalm 73:26**). The old hymn "It is Well With My Soul" is reflective of a life sold out to Jesus, realizing that whatever trials we experience this side of heaven are temporary. So often they are utilized to stretch and mold us into more of who we were created to be (**James 1:12**). There is great security in embracing the truth that, no matter what comes our way, we never face it alone. God designed us for dependence on Him; yet, in our human nature, we are prone to lean into self-sufficiency, which is so exhausting. Our Christian life is full of exchanging our perspective for His (**Romans 12:2**). May we *learn to be people who desire to receive all God offers* us in this life, including seeking Him, following His design for life, and having willing hearts that not only crave eternal life but crave Him here and now.

> *My health may fail, and my spirit may grow weak, but God remains the strength of my heart; he is mine forever.* — Psalm 73:26

> *God blesses those who patiently endure testing and temptation. Afterward they will receive the crown of life that God has promised to those who love him.* — James 1:12

> *Don't copy the behavior and customs of this world, but let God transform you into a new person by changing the way you think. Then you will learn to know God's will for you, which is good and pleasing and perfect.* — Romans 12:2

> *The one thing I ask of the Lord—the thing I seek most—is to live in the house of the Lord all the days of my life, delighting in the Lord's perfections and meditating in his Temple.* — Psalm 27:4

I WAS TALKING TO SOME YOUNG LADIES TODAY WHO WERE ASKING some great questions, such as, "What does it look like to walk in my new identity in Christ?" and "How do I discern how God is leading me in a certain situation?" (**Proverbs 20:12**). In our human nature we love black-and-white answers to our questions, but as believers we are called to daily reliance, growing in our confidence as we continually learn to be led (**1 John 3:22–23**). Beginning our days with proclamations such as, "God, I know who You are and who You say I am," or "I have new life in Christ and God is with me" can be life-changing habits that take less than ten seconds. We are all sheep in need of our good shepherd, and no matter how mature in our faith we are, we never outgrow our need to dress ourselves daily in surrender, identity, and gratitude. We should always *take our questions to the Lord* and have authentic conversations with leaders and friends. These ponderings of our hearts will lead us closer to Him as we realize He is the answer we seek.

> Ears to hear and eyes to see—both are gifts from the Lord.
> — Proverbs 20:12

> And we will receive from him whatever we ask because we obey him and do the things that please him. And this is his commandment: We must believe in the name of his Son, Jesus Christ, and love one another, just as he commanded us. — 1 John 3:22–23

> And we are confident that he hears us whenever we ask for anything that pleases him. And since we know he hears us when we make our requests, we also know that he will give us what we ask for. — 1 John 5:14–15

On the way to meet a special friend who was experiencing a bump in the road, my prayer was that I would listen well. The art of being a good listener is so valuable, not only in our human relationships but certainly in our relationship with the Lord (**Proverbs 4:20–21**). Being a good listener requires not being in a hurry and genuinely valuing the words being spoken. Paying attention to someone's words gives insight to how they are feeling and thinking, resulting in being able to pray more specifically. Being attentive during interactions also makes others feel valued and known, which is something we all crave (**John 13:35**). Listening well is a sign of humility before the Lord, realizing we need to be silent to hear His voice. So often I will pray, "Father, help me to open my mouth and shut my mouth when I need to, and give me the wisdom to respond well." (**Proverbs 2:6–8**). If you tend to be a talker, challenge yourself to listen more, and if you are quiet, *ask God* for confidence to communicate well. May we use our ears and mouths in a way that reflects Christ.

> *My child, pay attention to what I say. Listen carefully to my words. Don't lose sight of them. Let them penetrate deep into your heart . . .*
> *— Proverbs 4:20–21*

> *Your love for one another will prove to the world that you are my disciples.*
> *— John 13:35*

> *For the Lord grants wisdom! From his mouth come knowledge and understanding. He grants a treasure of common sense to the honest. He is a shield to those who walk with integrity. He guards the paths of the just and protects those who are faithful to him. — Proverbs 2:6–8*

Words I often find myself uttering are, "Lord, help me to stay in my lane." As followers of Christ, we are called to live in community, which includes sharing life, holding each other accountable, and encouraging each other in general (**Hebrews 10:24–25**). The Scriptures consistently call us to love well and speak truth but to likewise nurture our own spiritual health and exercise self-control (**Matthew 7:3**). While fellowship on deep levels can put us in difficult waters, seeking and trusting God is where we find wisdom (**Ephesians 4:2**). There are a multitude of verses in God's Word giving clear direction in how we can care for each other well. God knew how, in our broken human nature, we would need so much help in these sensitive areas. Distinguishing between our area of concern and responsibility is something we can only do with the Spirit's guidance. Once we have fulfilled our responsibility in a situation, we have the privilege of surrendering and *trusting God for the outcome* (**Psalm 37:5; Proverbs 3:5–6**). This is a privilege because we are not called to fix ourselves or each other; we are called to love well.

> *Let us think of ways to motivate one another to acts of love and good works. And let us not neglect our meeting together, as some people do, but encourage one another, especially now that the day of his return is drawing near.*
> *— Hebrews 10:24–25*

> *And why worry about a speck in your friend's eye when you have a log in your own? — Matthew 7:3*

> *Always be humble and gentle. Be patient with each other, making allowance for each other's faults because of your love. — Ephesians 4:2*

> *Commit everything you do to the Lord. Trust him, and he will help you.*
> *— Psalm 37:5*

> *Trust in the Lord with all your heart; do not depend on your own understanding. Seek his will in all you do, and he will show you which path to take.*
> *— Proverbs 3:5–6*

I LOVE THE IDEA OF LIVING A LIFESTYLE OF WORSHIP. Most often when we think of worship, our minds go directly to music, but it is so much more. We can begin by acknowledging how worthy our Lord and Savior is simply because He is our Lord and Savior (**Romans 10:9**). The reality that He made a way for us to have eternal life—that alone is reason enough for us to live sacrificially for Him. A heart posture of praise and gratitude is a powerful weapon against discouragement and despair (**Psalm 103:1**). We all need to cultivate that secret place with the Lord to which we can break away and be held by Him, even if only in our minds (**Psalm 63:8**). Worshiping through all circumstances can help us not fall into depression. This may look like focusing on how God is helping you navigate a situation, rather than focusing on the situation itself. Some days seem to reflect how broken our world is, but clinging to our hope in Christ is the gift that is ours now and always. We *worship through talking to God*, noticing His activity, meditating on His Word, singing His praises, and surrendering often. These are all habits that help us stand strong and live well.

> *If you openly declare that Jesus is Lord and believe in your heart that God raised him from the dead, you will be saved.* — Romans 10:9

> *Let all that I am praise the Lord; with my whole heart, I will praise his holy name.* — Psalm 103:1

> *I cling to you; your strong right hand holds me securely.* — Psalm 63:8

> *And so, dear brothers and sisters, I plead with you to give your bodies to God because of all he has done for you. Let them be a living and holy sacrifice—the kind he will find acceptable. This is truly the way to worship him.* — Romans 12:1

May 10

I was checking in on a friend the other day to see what she was up to, and her response was powerful. She said she was doing a deep dive in the book of Ephesians. She said it was a book she had read many times, but it's so rich that she always learns something different (**Ephesians 3:4**). The Scriptures can give us progressive revelation in that it is the Living Word, and the Holy Spirit will illuminate different ideas and truths for our continual growth (**1 Timothy 3:16–17**). God's written Word is one of the most valuable gifts known to man and is truly the gift that keeps giving. Scripture offers insight into many things, but, most importantly, it helps us to taste and see the heart of God (**Psalm 34:8**). Understanding that God created us in His image and He alone defines who we are shows us our identity in Christ (**Galatians 2:20**). *Being rooted in the Scriptures* gives hope and clarity in the midst of the world's discouragement and confusion. As followers of Christ, we should be in the Word daily. The same Spirit who is alive in these pages is His Spirit alive in us, teaching, encouraging, and motivating us to be all He created us to be.

> As you read what I have written, you will understand my insight into this plan regarding Christ. — Ephesians 3:4

> Without question, this is the great mystery of our faith: Christ was revealed in a human body and vindicated by the Spirit. He was seen by angels and announced to the nations. He was believed in throughout the world and taken to heaven in glory. — 1 Timothy 3:16–17

> Taste and see that the Lord is good. Oh, the joys of those who take refuge in him! — Psalm 34:8

> My old self has been crucified with Christ. It is no longer I who live, but Christ lives in me. So I live in this earthly body by trusting in the Son of God, who loved me and gave himself for me. — Galatians 2:20

> For we are God's masterpiece. He has created us anew in Christ Jesus, so we can do the good things he planned for us long ago. — Ephesians 2:10

May 11

A POWERFUL PRAYER LIFE IS AN ATTRIBUTE THAT CAN AND SHOULD BE one of the sweet spots of our faith. We should never neglect or put off the opportunity to pray, whether it's about a circumstance happening now or a friend in need. So often if we say, "I will pray for you," we are better off praying in the moment (**Matthew 18:20**). Our spiritual enemy knows how prayer empowers the believer and will do everything in his power to keep us from it; therefore, we need to push through distractions. God loves for us to communicate with Him, and the more we talk to Him, the more we will sense His presence (**Jeremiah 29:12**). We all have a desire to be known and heard, so there is no one we should go to first before God. When I was learning what it looked like to experience intimacy with the Lord, I had a wise friend who would not talk to me about certain subjects unless I had first gone to God. While this was difficult to understand at the time, it certainly worked for my good. Talk to Him. *Share your heart.* He is there for you now and forever.

> *For where two or three gather together as my followers, I am there among them.* — Matthew 18:20

> *In those days when you pray, I will listen.* — Jeremiah 29:12

> *The Lord is close to all who call on him, yes, to all who call on him in truth.* — Psalm 145:18

Mother's Day is such a beautiful reminder of God's faithfulness (**Psalm 25:10**). Today in church as we were worshiping I turned to embrace my daughter who was a miracle baby considering I was told I wouldn't be able to get pregnant. God had another opinion. As I held her in my arms, tears filled my eyes in gratitude because of her heart for the Lord (**Isaiah 54:13**). The first song we sang this morning was "Hallelujah Thank You for the Cross," and it is because of that cross that my mama is in heaven today and we will meet again (**John 5:24**). I never lose my awe of the reality that because of the sacrificial love of our Lord, we get to live with Him forever. It is imperative that we intentionally remind ourselves of the goodness of God and *reflect on the spiritual milestones* in our lives when we have witnessed His power and felt His love. He is worthy of our allegiance. All honor, praise, and glory be to God.

The Lord leads with unfailing love and faithfulness all who keep his covenant and obey his demands. — Psalm 25:10

I will teach all your children, and they will enjoy great peace. — Isaiah 54:13

I tell you the truth, those who listen to my message and believe in God who sent me have eternal life. They will never be condemned for their sins, but they have already passed from death into life. — John 5:24

Now all glory to God, who is able to keep you from falling away and will bring you with great joy into his glorious presence without a single fault. All glory to him who alone is God, our Savior through Jesus Christ our Lord. All glory, majesty, power, and authority are his before all time, and in the present, and beyond all time! Amen. — Jude 1:24–25

While talking with a group of women today, I mentioned the fact that so often our deepest pockets of pain are where God's love has the opportunity to shine the brightest. We began to talk through the "why" of that reality, learning in particular that any pain or suffering we experience grieves the heart of God (**Psalm 34:18–19**). Our heavenly Father can and will restore us as we turn to His healing power. For me personally, it was during a season of healing that the Lord drew me so close to His heart and I realized that is where I longed to stay (**Hebrews 10:22**). Another reality is that areas of weakness urge us to lean into the Lord for strength and are also a testimony to others of all God can do in and through a willing heart (**Philippians 2:13**). Sometimes the Lord allows circumstances in our lives because *He will provide opportunities for us* to minister to others and share the security and comfort we have found in our Father's arms. We need to always remember the best day here on earth pales in comparison to our eternal home, where there will be no tears or pain.

> The Lord is close to the brokenhearted; he rescues those whose spirits are crushed. The righteous person faces many troubles, but the Lord comes to the rescue each time. — Psalm 34:18–19

> "... let us go right into the presence of God with sincere hearts fully trusting him. For our guilty consciences have been sprinkled with Christ's blood to make us clean, and our bodies have been washed with pure water." — Hebrews 10:22

> For God is working in you, giving you the desire and the power to do what pleases him. — Philippians 2:13

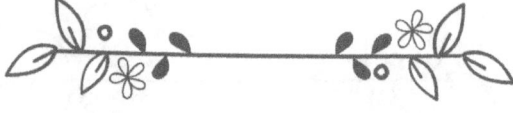

May 14

ONE OF THE BLESSINGS THAT WE ALL HAVE ACCESS TO IS THE opportunity to begin every day with an expectant heart. So often I find myself saying, "I wonder where God will show up today." (**Deuteronomy 29:29**). It never ceases to amaze me the way God will reveal Himself to a sensitive spirit. Since my parents have been in heaven, if I'm especially missing them, the Lord always seems to send something special that will remind me of them, like a person, a memory, or simply a sign of heaven that brings peace and comfort (**John 14:27**). We should all have a holy awe for the gift of such a personal God who desires to both strengthen us and care for us because He knows our individual weaknesses and sufferings (**Psalm 56:8**). It is a continual prayer of mine for the Lord to reveal Himself to me and others. We will notice what we are looking for, and the more we can *focus our hearts and minds on the things above*, the more we will have the privilege of seeing Him here on earth.

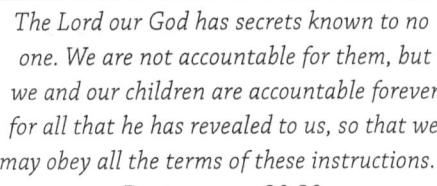

> *The Lord our God has secrets known to no one. We are not accountable for them, but we and our children are accountable forever for all that he has revealed to us, so that we may obey all the terms of these instructions.*
> *— Deuteronomy 29:29*

> *I am leaving you with a gift—peace of mind and heart. And the peace I give is a gift the world cannot give. So don't be troubled or afraid. — John 14:27*

> *You keep track of all my sorrows. You have collected all my tears in your bottle. You have recorded each one in your book. — Psalm 56:8*

> *Think about the things of heaven, not the things of earth. — Colossians 3:2*

May 15

OVER THE PAST FEW DAYS I HAVE HAD SEVERAL RANDOM INTERACTIONS with people that have highlighted the lack of margin in many of our lives. Margin by definition is simply the distance between our load and our limits. We all have different capacity levels, but no one can be spiritually, emotionally, and physically healthy without breathing room (**Psalm 46:10**). We need to learn how to seek, experience, and appreciate solitude. This is when we receive revelation and an awareness of God's desires and directions for our lives (**Galatians 5:25**). Solitude can certainly be difficult but beneficial at the same time. It may be difficult when conviction comes, as well as beneficial as God reveals steps to take. I love to reflect on our heroes of the faith and how closely they walked with God (**Hebrews 11:6**). We must first *believe by faith* it is worth it to create margin, seek solitude, and rest with God. It may be counter-cultural, but this way of abiding in Christ will help you accomplish more than you could imagine.

> Be still, and know that I am God! I will be honored by every nation. I will be honored throughout the world. — Psalm 46:10

> Since we are living by the Spirit, let us follow the Spirit's leading in every part of our lives. — Galatians 5:25

> And it is impossible to please God without faith. Anyone who wants to come to him must believe that God exists and that he rewards those who sincerely seek him. — Hebrews 11:6

> "... may he equip you with all you need for doing his will. May he produce in you, through the power of Jesus Christ, every good thing that is pleasing to him. All glory to him forever and ever! Amen." — Hebrews 13:21

May 16

WHAT DOES IT REALLY LOOK LIKE TO NOT ATTEMPT THINGS in our own power but instead to lean into God for His strength to navigate situations? We hear, "I can't do this on my own, I need God's power to do this or that" (**Philippians 2:13**). As we surrender situations to the Lord in prayer, seeking His guidance and wisdom, we are humbling ourselves under His authority, acknowledging our need for His insight. Through prayer and meditation, oftentimes God will soften our hearts, bending our will to His, enabling us to have a more Christlike perspective (**2 Corinthians 3:18**). It always provides *"Holy Spirit confidence"* for me as I bring conversations and situations to the Lord first, embracing the gift of His promptings and direction. Declaring out loud, "Father, I want your strength, not my own," is a great reminder of our human inadequacy (**Psalm 73:26**). Our burden should be light so we are free to live and love in a way that is uplifting to those around us. When we feel overwhelmed with the weight of circumstances and people, we are operating by the wrong power.

> *For God is working in you, giving you the desire and the power to do what pleases him.* — Philippians 2:13

> *So all of us who have had that veil removed can see and reflect the glory of the Lord. And the Lord—who is the Spirit—makes us more and more like him as we are changed into his glorious image.* — 2 Corinthians 3:18

> *My health may fail, and my spirit may grow weak, but God remains the strength of my heart; he is mine forever.* — Psalm 73:26

> *Then Jesus said, "Come to me, all of you who are weary and carry heavy burdens, and I will give you rest."* — Matthew 11:28

May 17

TODAY I HAD THE PRIVILEGE OF TAKING A YOUNG LADY TO LUNCH. I had a place in mind and thought I would pitch the idea when I picked her up. When I mentioned the restaurant, her eyes lit up and she was happy to tell me she woke up thinking of that type of food. It warmed my heart to know she was so excited. Afterwards, I mentioned a consignment store I wanted to show her, and she was overwhelmed, saying she always passed it and wanted to go in. The owner is a friend of mine and has a big heart for Jesus, and three of us, along with another friend, began talking of how the Lord had orchestrated the day (**Psalm 90:12**). This led to a lengthy conversation of the goodness of God. We all began swapping stories of how we have seen God move recently. We were all celebrating Jesus and His faithfulness (**Psalm 107:21–22**). I thought of how it warmed the Lord's heart listening to His daughters *find satisfaction and fulfillment in Him*, realizing His personal touch in our lives (**Ephesians 1:11**). God is constantly at work, moving in and around us in ways we cannot even imagine. How amazing it is to know the mighty God of the universe desires to share life with us every day.

> *Teach us to realize the brevity of life, so that we may grow in wisdom.*
> — Psalm 90:12

> Let them praise the Lord for his great love and for the wonderful things he has done for them. Let them offer sacrifices of thanksgiving and sing joyfully about his glorious acts.
> — Psalm 107:21–22

> Furthermore, because we are united with Christ, we have received an inheritance from God, for he chose us in advance, and he makes everything work out according to his plan. — Ephesians 1:11

May 18

ONE OF THE MOST POWERFUL TRUTHS TO HAVE ROOTED DEEP in our souls is how much Jesus truly cares for us. As we invite and embrace His supernatural love and provision, it builds the strong security of our identity (**1 Peter 5:7**). I often encourage people to research the Scriptures to find absolute truth to combat any lies they may be believing that produce insecurities. Unfortunately, due to abuse, negative environments, or lack of purpose, the foundations of our identity can be shattered, but never beyond repair (**Romans 6:4**). Jesus offers us new life with purpose and the opportunity to live, breathe, and move in resurrection power daily. In the morning, it is so powerful to proclaim, "This is the day the Lord has made; I will rejoice and be glad in it (**Psalm 118:24**). Life is genuinely so much more interesting walking with Jesus because we never know what He may have in store for us. Our lives will shift between joy and pain this side of heaven, but the loving arms of our Savior will hold us tight on the mountaintop and in the valley. May we *know, believe, and receive* His embrace.

> Give all your worries and cares to God, for he cares about you. — 1 Peter 5:7

> For we died and were buried with Christ by baptism. And just as Christ was raised from the dead by the glorious power of the Father, now we also may live new lives. — Romans 6:4

> This is the day the Lord has made.
> We will rejoice and be glad in it. — Psalm 118:24

> "... even there your hand will guide me, and your strength will support me."
> — Psalm 139:10

On the way to church this morning, I heard a message that pointed out God never gives a warning without offering a hope. I couldn't help but meditate on the reality of this idea. We could all quickly recall circumstances in our lives where this has played out (**1 Corinthians 10:13**). Look back and recall teetering between a good or bad choice, knowing full well God was offering a way out. Sometimes we choose well and sometimes we don't, which can result in us either grieving God's heart or bringing Him great pleasure (**Psalm 149:4**). The idea that we have opportunities every day to please the heart of our Father is both amazing and unending, meaning we have the rest of our lives to move towards this goal daily (**2 Corinthians 5:9–11**). *The more deeply we love Jesus*, the more our desire to please Him will outweigh the empty desire to gratify our flesh. So not only does He offer hope, but He offers more of Himself, because every victory we experience pulls us closer into the fold of His security, love, and purpose for our lives. When our heavenly Father is for us, whoever or whatever is against us has already lost.

> *The temptations in your life are no different from what others experience. And God is faithful. He will not allow the temptation to be more than you can stand. When you are tempted, he will show you a way out so that you can endure.* —1 Corinthians 10:13

> *For the Lord delights in his people;*
> *he crowns the humble with victory.* — Psalm 149:4

> *So whether we are here in this body or away from this body, our goal is to please him. For we must all stand before Christ to be judged. We will each receive whatever we deserve for the good or evil we have done in this earthly body. Because we understand our fearful responsibility to the Lord, we work hard to persuade others. God knows we are sincere, and I hope you know this, too.* — 2 Corinthians 5:9–11

> *What shall we say about such wonderful things as these? If God is for us, who can ever be against us?* — Romans 8:31

Take a few moments and ask yourself the question, "What assignment is God giving me right now?" Throughout our journey in this life, we can know God is always at work in and through our lives (**John 5:17**). God is consistently inviting us to internal assignments, urging us to cooperate with the Holy Spirit's work on a heart issue or alarm that He desires to heal (**Psalm 147:3**). His desire is for us to *walk in freedom and victory*. He knows when an area of hurt is holding us back, and in His perfect timing, He will provide steps to take towards restoration. Sometimes we have opportunities with external assignments, such as a project, ministry, or (most importantly) showing Christlike love and encouragement to someone He has placed along your path (**Proverbs 16:9**). These are divine interactions set up for us. God uses His people in mighty ways to bring the Good News of the Gospel to a hurting world. So often we don't feel equipped to be used by God and we can't do anything on our own, but all that He has predestined will come to pass.

"But Jesus replied, 'My Father is always working, and so am I.'" — John 5:17

He heals the brokenhearted and bandages their wounds. — Psalm 147:3

We can make our plans, but the Lord determines our steps. — Proverbs 16:9

Today I had the privilege to take a road trip to Asheville, North Carolina. Asheville has a significant sweet spot in my heart because that is where my personal relationship with Jesus came to life (**1 Corinthians 1:9**). This was the season of my life where God revealed to me my brokenness and offered a new way of living that didn't revolve around myself but around Him and His plans and purpose for me (**Luke 9:24**). It is radically counter-cultural to live a worship-filled life in a me-centered world, yet this is where we find satisfaction and joy beyond measure. When we wake up in the morning and ask, "Lord, how can I worship you today?" it immediately shifts our focus and frees us from the bondage of self-centeredness. When the Lord met me right where I was all those years ago, He wanted to rescue me from myself and show me a new reality of who He was and who I was called to be because of Him (**John 15:5**). I never lose my awe of looking back and recalling how faithful He has been and continues to be every day. His faithfulness should motivate us to *give Him our hearts*, our affection, our gratitude, and our lives for His glory.

> God will do this, for he is faithful to do what he says, and he has invited you into partnership with his Son, Jesus Christ our Lord. — 1 Corinthians 1:9

> If you try to hang on to your life, you will lose it. But if you give up your life for my sake, you will save it. — Luke 9:24

> Yes, I am the vine; you are the branches. Those who remain in me, and I in them, will produce much fruit. For apart from me you can do nothing.
> — John 15:5

> So whether you eat or drink, or whatever you do, do it all for the glory of God.
> — 1 Corinthians 10:31

As followers of Christ, we are called to be salt and light in the world (**Matthew 5:13–16**). While living this out is an exciting opportunity, it is also a responsibility we need to be intentional about. Stagnant, mundane Christianity is the enemy of representing salt and light. In order to be salty, our faith needs to have flavor and substance (**Hebrews 11:1**). We represent this when we are confident in the source of our hope and can encourage others towards Jesus with the assurance He is there for them. We can know, as these spiritual conversations present themselves, that the Holy Spirit is already at work (**Acts 1:8**). For lights to really shine, they must be present in the dark. All too often people want to surround themselves only with people just like them. We fall into rhythms of comfort, and we become disoriented around people who think and believe radically differently than we do. In these situations, it is critical that we are kind, compassionate, and inviting. We should all *pray daily for divine opportunities* to display love and hope in a chaotic, confused culture.

> You are the salt of the earth. But what good is salt if it has lost its flavor? Can you make it salty again? It will be thrown out and trampled underfoot as worthless. "You are the light of the world—like a city on a hilltop that cannot be hidden. No one lights a lamp and then puts it under a basket. Instead, a lamp is placed on a stand, where it gives light to everyone in the house. In the same way, let your good deeds shine out for all to see, so that everyone will praise your heavenly Father. — Matthew 5:13–16

> Faith shows the reality of what we hope for; it is the evidence of things we cannot see. — Hebrews 11:1

> But you will receive power when the Holy Spirit comes upon you. And you will be my witnesses, telling people about me everywhere—in Jerusalem, throughout Judea, in Samaria, and to the ends of the earth. — Acts 1:8

> Instead, be kind to each other, tenderhearted, forgiving one another, just as God through Christ has forgiven you. — Ephesians 4:32

May 23

CELEBRATING THE GOODNESS OF GOD HAS BEEN THE SONG of my heart today. One reason is today is one of my miracle babies' birthdays. Every child of God is a miracle, but she was conceived after a miscarriage that had already blown my doctor away, since I was told I would never conceive on my own, but God said differently (**Isaiah 55:8–9**). The reality is we serve a wonder-working God who has amazing things in store for His children (**Matthew 7:11**). I know the joy that fills my heart when my children are happy and also the sting of pain if they are struggling. There is such a comforting security to know God understands our emotions on a level we cannot even comprehend. We can also *rest in the assurance of His timing and* wisdom, realizing He is never late or early, but always right on time (**Ecclesiastes 3:1**). As we learn to surrender the control we think we have, our hearts become softer and our hands become open to receive His purposes and plans for our lives. Surrender and trust result in joy and peace.

> *"'My thoughts are nothing like your thoughts,' says the Lord. 'And my ways are far beyond anything you could imagine. For just as the heavens are higher than the earth, so my ways are higher than your ways and my thoughts higher than your thoughts.'" — Isaiah 55:8–9*

> *So if you sinful people know how to give good gifts to your children, how much more will your heavenly Father give good gifts to those who ask him.*
> *— Matthew 7:11*

> *For everything there is a season, a time for every activity under heaven. — Ecclesiastes 3:1*

> *So humble yourselves under the mighty power of God, and at the right time he will lift you up in honor. — 1 Peter 5:6*

May 24

I WOKE UP TODAY TO A TUNE IN MY HEART OF A CURRENT WORSHIP song by Matt Mayer called, "I Just Wanna Be in the Room." This song echoes the desire to see God move and celebrates welcoming whatever it takes to sense the presence of God (**Psalm 119:18**). The challenge has been on my heart all day as I've pondered the question, "Are we seeking, desiring, and expecting God to move?" Seeing the movement of God in people or situations is more than just believing or the assurance of eternity; it is recognizing that our God is a *waymaker*, and is as powerful right now as He ever has been or will be (**2 Samuel 22:33**). Looking and anticipating a move of God creates a zeal and passion in our faith. All too often we settle for less than God wants to show us because we lack the awe and wonder of His activity. I pray there will be an awakening of the places that have become dormant or dismissive to the vibrant reality of God's revelations to His people (**Ephesians 4:13**). We should *pray to receive all God has for His children.*

> *Open my eyes to see the wonderful truths in your instructions.* — Psalm 119:18

> *God is my strong fortress, and he makes my way perfect.* — 2 Samuel 22:33

> *This will continue until we all come to such unity in our faith and knowledge of God's Son that we will be mature in the Lord, measuring up to the full and complete standard of Christ.* — Ephesians 4:13

May 25

I RECEIVED A CALL TODAY FROM A YOUNG WOMAN I MET a few years ago. She was in distress and felt I was a safe place to reach out to. Although I hadn't seen or heard from her in a while, I vividly remember when we met and how the Holy Spirit prompted me to go to our church lobby, where we locked eyes (**John 16:13**). Shortly after we met, I was led to pray with her at what felt like a premature moment in our encounter, but I knew that's what God was calling me to do. God uses us as vessels of love and compassion in each other's lives in ways beyond our comprehension. Because of some of my experiences, I cannot in good conscience ignore a nudge of the Spirit towards someone. I'm sure I have been and will be wrong in my desire to be obedient, but I know that God even uses our mistakes for His glory (**Romans 8:28**). The reality is the Lord gives us opportunities to be His hands and feet, and as we *follow through in obedience*, the fruit from these not-so-random interactions is proof of how intimately God is involved in our ordinary lives that can and do make a difference.

> When the Spirit of truth comes, he will guide you into all truth. He will not speak on his own but will tell you what he has heard. He will tell you about the future. — John 16:13

> And we know that God causes everything to work together for the good of those who love God and are called according to his purpose for them. — Romans 8:28

> Let us think of ways to motivate one another to acts of love and good works. — Hebrews 10:24

THE IDEA THAT JESUS IS IN THE BUSINESS OF REVERSALS was emphasized this morning at my church. I meditated on this point throughout the day, thinking how true is the reality that He makes beauty from ashes and that in our humility is where we find strength (**Isaiah 61:3**). My mind began to wander to all the blessings I have seen in my life, as well as the lives of others in the midst of pain (**1 Peter 5:10**). Victory in our trials can be threefold. First, God meets us there, beginning a refining work in our heart. How often do we hear people say they met Jesus in the pit of despair (**Psalm 40:2**)? Second, through the healing of our woundedness, we get to experience the compassion and faithfulness of our Lord in His attentiveness to our circumstances (**Psalm 86:15**). Finally, the Lord never wastes our experiences or pain and sets us up to be able to share the comfort, mercy, and restoration of our suffering with others who may be navigating through similar waters (**2 Corinthians 1:4**). He is willing and able to reverse even the deepest places of pain as we *seek, trust, and invite Him in.*

> To all who mourn in Israel, he will give a crown of beauty for ashes, a joyous blessing instead of mourning, festive praise instead of despair. In their righteousness, they will be like great oaks that the Lord has planted for his own glory. — Isaiah 61:3

> In his kindness God called you to share in his eternal glory by means of Christ Jesus. So after you have suffered a little while, he will restore, support, and strengthen you, and he will place you on a firm foundation. — 1 Peter 5:10

> He lifted me out of the pit of despair, out of the mud and the mire. He set my feet on solid ground and steadied me as I walked along. — Psalm 40:2

> But you, O Lord, are a God of compassion and mercy, slow to get angry and filled with unfailing love and faithfulness. — Psalm 86:15

> He comforts us in all our troubles so that we can comfort others. When they are troubled, we will be able to give them the same comfort God has given us. — 2 Corinthians 1:4

May 27

Having lunch with a young lady today, the Lord revealed a common area of struggle. I was sharing with her how so often the places we find the most challenging are the ones in which we end up experiencing the most freedom seasons later (**Romans 5:3–4**). This strengthening is the result of learning to *lean into God for His direction* and healing. The struggle we shared was essentially the journey to trusting God. Trust is such a day-by-day, situation-by-situation choice, but as we put our faith in motion, we learn through experience that He is trustworthy (**Psalm 111:7**). Living life recognizing God's provision and faithfulness is a life-reflecting freedom and security (**Psalm 37:5**). We can all celebrate the promise that God knows exactly what He intends to accomplish in and through our lives. Thank goodness we do not hold the kind of power that we sometimes think we do. Embracing our position as God's creation and learning to relinquish control is a journey worthy of our effort.

> *We can rejoice, too, when we run into problems and trials, for we know that they help us develop endurance. And endurance develops strength of character, and character strengthens our confident hope of salvation.* — Romans 5:3–4

> *All he does is just and good, and all his commandments are trustworthy.* — Psalm 111:7

> *Commit everything you do to the Lord. Trust him, and he will help you.* — Psalm 37:5

> *I have told you all this so that you may have peace in me. Here on earth you will have many trials and sorrows. But take heart, because I have overcome the world.* — John 16:33

May 28

OUR RELATIONSHIP WITH THE LORD IS ACTUALLY the only one in our lives that will meet and surpass our expectations of intimacy and fulfillment (**Ephesians 3:19**). The tenderness in which God meets us in our desire is not to be understood but only embraced. Oftentimes, I have referred to my relationship with God as the hedge of protection around my heart. I say this in that with Him as my comfort, security, and identity, no situation or person can trump His ways or thoughts toward me (**2 Corinthians 5:17**). In order for God to be our safe place and refuge we have to put into practice running to Him first and staying as long as it takes for Him to renew our heart posture (**Psalm 51:10**). He will literally reorient our mindset as we *humble ourselves and seek His perspective*. I have found the more I run to Him the deeper my desire is to share life with the One who is worthy of my undivided heart.

> *May you experience the love of Christ, though it is too great to understand fully. Then you will be made complete with all the fullness of life and power that comes from God. — Ephesians 3:19*

> *This means that anyone who belongs to Christ has become a new person. The old life is gone; a new life has begun! — 2 Corinthians 5:17*

> *Create in me a clean heart, O God. Renew a loyal spirit within me. — Psalm 51:10*

> *Teach me your ways, O Lord, that I may live according to your truth! Grant me purity of heart, so that I may honor you. — Psalm 86:11*

Imagine waking up every day and the first question you ask yourself is, "How I can be on mission with God today?" The beauty is that this question in and of itself will drive you to seek God early as you offer your willing heart for service (**Exodus 35:21**). Another great benefit of this mindset is it quickly takes the focus off yourself and onto God. We can be on mission with God in the midst of our ordinary schedules and interactions. He is constantly putting opportunities in front of us to show His love and grace, or to comfort someone in a way that makes it obvious you are someone who has a personal relationship with Jesus (**1 John 4:7**). One solid fact we can be sure of: the more you live for God, the more you will desire to live for Him. We come to realize that a self-centered life leads to emptiness and frustration because we were not designed to glorify ourselves; *we were created to glorify God and* be on mission for His Kingdom. This is the heart posture that truly satisfies.

> *All whose hearts were stirred and whose spirits were moved came and brought their sacred offerings to the Lord. They brought all the materials needed for the Tabernacle, for the performance of its rituals, and for the sacred garments.* — Exodus 35:21

> *Dear friends, let us continue to love one another, for love comes from God. Anyone who loves is a child of God and knows God.* — 1 John 4:7

> *Because I am righteous, I will see you. When I awake, I will see you face to face and be satisfied.* — Psalm 17:15

I HAD THE PRIVILEGE OF TALKING TO A YOUNG LADY TODAY who has really grown in her personal relationship with the Lord over the past few years, and I asked her the question, "How are you experiencing God right now? What has he shown you?" (**Jeremiah 33:3**). She gave the most beautiful answer that He has impressed on her heart how He has been with her orchestrating events, people, and interactions to draw her closer to Himself. She spoke of the way she has recalled scenarios and realized His hand in not only calling her but simply being there with her (**Deuteronomy 31:8**). It is amazing to learn the creative ways God has wooed us to Himself when we weren't necessarily looking for Him (**Jeremiah 31:3**). I clearly remember the day the Holy Spirit literally stopped me in my tracks and I began to feel the pull of my heavenly Father in an opposite direction. However, the truth is that He was at work in my life long before I actually felt His call. We should all *pause and celebrate with a posture of gratitude* the ways our heavenly Father has fought for us at times when we didn't even know.

> *Ask me and I will tell you remarkable secrets you do not know about things to come.* — Jeremiah 33:3

> *Do not be afraid or discouraged, for the Lord will personally go ahead of you. He will be with you; he will neither fail you nor abandon you.* — Deuteronomy 31:8

> *"Long ago the Lord said to Israel: 'I have loved you, my people, with an everlasting love. With unfailing love I have drawn you to myself.'"* — Jeremiah 31:3

> *But you are not like that, for you are a chosen people. You are royal priests, a holy nation, God's very own possession. As a result, you can show others the goodness of God, for he called you out of the darkness into his wonderful light.* — 1 Peter 2:9

THE GIFT OF JESUS BEING HERE ON EARTH, modeling how we should live, love, and function in this life, is something we all need to hold close to our hearts and tap into daily (**Matthew 11:29**). How often do we take seriously the reality that Christ Himself is our role model for any given situation or relationship? Cultivating the self-control required to actually pause in an interaction and prayerfully seek Jesus for guidance takes intentionality and patience (**Ecclesiastes 7:9**). Our flesh is loud and impulsive, quick to respond, and doesn't always care for the hearts of those around us very well. As we grow in our relationship with God, *our flesh can be governed more by our Spirit*, which enables us to reflect the love of our Savior through our behavior (**Acts 1:8**). I love the reality that during Jesus' ministry He accomplished so much but was never frantic and out of control. This was a direct result of Him staying in step with God, trusting His timing, His ways, and His strength. So many lessons we can learn are available at our fingertips through the powerful living word of God.

> *Take my yoke upon you. Let me teach you, because I am humble and gentle at heart, and you will find rest for your souls.* — Matthew 11:29

> *Control your temper, for anger labels you a fool.* — Ecclesiastes 7:9

> *But you will receive power when the Holy Spirit comes upon you. And you will be my witnesses, telling people about me everywhere—in Jerusalem, throughout Judea, in Samaria, and to the ends of the earth.* — Acts 1:8

> *For the word of God is alive and powerful. It is sharper than the sharpest two-edged sword, cutting between soul and spirit, between joint and marrow. It exposes our innermost thoughts and desires.* — Hebrews 4:12

June 1

THE EARLY DAYS OF SUMMER ARE A GREAT OPPORTUNITY for us to create some new rhythms in our lives. It's so easy to get out of balance with our spiritual, emotional, and physical well-being, and being intentional to pause and create new habits is powerful. So often there are areas we try to keep from God almost out of fear of what His thoughts are on the subject. A great move forward spiritually would be bringing to God that issue so He can empower you to navigate through it according to His will (**Ephesians 3:16**). Speaking God's word out loud to ourselves in the early hours does wonders for our emotional well-being.

This month choose a scripture to encourage you where you need it and say it to yourself every morning. The Word of God is powerful emotional medicine (**Proverbs 4:20–22**). Some key power foods in the Bible are fish, flax, olive oil, fruits, vegetables, and honey. Incorporate these more regularly and enjoy the benefit of nurturing your physical body this way (**1 Corinthians 6:19–20**). *Prayerfully consider positive adjustments* you can make for your entire well-being. God cares about every part of who we are.

> I pray that from his glorious, unlimited resources he will empower you with inner strength through his Spirit. — Ephesians 3:16

> My child, pay attention to what I say. Listen carefully to my words. Don't lose sight of them. Let them penetrate deep into your heart, for they bring life to those who find them, and healing to their whole body. — Proverbs 4:20–22

> Don't you realize that your body is the temple of the Holy Spirit, who lives in you and was given to you by God? You do not belong to yourself, for God bought you with a high price. So you must honor God with your body.
> — 1 Corinthians 6:19–20

June 2

I HAD THE HONOR TODAY OF WITNESSING SEVERAL NEW BELIEVERS BE BAPTIZED. It was such a beautiful demonstration of the transformative power of Christ's love (**John 6:37**). We should never lose our awe of how the Lord found us and rescues us from a self-serving existence that ultimately leads to despair. Upon the end of my quiet time this morning I lifted my hands up as if God Himself was pulling me up and said, "Thank you, Father, for pulling me out of spiritual darkness into your loving arms of eternal purpose and security" (**Colossians 1:13–14**). Our rescue is obviously the tip of the iceberg for our journey of spiritual maturity and learning how to practically work out our salvation, but choosing to move from darkness to light is a supernatural start (**Ecclesiastes 2:13**). *Choosing Jesus' way* for our lives will always be the right answer, but building spiritual disciplines into our lives in order that He is the foundation on which we stand has to be our priority and mission.

> *However, those the Father has given me will come to me, and I will never reject them.* — John 6:37

> *For he has rescued us from the kingdom of darkness and transferred us into the Kingdom of his dear Son, who purchased our freedom and forgave our sins.*
> — Colossians 1:13–14

> *"I thought, 'Wisdom is better than foolishness, just as light is better than darkness.'"*
> — Ecclesiastes 2:13

June 3

IN THE MIDST OF A COUPLE OF RICH CONVERSATIONS WITH two different people, I found myself emphasizing the concept that we need to be seeking Jesus himself, not what He has for us (**Psalm 14:2**). All too often questions such as, "What are God's plans for me?" or "What gifts will God allow me to experience?" create distractions from us learning more about the character and heart of Jesus and experiencing deeper intimacy with Him (**Psalm 27:8**). God has the details and seasons of our lives covered. Our responsibility is to cling to His direction and wisdom while He helps us navigate through (**Psalm 119:105**). If we *wake up in the morning and declare*, "Jesus, I will move towards you today," there is no person or circumstance that can stand in our way. He is there with us through everything, our mighty rock, our fortress, our deliverer, our comforter, and our most precious supporter. His love, mercy, and companionship is the ultimate gift, plan, and prize.

> The Lord looks down from heaven on the entire human race; he looks to see if anyone is truly wise, if anyone seeks God. — Psalm 14:2

> "My heart has heard you say, 'Come and talk with me.' And my heart responds, 'Lord, I am coming.'" — Psalm 27:8

> Your word is a lamp to guide my feet and a light for my path. — Psalm 119:105

> I press on to reach the end of the race and receive the heavenly prize for which God, through Christ Jesus, is calling us. — Philippians 3:14

June 4

ALMOST DAILY I FIND MYSELF UTTERING THE WORDS, "FATHER, I acknowledge You are God and I am not." This verbal declaration frees me to be a follower, not an orchestrator, of situations and timing in my own and others' lives that I long to see come to fruition (**Jeremiah 32:17**). As we embrace God being the creator, establisher, and finisher of all things, it becomes clearer how critical it is for us to humble ourselves and follow His lead (**1 Peter 5:6–7**). Why do we struggle to truly surrender the things that deep down we know only He can change? Obviously there is not a one-size-fits-all answer, but all too often it's because our flesh craves immediate results or we aren't sure God is going to move the way we would like (**Isaiah 43:16**). We have to *preach to ourselves that God* will move if it needs to happen, when it needs to happen, and how it needs to happen. The beauty found in trusting Him leads us to that peace that surpasses all understanding.

> *O Sovereign Lord! You made the heavens and earth by your strong hand and powerful arm. Nothing is too hard for you!* — Jeremiah 32:17

> *So humble yourselves under the mighty power of God, and at the right time he will lift you up in honor. Give all your worries and cares to God, for he cares about you.*
> — 1 Peter 5:6–7

> *I am the Lord, who opened a way through the waters, making a dry path through the sea.* — Isaiah 43:16

> *Then you will experience God's peace, which exceeds anything we can understand. His peace will guard your hearts and minds as you live in Christ Jesus.*
> — Philippians 4:7

June 5

Today I have been in awe of the creativity in which the Lord orchestrates our paths to cross with others for our benefit, their benefit, and His glory (**Proverbs 16:9**). Coincidences don't have a place in the life of a believer. It's all about divine appointments, blessings that remind us of God's goodness and involvement in our daily comings and goings (**Psalm 121:8**). The way in which the Lord has us run into or meet the right person at the right time is simply a manifestation of His provision. God knows how deeply we need each other to spur one another on in our faith and navigate through what can be a complicated journey this side of heaven. Our spiritual enemy works overtime in the areas of pride and isolation, seeking to convince people to be self-protective and not letting others in. We need to prayerfully *seek God's guidance* towards relationships where we can love, support, and edify each other, as well as encouraging one another more towards Christ. We need to be open to the community that God provides for us.

> We can make our plans, but the Lord determines our steps. —Proverbs 16:9

> The Lord keeps watch over you as you come and go, both now and forever. — Psalm 121:8

> Let us think of ways to motivate one another to acts of love and good works. And let us not neglect our meeting together, as some people do, but encourage one another, especially now that the day of his return is drawing near. — Hebrews 10:24–25

June 6

TODAY I GOT TO CELEBRATE MY BIRTHDAY, AND GOD WOKE ME UP with these worship lyrics, "Go let all the people know anything is possible." This could not be a more appropriate message to reflect the passion of my heart to point others to the loving embrace of Christ's arms and to live in the sweet spot of relationship with Him (**Psalm 16:11**). The enemy of my soul tried to destroy who God created me to be early in my life, and he failed miserably. God pursued, rescued, and healed me, securing me into the abundant life He has for me (**John 10:10**). I never grow weary of worshiping Him and *being on mission with Him daily*, relying on His strength and guidance to love others and to encourage them to move towards Him, where their true salvation, joy, satisfaction, and purpose will be found (**Ephesians 3:20**). The gift of abiding, celebrating, and resting in the presence of my heavenly Father forever brings me an everlasting joy that will never change or grow dim. Hallelujah!

> *You will show me the way of life, granting me the joy of your presence and the pleasures of living with you forever.*
> *— Psalm 16:11*

> *The thief's purpose is to steal and kill and destroy. My purpose is to give them a rich and satisfying life. — John 10:10*

> *Now all glory to God, who is able, through his mighty power at work within us, to accomplish infinitely more than we might ask or think. —Ephesians 3:20*

> *For the Lord your God is living among you. He is a mighty savior. He will take delight in you with gladness. With his love, he will calm all your fears. He will rejoice over you with joyful songs.*
> *— Zephaniah 3:17*

June 7

My parents have both moved from this life into eternity. Although my parents and I experienced our struggles, especially early in my life, I was and remain very emotionally attached to them. It brings me unspeakable joy knowing I will see them again (**2 Samuel 12:23**). A sweet friend of mine asked me just the other day, "How are you with your mama and daddy being gone?" I just thought for a minute how to communicate the peace that fills my heart, and before I could speak she said, "They are still very much alive to you, aren't they?" And I immediately responded yes, with a sense of contentment filling my heart (**Philippians 4:7**). Not only does our amazing God grant us the gift of eternal life, but He will also stand in the gap for us wherever we are lacking. He will be our mother, father, husband, and friend in supernatural, creative ways if we will only *open our eyes, ears, and hearts* to experience Him (**Ephesians 1:18**). He is always with us and is more than able to offer the comfort we seek.

> *But why should I fast when he is dead? Can I bring him back again? I will go to him one day, but he cannot return to me.* — 2 Samuel 12:23

> *Then you will experience God's peace, which exceeds anything we can understand. His peace will guard your hearts and minds as you live in Christ Jesus.* — Philippians 4:7

> *I pray that your hearts will be flooded with light so that you can understand the confident hope he has given to those he called—his holy people who are his rich and glorious inheritance.* — Ephesians 1:18

June 8

I HEARD THE MOST BEAUTIFUL WORDS FROM A SPECIAL LADY while we were discussing her journey with the Lord. She declared, "I just want more of Jesus! I want to love Him and love others and want people to see the light of Christ in me." I encouraged her immediately that she just articulated what life is all about (**Matthew 22:37–39**). It is easy to get distracted by the things we desire from God. His plans, His purpose, even gifts from God are all wonderful and worthy of our excitement, but they cannot overshadow our desire for God Himself (**John 3:16**). It is absolutely critical that we are confident in the reality that, as we seek Jesus and abide in Him, He will supply all we need. He may bless us with gifts or reveal a path or plan, but only in His time, and we can rest assured He knows how to communicate with us in ways we will understand. *Continually moving towards Jesus* means continually moving towards any and all things He has in store for our lives on earth and in heaven.

> *"Jesus replied, 'You must love the Lord your God with all your heart, all your soul, and all your mind.' This is the first and greatest commandment. A second is equally important: 'Love your neighbor as yourself.'" — Matthew 22:37–39*

> *For this is how God loved the world: He gave his one and only Son, so that everyone who believes in him will not perish but have eternal life. — John 3:16*

> *God saved you by his grace when you believed. And you can't take credit for this; it is a gift from God. Salvation is not a reward for the good things we have done, so none of us can boast about it. For we are God's masterpiece. He has created us anew in Christ Jesus, so we can do the good things he planned for us long ago.*
> *— Ephesians 2:8–10*

June 9

NAVIGATING THE MULTITUDE OF RELATIONSHIPS I HAVE is something I could never do in my own strength (**Proverbs 3:5–6**). I am constantly seeking God's wisdom as to how to love well, because I believe loving God, loving others, and nurturing our own love affair with the Lord is of the utmost importance (**Luke 10:27**). There are three critical ways I find myself being led to show love. First is to speak or point out truth gently. Speaking truth in love makes others feel safe, not attacked (**Ephesians 4:15**). This could look like comforting someone the same way God has comforted you. Second is making the other person aware of their value and God's relentless love for them, emphasizing that struggles will pass and that there is hope. Finally, the most important way to love well is to encourage movement toward Christ (**Hebrews 10:24–25**). He is always the answer, and *pointing others toward Jesus* is only influential when He is reigning and ruling in our own lives. Knowing Him and being known is the path to real love.

> Trust in the Lord with all your heart; do not depend on your own understanding. Seek his will in all you do, and he will show you which path to take.
> — Proverbs 3:5–6

> "The man answered, 'You must love the Lord your God with all your heart, all your soul, all your strength, and all your mind.' And, 'Love your neighbor as yourself.'"
> — Luke 10:27

> Instead, we will speak the truth in love, growing in every way more and more like Christ, who is the head of his body, the church.
> — Ephesians 4:15

> Let us think of ways to motivate one another to acts of love and good works. And let us not neglect our meeting together, as some people do, but encourage one another, especially now that the day of his return is drawing near.
> — Hebrews 10:24–25

June 10

ONCE WE HAVE INVITED CHRIST TO LIVE IN OUR HEARTS, we have the opportunity to allow the Holy Spirit to invade every part of who we are (**Galatians 5:16**). We can choose to agree and cooperate with the way the Holy Spirit manifests in our attitudes, interactions, and the fruit in our lives, creating evidence that Christ lives in our hearts (**Galatians 5:22–23**). Although none of us would set out to grieve the Spirit intentionally, we all do when we fall short. When we give in to the temptation of complaining, gossiping, slandering, or being prideful, our spirit will feel heavy, indicating unrest with our behavior (**Ephesians 4:31**). On the other hand, when we are allowing the Holy Spirit to bear fruit in the ways of kindness, gentleness, and joy, there is a pep in our step and a sense of freedom (**Ephesians 4:32**). Starting the day *saying out loud, "Holy Spirit,* have your way in me today" definitely increases our sensitivity to how God is leading, helping us to live in a way that pleases Him.

> *So I say, let the Holy Spirit guide your lives. Then you won't be doing what your sinful nature craves.* — Galatians 5:16

> *But the Holy Spirit produces this kind of fruit in our lives: love, joy, peace, patience, kindness, goodness, faithfulness, gentleness, and self-control. There is no law against these things!* — Galatians 5:22–23

> *Get rid of all bitterness, rage, anger, harsh words, and slander, as well as all types of evil behavior. Instead, be kind to each other, tenderhearted, forgiving one another, just as God through Christ has forgiven you.*
> — Ephesians 4:31–32

June 11

WALKING ON THE TRAIL NEAR MY HOUSE, LISTENING TO WORSHIP MUSIC, I looked up and there was the most beautiful light coming through the trees in the shape of a cross. In that moment I was meditating on God's goodness, and to look up and see that cross stopped me in my tracks (**Jeremiah 29:13**). As we cultivate our love relationship with the Lord, we are more connected and aware of how creative He is in revealing Himself. He knows when we are making an effort to move towards Him and wants to give us encouragement. God's desire is for us to have the assurance He is present and available (**Ephesians 3:12**). Such a beneficial prayer for us is to *stay in the moment with God*, abiding with expectant hearts. In our human nature, we tend to get distracted by the past or future, but in the present we can experience peace as we stay focused on the one who holds it all in His capable hands.

If you look for me wholeheartedly, you will find me. — Jeremiah 29:13

Because of Christ and our faith in him, we can now come boldly and confidently into God's presence. — Ephesians 3:12

You will keep in perfect peace all who trust in you, all whose thoughts are fixed on you! — Isaiah 26:3

June 12

WE CAN ALL EMBRACE WITH CONFIDENCE THE REALITY THAT GOD speaks to His people. The most common way He speaks, for most people, is through His Word (**2 Timothy 3:16**). It is amazing the way the Holy Spirit will illuminate messages in Scripture to enact real heart transformation in us. The Scriptures are indeed the living Word of God, which is, always has been, and always will be the most powerful resource in the world. As believers, we should take advantage of reading the Word daily for encouragement, direction, and, most importantly, getting to know better the heart of our Father (**1 Corinthians 2:9–10**). God also desires for us to know ourselves and others through the lens of His truth, and to experience life's ups and downs with His Word on our hearts (**Psalm 119:18**). I never lose my awe of how one idea or truth from the Bible can cause peace to wash over us in a way that radically changes our perspective. *Read His Word, search it*, and marinate in it, and you will develop a hunger because it's just that powerful.

> *All Scripture is inspired by God and is useful to teach us what is true and to make us realize what is wrong in our lives. It corrects us when we are wrong and teaches us to do what is right. — 2 Timothy 3:16*

> *That is what the Scriptures mean when they say, 'No eye has seen, no ear has heard, and no mind has imagined what God has prepared for those who love him.' But it was to us that God revealed these things by his Spirit. For his Spirit searches out everything and shows us God's deep secrets. — 1 Corinthians 2:9–10*

> *Open my eyes to see the wonderful truths in your instructions. — Psalm 119:18*

> *For the word of God is alive and powerful. It is sharper than the sharpest two-edged sword, cutting between soul and spirit, between joint and marrow. It exposes our innermost thoughts and desires. — Hebrews 4:12*

June 13

PEOPLE OFTEN SAY, "I FEEL LIKE GOD IS DISTANT." It could be from unanswered prayers or a lack of sensing His presence, but either way leaves us wondering if He is listening and why we are not seeing or hearing a response. David, who is often referred to as "a man after God's own heart," describes a feeling of abandonment in Psalm 13, but the reality is God was there just as He is here with us (**Psalm 23:4**).

During seasons when we feel God is distant, the best thing we can do is *continue seeking Him* and focus on cultivating a heart posture that is ready to receive and be attentive to His activity. We are not always going to feel the feelings we are looking for, and our faith cannot be based on emotional highs or lows. Feelings and emotions are inconsistent, contrary to the unshakeable truth of Christ. We need to remind ourselves of the promise that God is with us. He is for us, and His activity is constantly at work in and around us. We can trust that we are known, seen, and heard, and He will provide answers if we need them along the way.

> Even when I walk through the darkest valley, I will not be afraid, for you are close beside me. Your rod and your staff protect and comfort me. — Psalm 23:4

> If you need wisdom, ask our generous God, and he will give it to you. He will not rebuke you for asking. But when you ask him, be sure that your faith is in God alone. Do not waver, for a person with divided loyalty is as unsettled as a wave of the sea that is blown and tossed by the wind. — James 1:5–6

June 14

ON THIS SIDE OF ETERNITY, WE ARE ALL A WORK IN PROGRESS. Our heavenly Father is so patient and brings His work in us to fruition at His perfect pace (**Ephesians 3:20**). As God transforms our hearts, it is our willingness to follow in obedience and trust His process. We can become impatient when we don't see the changes in ourselves or loved ones happening as quickly as we would like. However, instant gratification tends to be temporary, whereas God's work is strong and eternal (**Philippians 1:6**). Along the way it is beneficial for us to *celebrate the movement we notice* in ourselves and others. We all learn invaluable lessons that are medicine for our souls and for the souls of others God brings across our path (**Psalm 25:8–9**). Having a front row seat to the Lord's work of a brother or sister in Christ's life should be one of our greatest joys this side of heaven. Once that seed is sown, He will complete His work. His timing is always right and His way is always best.

> *Now all glory to God, who is able, through his mighty power at work within us, to accomplish infinitely more than we might ask or think.* — Ephesians 3:20

> *And I am certain that God, who began the good work within you, will continue his work until it is finally finished on the day when Christ Jesus returns.* — Philippians 1:6

> *The Lord is good and does what is right; he shows the proper path to those who go astray. He leads the humble in doing right, teaching them his way.* — Psalm 25:8–9

> *You can make many plans, but the Lord's purpose will prevail.* — Proverbs 19:21

June 15

THERE ARE SEASONS DURING OUR WALK WITH GOD WHEN we have the opportunity to build spiritual muscle. Much like physical muscle, this process does not happen overnight and we need the right guidance. God has creative ways to strengthen areas where we need work. Our faith is built gradually and is heavily impacted by our upbringing, experiences, and how we are wired (**Joshua 1:8**). Sometimes we have big mountaintop experiences of revelation and change, but so often it's more of a slow burn where God is teaching us perseverance and faithfulness. Spiritual stability is a result of revelation coupled with continued discipleship (**Colossians 1:23**). We may find ourselves facing an old temptation more frequently, but the more victory we experience over that temptation, the stronger we become (**Isaiah 54:17**). We can all celebrate that, as long as *we are seeking holiness* and allowing God to have His way in and through our lives, we are being daily refined into all God has created us to be.

> *Study this Book of Instruction continually. Meditate on it day and night so you will be sure to obey everything written in it. Only then will you prosper and succeed in all you do.* — Joshua 1:8

> *But you must continue to believe this truth and stand firmly in it. Don't drift away from the assurance you received when you heard the Good News. The Good News has been preached all over the world, and I, Paul, have been appointed as God's servant to proclaim it.* — Colossians 1:23

> *But in that coming day no weapon turned against you will succeed. You will silence every voice raised up to accuse you. These benefits are enjoyed by the servants of the Lord; their vindication will come from me. I, the Lord, have spoken!* — Isaiah 54:17

> *I pray that from his glorious, unlimited resources he will empower you with inner strength through his Spirit.* — Ephesians 3:16

June 16

CELEBRATING FATHER'S DAY IS VERY CLOSE TO MY HEART. My sweet daddy is in his heavenly home, and I hold dear the many conversations we had about heaven and Jesus prior to him moving on from life as he knew it (**2 Corinthians 5:1**). I love when people long to talk about eternity and realize the lavish gift of everlasting life. I had an imperfect earthly father just like everybody else, but the more I grew in my relationship with my heavenly Father, I saw everyone through a different lens (**2 Corinthians 5:16**). We should all embrace the reality that every one of us has access to the perfect Father and that learning to be held by *His love changes everything*. We desperately need the security, guidance, and boundaries God provides for our good. Our lives can be rescued, our souls fought for, and the purpose for which we were created, coached by the Almighty King of the Universe. He delights in who He created us to be and equips us with all we need to succeed. He is a good Father and we are His children.

> *For we know that when this earthly tent we live in is taken down (that is, when we die and leave this earthly body), we will have a house in heaven, an eternal body made for us by God himself and not by human hands.*
> *— 2 Corinthians 5:1*

> *So we have stopped evaluating others from a human point of view. At one time we thought of Christ merely from a human point of view. How differently we know him now! — 2 Corinthians 5:16*

> *And I will be your Father, and you will be my sons and daughters, says the Lord Almighty. —2 Corinthians 6:18*

June 17

WHEN I REFLECT ON THE ATTRIBUTES OF MY EARTHLY PARENTS, which made me feel the most loved, I think of the ways they mirrored Christ's love to me (**Ephesians 5:1**). I valued how they supported and encouraged who God created me to be by not comparing me to others. Comparison is a deadly trap that makes it impossible for us to embrace our authentic selves. We have to *remember God created us on purpose for a purpose* and has worthwhile roles for us that have eternal benefits (**Jeremiah 1:5**). My parents also seemed to know there was woundedness and brokenness covering who I really was and, even though they didn't understand, showed me unconditional love. Our heavenly Father knows what lies beneath any pain or suffering we have experienced and is willing and ready to begin a restorative, healing work in our hearts (**1 Peter 5:10**). The bright light God had in mind as He knitted us together in our mother's womb can shine and make the difference it was created to make.

> *Imitate God, therefore, in everything you do, because you are his dear children.*
> — Ephesians 5:1

> *I knew you before I formed you in your mother's womb. Before you were born I set you apart and appointed you as my prophet to the nations.*
> — Jeremiah 1:5

> *In his kindness God called you to share in his eternal glory by means of Christ Jesus. So after you have suffered a little while, he will restore, support, and strengthen you, and he will place you on a firm foundation.*
> — 1 Peter 5:10

A YOUNG LADY ASKED THE MOST HONEST, VULNERABLE QUESTION yesterday as I was meeting with a group of ladies growing in their faith. She said, "What does it look like to commit my way to the Lord?" (**Psalm 37:5**). Making the transition from a self-centered life to a God-centered life is the best decision any of us can make, but it doesn't happen in the blink of an eye and requires the belief that God's way is best (**Psalm 18:30**). You may have heard it said that love is a choice, not a feeling, and I would suggest the same is true about belief. We decide to believe God is good and His ways are best.

As we surrender our will to His, the Holy Spirit will illuminate our path and our spiritual confidence will grow (**Psalm 32:8**). I made the suggestion to my sweet friend to *begin every morning thanking God* for His hand on her life, as evidenced by her asking the question, reflecting her spiritual desire. I also encouraged her to pray, "Father, I will move towards you today, whatever that looks like." Committing our day to Him is always a bright start to a good day!

> *Commit everything you do to the Lord. Trust him, and he will help you.*
> *— Psalm 37:5*

> *God's way is perfect. All the Lord's promises prove true. He is a shield for all who look to him for protection. — Psalm 18:30*

> *"The Lord says, 'I will guide you along the best pathway for your life. I will advise you and watch over you.'" — Psalm 32:8*

June 19

ONE OF THE BEST FERTILIZERS FOR SPIRITUAL GROWTH IS OBEDIENCE (**Luke 11:28**). So often we don't realize the difference one simple act of obedience can make, whether it be in our own life or the life of another. Last night my beautiful niece joined me in our care and recovery ministry at church. This was her first visit, and she was in a group learning more about the program. She was nudged by the Holy Spirit to give one of the young ladies in her group a hug, which was a little out of her comfort zone, considering they had just met. She was prompted again, stepped out of her comfort zone, and asked permission for a hug. The young lady responded warmly and it was a special moment (**John 13:34**). God will give us opportunities to spontaneously show love if we are sensitive to His voice. It could be a hug, a smile, or a phone call, but any time we act in obedience, it's a blessing. Following the Spirit's lead comes more naturally the more you do it. *Seeking God and responding in obedience* can become the heartbeat of your life, and that's a peaceful, fulfilling way to live.

> *"Jesus replied, 'But even more blessed are all who hear the word of God and put it into practice.'" — Luke 11:28*

> *So now I am giving you a new commandment: Love each other. Just as I have loved you, you should love each other. — John 13:34*

> *Submit to God, and you will have peace; then things will go well for you.*
> *— Job 22:21*

June 20

Sometimes we will hear the phrase, "Pray in faith." I can clearly remember pondering, "What exactly does that mean?" When we pray, there are several different responses we could receive from God, but we can know He does hear our prayers. And whether it's yes, no, slow, or grow, His response is for our good (**Isaiah 65:24**). Slow means our prayer is not His timing yet, and grow means we need some refining heart work. Praying in faith says, "Lord, I know you know better than I do, so I trust your answer is right" (**James 1:5–6**). We often pray to give something to God, only to take it back and doubt His divine wisdom. As we learn the freedom of surrendering our will, people, and circumstances to God, it moves us into a lifestyle of dependence (**John 15:4**). Settling into the comfort and security of *God's provision is essential* to experiencing abundant life. The world will attempt to influence us to doubt God and handle life on our own, but embracing the reality that we are in better hands with God is just a part of the beauty of being His children.

> *I will answer them before they even call to me. While they are still talking about their needs, I will go ahead and answer their prayers!* — Isaiah 65:24

> *If you need wisdom, ask our generous God, and he will give it to you. He will not rebuke you for asking. But when you ask him, be sure that your faith is in God alone. Do not waver, for a person with divided loyalty is as unsettled as a wave of the sea that is blown and tossed by the wind.* — James 1:5–6

> *Remain in me, and I will remain in you. For a branch cannot produce fruit if it is severed from the vine, and you cannot be fruitful unless you remain in me.* — John 15:4

> *You have been set apart as holy to the Lord your God, and he has chosen you from all the nations of the earth to be his own special treasure.* — Deuteronomy 14:2

June 21

I CLING TO THE COMFORT AND EXPECTATION THAT MY heavenly Father has good plans for me (**Jeremiah 29:11**). The ultimate, eternal plan is our greatest gift, and the more we can focus on the divine destination of heaven, the more tolerable this world becomes (**Revelation 21:4**). We can come to the Lord in the morning with open hearts and hands, waiting to see what He may have in store for today. He orchestrates divine appointments that we have no prior knowledge of (**Proverbs 16:9**). Today a young lady noticed my outfit in a thrift store and wanted to show it to her mom. As we were chatting, I mentioned a ministry I'm involved in and she said her mom was also involved in it. We celebrated our common ground, and the employees of the store overheard. After they left, the employees and I discussed how cool it was that God crossed our paths. He is so intentional and creative (**Psalm 37:23**). He is a real and personal God. What a privilege it is to be His vessels. When we *keep our eyes open and alert*, we will see His hand.

> "'For I know the plans I have for you,' says the Lord. 'They are plans for good and not for disaster, to give you a future and a hope.'" — Jeremiah 29:11

> He will wipe every tear from their eyes, and there will be no more death or sorrow or crying or pain. All these things are gone forever. — Revelation 21:4

> We can make our plans, but the Lord determines our steps. — Proverbs 16:9

> The Lord directs the steps of the godly. He delights in every detail of their lives. — Psalm 37:23

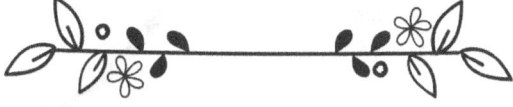

June 22

DURING THE EARLY HOURS OF THE DAY, I WILL OFTEN SAY, "Lord, open the eyes of my heart, that I may see you today." We can feel confident knowing this is a prayer the Lord loves to hear (**Ephesians 1:18, Psalm 119:18**). The God of the universe reveals things to His children in many ways, but we do need to cultivate spiritual sensitivity. The more we strive to satisfy our flesh, the weaker our spiritual eyes become. The world views fulfillment as vacations, hobbies, or whatever else brings us pleasure. These fun things are not wrong, but they cannot be the goal of our existence (**Romans 8:5**). As we *live more according to the Spirit*, the desires of our flesh actually shift. We may find the things we once craved begin to fade as we experience God more fully and become more preoccupied with His agenda. Living a self-focused life can turn empty and exhausting, whereas a God-centered life is challenging, fulfilling, and, most importantly, everlasting.

> *I pray that your hearts will be flooded with light so that you can understand the confident hope he has given to those he called—his holy people who are his rich and glorious inheritance.* — Ephesians 1:18

> *Open my eyes to see the wonderful truths in your instructions.* — Psalm 119:18

> *Those who are dominated by the sinful nature think about sinful things, but those who are controlled by the Holy Spirit think about things that please the Spirit.* — Romans 8:5

> *By his divine power, God has given us everything we need for living a godly life. We have received all of this by coming to know him, the one who called us to himself by means of his marvelous glory and excellence.*
> — 2 Peter 1:3

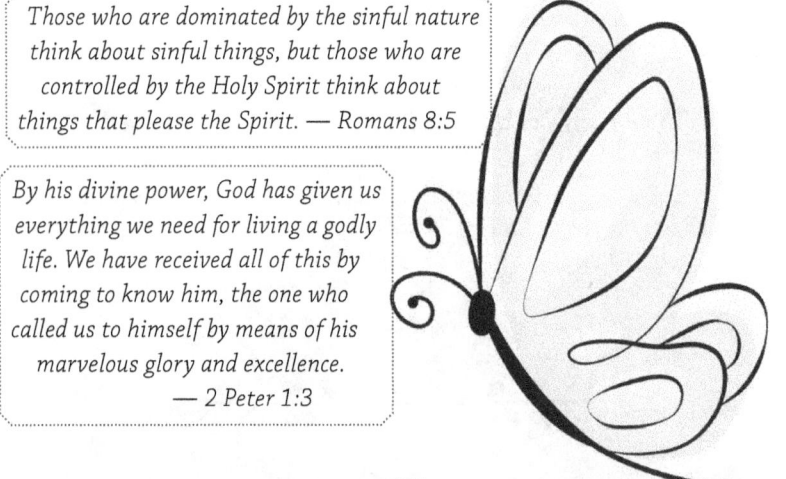

June 23

THE DRIVING FORCE IN OUR LIVES IS REFLECTED IN WHERE WE FIND our identity. Our culture screams two distinct lies about identity. The first is that our identity is up for grabs and we get to decide what that is. The second is that we are defined by our past mistakes or current struggles. Contrary to culture, the truth of who we are is rooted in the heart of God (**Ephesians 1:5, 2 Corinthians 5:17**). We are children of the Most High God, and there is absolutely nothing too hard or tragic for His healing, restorative power (**Jeremiah 32:17**). People often feel they need to clean up to come to, or back to God, but that could not be further from the truth. He is the author and finisher of our cleansing and sanctification, and he delights to be right with us through the entire process. One of the most beautiful comforts of my life is that *my heavenly Father is for me* and with me, and His thoughts toward me are true, everlasting, and sweeter than I could ever imagine. We are made in His image to carry out His mission.

> God decided in advance to adopt us into his own family by bringing us to himself through Jesus Christ. This is what he wanted to do, and it gave him great pleasure.
> — Ephesians 1:5

> This means that anyone who belongs to Christ has become a new person. The old life is gone; a new life has begun!" — 2 Corinthians 5:17

> O Sovereign Lord! You made the heavens and earth by your strong hand and powerful arm. Nothing is too hard for you!
> — Jeremiah 32:17

> "Then God said, 'Let us make human beings in our image, to be like us. They will reign over the fish in the sea, the birds in the sky, the livestock, all the wild animals on the earth, and the small animals that scurry along the ground.' So God created human beings in his own image. In the image of God he created them; male and female he created them. Then God blessed them and said, 'Be fruitful and multiply. Fill the earth and govern it. Reign over the fish in the sea, the birds in the sky, and all the animals that scurry along the ground.'" — Genesis 1:26–28

June 24

I OFTEN MARVEL AT THE EXCHANGE THAT TAKES PLACE BETWEEN GOD and His children. He offers His holiness, unwavering love, victory, and power (**Leviticus 20:26, John 3:16, Luke 10:19**). We should never lose sight of the magnitude of these amazing gifts available to us because of Christ. What does it look like for us to respond in such a way that reflects our gratitude towards the God of our salvation? We can offer our hearts, our devotion, and a willingness to be changed, guided, and used by God (**2 Corinthians 3:16, Ephesians 3:12**). Giving our heart to the Lord looks like being vulnerable and transparent with all that we think, feel, and even doubt. He already knows it all but longs to be invited in by us. We can *choose daily to be devoted to Him*, living for Him rather than ourselves, as we learn that real fulfillment comes through the Holy Spirit, not our flesh (**Galatians 5:16**). We can approach the Lord with open hands, saying, "Here I am, send me," knowing that what He has in store is better than anything we do on our own.

> You must be holy because I, the Lord, am holy. I have set you apart from all other people to be my very own. — Leviticus 20:26

> For this is how God loved the world: He gave his one and only Son, so that everyone who believes in him will not perish but have eternal life. — John 3:16

> Look, I have given you authority over all the power of the enemy, and you can walk among snakes and scorpions and crush them. Nothing will injure you. — Luke 10:19

> But whenever someone turns to the Lord, the veil is taken away. — 2 Corinthians 3:16

> Because of Christ and our faith in him, we can now come boldly and confidently into God's presence. — Ephesians 3:12

> So I say, let the Holy Spirit guide your lives. Then you won't be doing what your sinful nature craves. — Galatians 5:16

June 25

When we choose to share life with Jesus this side of heaven, we can posture ourselves firmly in the reality that we never stand alone (**1 Corinthians 16:13**). As believers, we have the opportunity to dress ourselves in the armor of God every day. It is actually beneficial for us to verbalize these pieces of armor to remind ourselves what we possess as children of God (**Ephesians 6:13**). Recognizing that absolutely nothing can penetrate God's covering over your life results in strengthened Holy Spirit confidence (**Isaiah 54:17**). We can ultimately *make the decision to trust God*, but this is a state of mind we have to cultivate daily. Praying God's promises back to Him out loud can bolster our faith in amazing ways. Anytime we feel alone, we can know that is a lie from our spiritual enemy. God is always with us, always for us, and has already equipped us with all we need to navigate any situation. We never stand alone.

> *Be on guard. Stand firm in the faith. Be courageous. Be strong.*
> *— 1 Corinthians 16:13*

> *Therefore, put on every piece of God's armor so you will be able to resist the enemy in the time of evil. Then after the battle you will still be standing firm.*
> *— Ephesians 6:13*

> *But in that coming day no weapon turned against you will succeed. You will silence every voice raised up to accuse you. These benefits are enjoyed by the servants of the Lord; their vindication will come from me. I, the Lord, have spoken! — Isaiah 54:17*

> *So be strong and courageous! Do not be afraid and do not panic before them. For the Lord your God will personally go ahead of you. He will neither fail you nor abandon you. — Deuteronomy 31:6*

June 26

Navigating life believing the mighty God of the universe is our power source enables us to have stability and security in an otherwise chaotic world (**Psalm 121:2**). We know that the ultimate battle has already been won, and when we accept Jesus into our hearts, we are automatically a part of the winning team. This reality should motivate us towards holiness and create momentum to prioritize working out our salvation living for Christ (**Philippians 2:12–13**). Even in the midst of seasons of discouragement or what feels like defeat, we can *cling to light at the end of the tunnel because He is the light* that will forever shine. Especially during trials and suffering or even doubt, God Himself will help reorient our focus back to hope and victory (**Romans 5:3–5**). The mere fact that our home is in heaven gives us reason to celebrate during periods of joy or pain. The greatest satisfaction we experience here on this earth is nothing compared to the joys of heaven, and as we move through hard things, we can know they will pass. Our powerful Lord and Savior is forever victorious, and we get to walk in that same victory every day.

> *My help comes from the Lord, who made heaven and earth!* — Psalm 121:2

> *Dear friends, you always followed my instructions when I was with you. And now that I am away, it is even more important. Work hard to show the results of your salvation, obeying God with deep reverence and fear.*
> *For God is working in you, giving you the desire and the power to do what pleases him."* — Philippians 2:12–13

> *We can rejoice, too, when we run into problems and trials, for we know that they help us develop endurance. And endurance develops strength of character, and character strengthens our confident hope of salvation. And this hope will not lead to disappointment. For we know how dearly God loves us, because he has given us the Holy Spirit to fill our hearts with his love.*
> — Romans 5:3–5

> *For the Lord your God is going with you! He will fight for you against your enemies, and he will give you victory!* — Deuteronomy 20:4

June 27

THE GIFT OF OUR ETERNAL SALVATION IS AVAILABLE TO US ONLY BECAUSE of Christ's sacrifice at the cross. The same power that raised Christ from the grave puts us as believers in position to respond to the various callings God has on our lives (**2 Corinthians 9:8**). Whatever our individual roles may be in Kingdom work, there are steps we can take daily to stay in step with God. This looks like seeking Holy Spirit direction and wisdom daily (**Psalm 16:7–8**). His desire is that we remain reliant on Him and not attempt to move in front of Him, forging our own path. Moving forward in faith gives us the opportunity to build our trust in God's provision. The risks of uncertainty can even begin to feel safe, knowing that ultimately we are in God's hands.

Embracing God's unique purpose and plan for our lives is certainly critical to living out an abundant life, but accepting and appreciating His timing is equally important (**Psalm 27:14**). I love to regularly remind myself that God sees the big picture so I don't have to. Our role is to *seek, follow, abide, rest, and (so often) wait*, but wherever, however, or whenever He is guiding us in the right direction. May we be alert and obedient.

> And God will generously provide all you need. Then you will always have everything you need and plenty left over to share with others.
> — 2 Corinthians 9:8

> I will bless the Lord who guides me; even at night my heart instructs me. I know the Lord is always with me. I will not be shaken, for he is right beside me.
> — Psalm 16:7-8

> Wait patiently for the Lord. Be brave and courageous. Yes, wait patiently for the Lord. — Psalm 27:14

June 28

OFTENTIMES WE DEEPLY DESIRE TO BE IN A SWEET SPOT OF FEELING really close and connected to the Lord and don't realize we aren't making room for that intimacy to occur (**Psalm 73:28**). We may believe the lie that God has greater things to be concerned about or that we should deal with minor details on our own. The truth is the more we *learn about the heart of God*, the more clear it becomes that He longs for our companionship, and part of building that intimacy is indeed bringing Him the details we minimize (**Psalm 33:18**). When we bring every part of ourselves to Him in prayer, it creates the atmosphere of being fully known. Realizing we are fully loved and known by God creates an inner sanctuary in our hearts where we can escape instead of turning to lesser things (**Psalm 119:114**). He is a present, loving Father who wants to hold you and hear about your day. Our thoughts, feelings, and desires matter to Him, and the more vulnerable and transparent we are willing to be, the deeper we can sense His everlasting love.

> *But as for me, how good it is to be near God! I have made the Sovereign Lord my shelter, and I will tell everyone about the wonderful things you do.*
> *— Psalm 73:28*

> *But the Lord watches over those who fear him, those who rely on his unfailing love. — Psalm 33:18*

> *You are my refuge and my shield; your word is my source of hope. — Psalm 119:114*

> *And may you have the power to understand, as all God's people should, how wide, how long, how high, and how deep his love is. — Ephesians 3:18*

June 29

Running into an old friend at the gym this morning, I was reminded of how I used to try to motivate her towards spiritual, emotional, and physical health 25 years ago. I revisited in my mind how that was the season in my life right after God had captivated my imagination with His love (**Romans 5:8**). I remember how He reached for me and rescued me from myself, bringing me into the fold of His secure arms. Remembering that season brings an amazing peace, seeing how strong and mighty His pursuit of His children is as He Himself transforms our hearts (**Deuteronomy 30:6**). As we *allow the Holy Spirit to have access* to our spirit, mind, and body, we are reoriented to our authentic selves and can enjoy the love relationship with our Savior we were created for. Once we have really allowed ourselves to encounter Jesus, we will never want to be without Him. Although we all have mountaintops and valleys, His presence remains the same (**Psalm 23:4**). Our joy and satisfaction is found in the shelter of His love, and as we continue to desire more of Him, He shows up in such creative ways. What really made my heart smile remembering that season is that I have Him more now than I did then, and I am continually expectant of how that love will continue to grow.

> But God showed his great love for us by sending Christ to die for us while we were still sinners. — Romans 5:8

> The Lord your God will change your heart and the hearts of all your descendants, so that you will love him with all your heart and soul and so you may live! — Deuteronomy 30:6

> Even when I walk through the darkest valley, I will not be afraid, for you are close beside me. Your rod and your staff protect and comfort me. — Psalm 23:4

> This is my second letter to you, dear friends, and in both of them I have tried to stimulate your wholesome thinking and refresh your memory. — 2 Peter 3:1

June 30

BY HIS DIVINE GRACE, GOD ALLOWS US TO CROSS PATHS WITH PEOPLE who have experienced similar harms to us or by us. While having dinner with a dear friend of mine who fits this category, she asked, "How do you reconcile pieces of your past to feel free from it?" My response to this can be summarized by, "I don't, but Jesus does" (**Colossians 1:22**). We can stand firm in the victory and freedom we have from our past only because of what Christ did for us on the cross. Our sufferings or mistakes have no power to define us. We are truly made new (**2 Corinthians 5:17**). When a painful memory surfaces, instead of dwelling in the quicksand of discouragement, we can *say, "Look at God"* (**Ephesians 2:4–5**). It is spiritually energizing to remind ourselves that our lives are no longer revolving around the flesh that leads to emptiness, but the Spirit that leads us is everlasting life (**Galatians 6:8**). So often, if our spiritual enemy can't find any other tactic, he will use our past, but we can confidently remind him his time is over and our God is doing a new thing that no one or nothing has the power to reverse or take away.

> *Yet now he has reconciled you to himself through the death of Christ in his physical body. As a result, he has brought you into his own presence, and you are holy and blameless as you stand before him without a single fault. — Colossians 1:22*

> *This means that anyone who belongs to Christ has become a new person. The old life is gone; a new life has begun! — 2 Corinthians 5:17*

> *But God is so rich in mercy, and he loved us so much, that even though we were dead because of our sins, he gave us life when he raised Christ from the dead. (It is only by God's grace that you have been saved!) — Ephesians 2:4-5*

> *For I am about to do something new. See, I have already begun! Do you not see it? I will make a pathway through the wilderness. I will create rivers in the dry wasteland. — Isaiah 43:19*

July 1

THE FIRST OF THE MONTH PRESENTS US WITH THE OPPORTUNITY TO REFRESH and reboot our spiritual, emotional, and physical health journeys. We all have to be intentional with these critical areas, and accountability always helps. Choose someone to share a similar goal with, to motivate and encourage one another (**Proverbs 27:17**). Prayerfully decide three beneficial goals for the month. Think of one act of obedience you have been procrastinating on and take action. Obedience makes our spirits flourish (**1 Thessalonians 5:19**). The Word of God transforms our minds, and as we read the Scriptures daily, it is the best medicine for emotional health (**Isaiah 26:3**).

We all have to move out of our comfort zones with our bodies. This morning I took a foam roller class at the gym, which is a form of massage focusing on pressure points. It's not part of my regular routine, but I know its benefits, so I've committed to adding that this month; painful but helpful. *Setting goals and following through* is a critical part of stamina building. We can be expectant as the Lord continues to shape and refine us this side of heaven.

> As iron sharpens iron, so a friend sharpens a friend. — Proverbs 27:17

> Do not stifle the Holy Spirit. — 1 Thessalonians 5:19

> You will keep in perfect peace all who trust in you, all whose thoughts are fixed on you! — Isaiah 26:3

> "I will bring that group through the fire and make them pure. I will refine them like silver and purify them like gold. They will call on my name, and I will answer them. I will say, 'These are my people,' and they will say, 'The Lord is our God.'" — Zechariah 13:9

July 2

THE WAY IN WHICH OUR CULTURE GLAMORIZES THE IDEA of being independent, self-reliant, and individualistic carries with it a very dark reality. It portrays a lifestyle that has no need for God because you are the one in charge and calling all the shots. Along with being in charge comes carrying burdens we were never meant to carry (**Matthew 11:28–30**). Our human nature can be incredibly stubborn, stemming from a heart posture of pride, a belief that we know how to do things better than our Creator does. Allowing God to take the reins of our life is a daily decision and one that is best made within the first few minutes of being awake (**Philippians 4:6–7**). When we can fill our minds with peace before anxious thoughts begin, the odds are in our favor to have a victorious day (**Colossians 3:15**).

We have the privilege, as Christ's followers, to lean into Him for everything, including our emotions, thoughts, and plans. God delights in us expressing our reliance on Him and honors those prayers (**Psalm 34:15**). May we be people who *embrace all the blessings* our heavenly Father desires for us, especially love and peace.

> "Then Jesus said, 'Come to me, all of you who are weary and carry heavy burdens, and I will give you rest. Take my yoke upon you. Let me teach you, because I am humble and gentle at heart, and you will find rest for your souls. For my yoke is easy to bear, and the burden I give you is light.'"
> — Matthew 11:28–30

> Don't worry about anything; instead, pray about everything. Tell God what you need, and thank him for all he has done. Then you will experience God's peace, which exceeds anything we can understand. His peace will guard your hearts and minds as you live in Christ Jesus.
> — Philippians 4:6–7

> And let the peace that comes from Christ rule in your hearts. For as members of one body you are called to live in peace. And always be thankful.
> — Colossians 3:15

> The eyes of the Lord watch over those who do right; his ears are open to their cries for help. — Psalm 34:15

July 3

As followers of Christ, we have to be intentional every day to pursue holiness (**Hebrews 12:14**). Living in a world that encourages and glamorizes unholiness makes this seem difficult, but it is critical to decide, before temptation comes, to be led by the Spirit instead of by our flesh (**Romans 12:1–2**). It is important for us to understand how valuable we are to our heavenly Father and how He desires only the best for His children. There have been many times in my life that I have sought wise counsel from a pastor when navigating a decision. I'll never forget a particular discussion in which someone emphasized to me that God wants what is best for me and that I should never settle for less. So often we seek the comfort of mediocrity when God has far better in store for us (**Ephesians 3:19**). When we consider ourselves valuable because we identify as God's holy possession, our behavior is more likely to reflect godliness. Denying ourselves and following Christ's leadership is counter-cultural, but are we not called to be set apart? (**1 Peter 2:9**) Sacrificial living is truly the path to satisfaction and fulfillment this side of heaven. We will never regret making the most of the opportunities and time God has given us to *represent Him well through our choices* and lifestyle.

> Work at living in peace with everyone, and work at living a holy life, for those who are not holy will not see the Lord. — Hebrews 12:14

> And so, dear brothers and sisters, I plead with you to give your bodies to God because of all he has done for you. Let them be a living and holy sacrifice—the kind he will find acceptable. This is truly the way to worship him. Don't copy the behavior and customs of this world, but let God transform you into a new person by changing the way you think. Then you will learn to know God's will for you, which is good and pleasing and perfect. — Romans 12:1–2

> May you experience the love of Christ, though it is too great to understand fully. Then you will be made complete with all the fullness of life and power that comes from God. — Ephesians 3:19

> But you are not like that, for you are a chosen people. You are royal priests, a holy nation, God's very own possession. As a result, you can show others the goodness of God, for he called you out of the darkness into his wonderful light. — 1 Peter 2:9

July 4

PRAYERFULLY I ASK THE LORD BEFORE I GO TO SLEEP to please wake me up with a song in my heart and a thought in my head. This morning the song was "Lord, I Need You" by Matt Mahr, and with it being July 4th, the thought was gratitude for freedom in Christ (**2 Corinthians 3:17**). As I meditate on the freedom God offers, I love the security that accompanies this freedom within the boundaries of His design for life. The world teaches that boundaries are stifling and negative. The truth is His ways lead to healing, freedom, joy, and peace (**Isaiah 57:18–19**). We know God sees the chaos that results from attempting to do life on our terms. We have all experienced the consequences of stubbornness and rebellion (**1 Samuel 15:23**). *We all so desperately need God.* We need His Lordship over our lives in every area. Oftentimes, when we realize our need, we are immediately able to sense the peace that follows, submitting to His authority with the confidence that He is stronger, wiser, and more powerful than anything this world has to offer.

> *"'I have seen what they do, but I will heal them anyway! I will lead them. I will comfort those who mourn, bringing words of praise to their lips. May they have abundant peace, both near and far,' says the Lord, who heals them."*
> *— Isaiah 57:18–19*

> *Rebellion is as sinful as witchcraft, and stubbornness as bad as worshiping idols. — 1 Samuel 15:23*

> *This foolish plan of God is wiser than the wisest of human plans, and God's weakness is stronger than the greatest of human strength.*
> *— 1 Corinthians 1:25*

July 5

SPENDING TIME WITH FAMILY CAN BE A GREAT REMINDER of the special relationships God has woven into our lives (**Mark 12:31**). God uses the relationships in our lives to teach us valuable lessons about real love, humility, and even perseverance. Obviously not everyone in our lives is going to be easy to love, and neither are we, from time to time. This is why we need divine guidance as we navigate life with others. Oftentimes connections are severed due to such insignificant arguments (**Colossians 3:13**). When we become frustrated with each other, it can be helpful to remind ourselves that this brother or sister in Christ is a work-in-progress just as we are. Having this heart posture allows us to be less judgmental and more forgiving. Although we need to be prayerful about boundaries, we cannot rely on avoidance for conflict resolution (**Hebrews 12:14**). We are all wired beautifully different and, as *we depend on Christ's ways* to live in harmony with one another, it not only strengthens our spirits but it puts Christ's love in our heart on full display.

> *The second is equally important: 'Love your neighbor as yourself.' No other commandment is greater than these.*
> — Mark 12:31

> *Make allowance for each other's faults, and forgive anyone who offends you. Remember, the Lord forgave you, so you must forgive others.*
> —Colossians 3:13

> *Work at living in peace with everyone, and work at living a holy life, for those who are not holy will not see the Lord.* — Hebrews 12:14

July 6

MOST OF US ARE FAMILIAR WITH THE CLASSIC SONG, "He's Got the Whole World in His Hands," which is typically introduced very early in our lives. Our church has recently started singing a worship song "Better Hands," and today I have been reflecting on both of these songs (**Psalm 24:1–2**). How much more accepting of this reality were most of us as children? Even for the skeptical and inquisitive, we would most likely embrace the comfort of His power and shelter. I cling to the relief that, even though I am responsible for my God-given tasks, ultimately the design and outcome of scenarios are not in my hands (**Psalm 37:5**). Having Holy Spirit confidence, not in ourselves but in God's wisdom and deity, is the foundation of a healthy heart posture (**Psalm 28:7**). This unquestionable trust is stable, tranquil, and the epitome of peace (**Romans 15:13**). When I think of the faith of a child, I think of acceptance of what simply is. I think of not needing proof and the sense of being authentically, undeniably safe. *Thank goodness we can experience the assurance* of being in His hands now and forever.

> *The earth is the Lord's, and everything in it. The world and all its people belong to him. For he laid the earth's foundation on the seas and built it on the ocean depths.* — Psalm 24:1–2

> *Commit everything you do to the Lord. Trust him, and he will help you.* — Psalm 37:5

> *The Lord is my strength and shield. I trust him with all my heart. He helps me, and my heart is filled with joy. I burst out in songs of thanksgiving.* — Psalm 28:7

> *I pray that God, the source of hope, will fill you completely with joy and peace because you trust in him. Then you will overflow with confident hope through the power of the Holy Spirit.* — Romans 15:13

> *I cling to you; your strong right hand holds me securely.* — Psalm 63:8

July 7

DISCOVERING OUR VALUE AND WORTH NESTLED WITHIN THE TRUTH of who we are in Christ is beneficial for so many reasons (**Psalm 139:13–14**). Even our struggles, idiosyncrasies, or sensitivities can be learning tools for the complexity of how we are knit together. As the Holy Spirit brings to mind tough areas for us, it's always an opportunity for refinement, not discouragement. We are valuable because of Christ, and we have the privilege of sharing life with Him and others. As we learn to see others through the lens of this kinship with Christ, it can help us have the grace needed for kindness and compassion (**1 John 4:16**). Our goal should always be to reflect God's love. One of the biggest ways God continues to weave this lesson into my life is through restraint, instead of acting or speaking impulsively. So often I will ask myself, "How would God have me respond to this?" (**Ephesians 4:1–2**). When we value one another as brothers and sisters in Christ, *we can move past differences* or conflict, remain connected, and even learn valuable lessons along the way.

> You made all the delicate, inner parts of my body and knit me together in my mother's womb. Thank you for making me so wonderfully complex! Your workmanship is marvelous—how well I know it. — Psalm 139:13–14

> We know how much God loves us, and we have put our trust in his love. God is love, and all who live in love live in God, and God lives in them. — 1 John 4:16

> Therefore I, a prisoner for serving the Lord, beg you to lead a life worthy of your calling, for you have been called by God. Always be humble and gentle. Be patient with each other, making allowance for each other's faults because of your love. — Ephesians 4:1–2

> A gentle answer deflects anger, but harsh words make tempers flare. — Proverbs 15:1

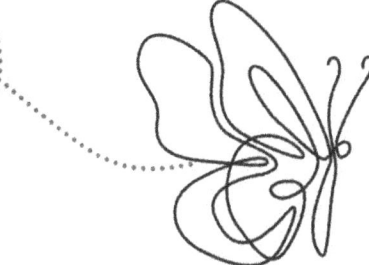

July 8

TONIGHT I HAVE THE PRIVILEGE OF HEARING THE TESTIMONIES of three young ladies who will be graduating from a Christ-centered program that I have the honor of being a part of. Having a front row seat to watching and witnessing God's transformative power is something that never fails to inspire awe (**Ephesians 4:23-24**). While these three ladies are very different, they share common ground in the way they have agreed with the Holy Spirit's promptings in their lives towards change. As we agree with God, seeking His way, it unleashes the power to live the victorious, abundant life we were created for (**Ephesians 6:16**). As we grow in our faith we realize more and more that we actually live by resurrection power (**Philippians 4:13**). God wages war on anything set out to destroy us. The enemy lost its battle with these three women tonight, and God will receive all the glory for this transformation. We are all going through our own transformations every day as we are presented with opportunities to agree with, or grieve, the Spirit of God. It can be so beneficial for us to *proclaim, "Father, I am going to agree with you today. Whatever you desire to do in and through my life—I am yours."*

> *Instead, let the Spirit renew your thoughts and attitudes. Put on your new nature, created to be like God—truly righteous and holy. — Ephesians 4:23-24*

> *In addition to all of these, hold up the shield of faith to stop the fiery arrows of the devil. — Ephesians 6:16*

> *Each of you should continue to live in whatever situation the Lord has placed you, and remain as you were when God first called you. This is my rule for all the churches. —1 Corinthians 7:17*

July 9

TODAY IS MY EARTHLY FATHER'S BIRTHDAY, AND I AM RESTING in the gratitude that he is with my heavenly Father in eternity (**John 3:16**). As a child, I remember how I feared losing my daddy to death. I tended to be emotionally attached to him, and although our relationship wasn't perfect, it certainly provided security. So often over the years I have witnessed God turning areas of weakness into the places His light shines the brightest (**2 Corinthians 12:9**). *Taking the time* to cultivate an intimate love connection to our heavenly Father allows His strength and perspective to pour over all other relationships (**Psalm 73:26**). I can peacefully grieve my loss here on earth, celebrating the eternal life my Jesus has provided. The meditations of my heart can shift to heaven, where my earthly father gets to celebrate every day with those he loves while he waits for the rest of us to join him in our miraculous heavenly home.

> *For this is how God loved the world: He gave his one and only Son, so that everyone who believes in him will not perish but have eternal life.* — John 3:16

> *Each time he said, 'My grace is all you need. My power works best in weakness.' So now I am glad to boast about my weaknesses, so that the power of Christ can work through me.* — 2 Corinthians 12:9

> *My health may fail, and my spirit may grow weak, but God remains the strength of my heart; he is mine forever.* — Psalm 73:26

> *There is more than enough room in my Father's home. If this were not so, would I have told you that I am going to prepare a place for you? When everything is ready, I will come and get you, so that you will always be with me where I am.* — John 14:2–3

July 10

What would your response be to the question, "Do you crave time focusing on the Lord?" It's a good question to ponder. This focused time doesn't only have to be spent in prayer or reading His Word. It could be reflecting on nature or talking about His goodness with others (**Psalm 119:36–37**). I was recalling the last couple of weeks my daddy was here and how he had such a desire to discuss Jesus and heaven with me. If we are not craving fellowship with the Lord, we are missing out on the sweet spot of that deep desire (**Psalm 27:4**). Simply keeping His name on the forefront of our minds can enable us to feel connected on a more intimate level. One of the most beautiful attributes of a vibrant love relationship with the Lord is that He is always right there with us, available and eager to listen, providing refuge as only He can (**Psalm 91:4**). Our safe place with God isn't only for issues, it's for celebrating, rejoicing, *thanking Him for everything He is* and all He continually helps us to be and do. The more we seek Him the more we crave Him and satisfaction in Him never runs dry.

> Give me an eagerness for your laws rather than a love for money! Turn my eyes from worthless things, and give me life through your word. — Psalm 119:36–37

> The one thing I ask of the Lord—the thing I seek most—is to live in the house of the Lord all the days of my life, delighting in the Lord's perfections and meditating in his Temple. — Psalm 27:4

> He will cover you with his feathers. He will shelter you with his wings. His faithful promises are your armor and protection. — Psalm 91:4

> The Lord will guide you continually, giving you water when you are dry and restoring your strength. You will be like a well-watered garden, like an ever-flowing spring. — Isaiah 58:11

July 11

A SWEET FRIEND OF MINE SHARED THE MOST BEAUTIFUL PHRASE that she is feeling led to pray daily: "Lord, have your way in me." My heart overflowed with joy imagining what music that is to His ears (**Psalm 86:11**). These words reflect a surrendered heart posture, a willing spirit, and an anticipation of God moving. A statement like this one has the undertone of humility, an awareness that God is on the throne and is all-wise, all-powerful, and trustworthy with every part of our being. This perspective overflows with vulnerability and an open-handed attitude (**Ephesians 3:20**). Oftentimes there are many opportunities the Lord desires to work in and through us, but He is waiting for our cooperation or invitation (**James 4:8**). As we invite the Holy Spirit to invade all we are, we position ourselves at the feet of Jesus. We should all *ask ourselves*, *"Have I* spent time at His feet today, listening, learning, allowing Him to empower and strengthen me?" Spending time in His presence leads us to say, "Lord, have your way in me," with Holy Spirit confidence.

Teach me your ways, O Lord, that I may live according to your truth! Grant me purity of heart, so that I may honor you. — Psalm 86:11

Now all glory to God, who is able, through his mighty power at work within us, to accomplish infinitely more than we might ask or think. — Ephesians 3:20

Come close to God, and God will come close to you. Wash your hands, you sinners; purify your hearts, for your loyalty is divided between God and the world. — James 4:8

For in him we live and move and exist. As some of your own poets have said, 'We are his offspring.' — Acts 17:28

July 12

I HAD AN OPPORTUNITY AT THE GYM THIS MORNING to have such a meaningful conversation with a sister in Christ who is a mother of five. She and I talked and celebrated a mutual lesson God has shown us of the beauty of surrendering those we love into His hands (**Philippians 4:6**). God has unequivocally shown me that, as I surrender loved ones to Him, this frees me to love in a way that is pure and inviting. We all have people in our lives we love and desire the best for, but all too often good intentions move into worry and control. We are stifling our ability to love by attempting to fix. This is simply not what we are called to do, nor is it effective for the person of our concern. God loves our loved ones more than we can imagine, and He knows the time and the way to pursue them (**Psalm 62:11–12**). The truth is we are not guaranteed anyone else's salvation, but that cannot be where we place our hope. Our hope lies in the capable arms of Jesus, and as we *keep Him number one in our lives*, He will lead us to love well, speak life, and stay in our lane when it comes to work only He can do.

> *Don't worry about anything; instead, pray about everything. Tell God what you need, and thank him for all he has done.*
> *— Philippians 4:6*

> *God has spoken plainly, and I have heard it many times: Power, O God, belongs to you; unfailing love, O Lord, is yours. Surely you repay all people according to what they have done.*
> *— Psalm 62:11–12*

> *The king's heart is like a stream of water directed by the Lord; he guides it wherever he pleases. — Proverbs 21:1*

July 13

NEXT WEEK MY DAUGHTER AND I BOTH HAVE SEPARATE OPPORTUNITIES to serve that are out of the rhythm of our norm. We both love discipleship, but we also love the ministries we are taking the week away from to serve in a different way (**Deuteronomy 15:11**). Three powerful words keep coming to my spirit: expectancy, willingness, and obedience. When we have an expectant heart, we are more curious to see what God has in store and how He is working. This perspective creates an atmosphere of adventure and an awe that we get to witness God's activity (**Matthew 16:24**). When we are available and willing to follow God into uncertain waters, relying on His strength and guidance, our eyes are opened in amazing ways (**2 Corinthians 5:7**). Answering opportunities with a heart posture of obedience looks like being more interested in God's agenda than our comfort. What an incredible privilege to be on mission for Christ, *pursuing, encouraging, and loving His children*, pointing them into the arms of the Father.

There will always be some in the land who are poor. That is why I am commanding you to share freely with the poor and with other Israelites in need.
— *Deuteronomy 15:11*

"Then Jesus said to his disciples, 'If any of you wants to be my follower, you must give up your own way, take up your cross, and follow me.'" — *Matthew 16:24*

For we live by believing and not by seeing.
— *2 Corinthians 5:7*

Instead, you must worship Christ as Lord of your life. And if someone asks about your hope as a believer, always be ready to explain it. — *1 Peter 3:15*

July 14

When my son was about four years old, he told me, "If I was a superhero, my power would be loving people." I remember thinking that was one of the most meaningful things anyone could say (**1 Corinthians 13:7**). There is really no better request we can make than to pray to love well. I know we can all recall times and situations where we have not loved well and the consequences that followed. Not loving well typically results from pride, control, or fear, which are all fueled by our flesh (**1 Corinthians 13:4–5**). Christlike love embodies humility, surrender, and grace, which are all cultivated by the Spirit. We have all been called by God to love. When we do it well, we shine the light of Christ. When we don't, we are not operating as God's image bearers (**Ephesians 4:2**). No matter what season we are in or the calling on our life, this idea of loving well needs to be a top priority. May we all *invite the love of Christ to flow in and out* of us in a way that draws the world to the heart of the Father in this lifetime and into eternity.

> *Love never gives up, never loses faith, is always hopeful, and endures through every circumstance.* — 1 Corinthians 13:7

> *Love is patient and kind. Love is not jealous or boastful or proud or rude. It does not demand its own way. It is not irritable, and it keeps no record of being wronged.* — 1 Corinthians 13:4–5

> *Always be humble and gentle. Be patient with each other, making allowance for each other's faults because of your love.* — Ephesians 4:2

> *I pray that your love will overflow more and more, and that you will keep on growing in knowledge and understanding.* — Philippians 1:9

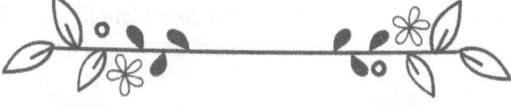

July 15

I HAD AN INCREDIBLE OPPORTUNITY TO TALK WITH SOME CHILDREN today about the story of the woman at the well (**John 4:13–14**). This is one of the most beautiful depictions of the truth, that God knows our story and knows exactly when to make Himself known to us. The Samaritan woman's encounter with Jesus changed the entire trajectory of her life (**John 4:26**). Jesus communicated that He knew of her struggles and offered her life in the One who would never fail her, whose love would never run out. This divine meeting was not happenstance; it was orchestrated by God to reorient this woman to new life and living water. She was so amazed by her encounter she could not wait to share her news (**John 4:28–30**). As Jesus captivates our heart, there is an overflow of that divine living water into everyone around us. When we can finally embrace the resurrection power available to us—*as we live in Him, through Him, and for Him*—not only will our lives change but others' lives as well.

> "Jesus replied, 'Anyone who drinks this water will soon become thirsty again. But those who drink the water I give will never be thirsty again. It becomes a fresh, bubbling spring within them, giving them eternal life.'" — John 4:13–14

> "Then Jesus told her, 'I AM the Messiah!'" — John 4:26

> "The woman left her water jar beside the well and ran back to the village, telling everyone, 'Come and see a man who told me everything I ever did! Could he possibly be the Messiah?' So the people came streaming from the village to see him." — John 4:28–30

July 16

TODAY I WAS REMINDED OF HOW ESSENTIAL THE PRACTICE OF "preaching to myself" has been over the years; especially preaching God's Word to myself. Scripture is where we can find encouragement about virtually everything (**Romans 10:17**). When we are feeling unloved, unwanted, or unseen, we can remind ourselves we are loved, valued, and seen by the Almighty God of the Universe (**Ephesians 3:19**). I shared with a group of children today how, if I'm struggling in any way, I will pray, "Father, I thank you that you love me, you are with me, and You will provide all I need" (**2 Corinthians 12:9**). He is always available and always shows up. As we lean into His thoughts towards us, other opinions don't rattle our confidence, because it is God's opinion that rules over all (**Psalm 139:17**). As we *learn to pray His Word over ourselves* or situations, it enables His thoughts to override our own, which we all need sometimes. Hiding God's Word in our hearts allows us to never be without the most powerful secret weapon: the assurance that nothing and nobody can come against us. All glory be to God, who has provided all we need.

> *So faith comes from hearing, that is, hearing the Good News about Christ. — Romans 10:17*

> *May you experience the love of Christ, though it is too great to understand fully. Then you will be made complete with all the fullness of life and power that comes from God. — Ephesians 3:19*

> *Each time he said, 'My grace is all you need. My power works best in weakness.' So now I am glad to boast about my weaknesses, so that the power of Christ can work through me. — 2 Corinthians 12:9*

> *How precious are your thoughts about me, O God. They cannot be numbered! — Psalm 139:17*

> *And this same God who takes care of me will supply all your needs from his glorious riches, which have been given to us in Christ Jesus. — Philippians 4:19*

July 17

ONE OF THE MOST DIFFICULT EMOTIONS TO FEEL IS LONELINESS. We have all heard others say, or have uttered the words ourselves, "I feel alone in this." It could be a situation, a season of life, or a struggle that seems will never go away (**Psalm 25:16–17**). We may even attempt to surround ourselves with others and still feel alone. The enemy of our souls will actually attempt to push us toward isolation, toward the lie that no one else deals with what we are dealing with. God says that, no matter our situation or state of mind, we are never alone. In fact, we cannot escape His ability to see us (**Psalm 121:8**). Powerful words from the Scriptures we can stand on are, "Father, I thank you, for you are always with me" (**Joshua 1:5**). Saying a promise over and over helps us *marinate in His truth and rest there.* There is a very special woman in my life who lives alone. She has a loving family and a church community who check on her regularly. Walking into her house, you can almost tangibly feel the Holy Spirit. She will smile and say, "Me and Jesus do just fine."

Turn to me and have mercy, for I am alone and in deep distress. My problems go from bad to worse. Oh, save me from them all!
— Psalm 25:16-17

The Lord keeps watch over you as you come and go, both now and forever. — Psalm 121:8

No one will be able to stand against you as long as you live. For I will be with you as I was with Moses. I will not fail you or abandon you.
— Joshua 1:5

You will show me the way of life, granting me the joy of your presence and the pleasures of living with you forever. — Psalm 16:11

July 18

SOME DAYS THE UNEXPECTED HAPPENS, and these are the kind of days we describe as life throwing us a curve ball (**John 16:33**). Today was one of those days: a friend of mine was involved in what could have been a fatal accident, when just earlier in the day we had been laughing together! While prayerfully it seems she will recover, there were lots of moving parts to the day, but God already had everything covered (**Matthew 6:8**). I often emphasize that God has already "seen the movie." He knows what this day holds, and for Him there are no curve balls. Our dependence on Him to navigate difficult waters is key. Not only does He know what's coming, but He has already made provision for those involved. As we live by faith when these hard things come, it strengthens us to not be un-stabilized in the storm, but to faithfully focus on the One who will lead us through it (**Psalm 46:1–3**). With our heavenly Father as our refuge, safe place, and hope, there is no circumstance He is not ready for; He is available and waiting to carry us through when we cling to Him. May we learn to be people who *run into His arms first* for refuge, direction, and hope.

> *I have told you all this so that you may have peace in me. Here on earth you will have many trials and sorrows. But take heart, because I have overcome the world.* — John 16:33

> *". . . your Father knows exactly what you need even before you ask him!"* — Matthew 6:8

> *God is our refuge and strength, always ready to help in times of trouble. So we will not fear when earthquakes come and the mountains crumble into the sea. Let the oceans roar and foam. Let the mountains tremble as the waters surge!*
> — Psalm 46:1–3

> *The name of the Lord is a strong fortress; the godly run to him and are safe.* — Proverbs 18:10

July 19

How amazing is it that the Almighty God of the Universe invites us to be on mission with Him, sharing His love (**Matthew 28:18-20**). As we allow the Holy Spirit to reorient our hearts and minds, He will lead us to areas of opportunity to spread His redemptive power. One time a young lady shared she was going through a dark season of depression. I challenged her to help, volunteer, or serve once a week somewhere that would expose her to some new environments (**Proverbs 19:17**). When we are able to take our focus off ourselves and focus on Jesus directing us to serve Him by loving others well, it can be a game changer. Oftentimes, pivoting in our spiritual and emotional well-being can lead to improved physical health. The best compliment that any of us can receive is that we love well (**John 13:34–35**). Every human has a desire to be cherished and truly loved. As we *receive that love from our Father in heaven*, it releases us to draw others towards Him by the way we love.

> "Jesus came and told his disciples, 'I have been given all authority in heaven and on earth. Therefore, go and make disciples of all the nations, baptizing them in the name of the Father and the Son and the Holy Spirit. Teach these new disciples to obey all the commands I have given you. And be sure of this: I am with you always, even to the end of the age.'"
> — Matthew 28:18–20

> If you help the poor, you are lending to the Lord—and he will repay you!
> — Proverbs 19:17

> So now I am giving you a new commandment: Love each other. Just as I have loved you, you should love each other. Your love for one another will prove to the world that you are my disciples. — John 13:34–35

> Above all, clothe yourselves with love, which binds us all together in perfect harmony. — Colossians 3:14

July 20

As Christ followers, people who love Jesus and desire to be on mission with Him, how should we show love to people who don't believe like we do (**Romans 5:8**)? The first step is choosing to love, whether people agree with us or not. The Bible doesn't say to love people who are like you or agree with how you believe. It says to love others (**John 15:12**). We can be motivated to choose love as we remind ourselves how our heavenly Father has loved us (**John 3:16**). I know beyond a shadow of a doubt that, as the Lord was pursuing me, He strategically placed people in my path who were gentle, kind, and inviting for no other reason than that they were led by the Spirit (**Luke 19:10**). We need to prayerfully navigate hard conversations but not be harsh or demanding. The Scriptures tell us love does not demand its own way (**1 Corinthians 13:4–5**). We would love to see people come to know Jesus, but that's not our decision. It is theirs. Our command is to *live and walk in love* and trust God with the outcome.

> But God showed his great love for us by sending Christ to die for us while we were still sinners. — Romans 5:8

> This is my commandment: Love each other in the same way I have loved you. — John 15:12

> For the Son of Man came to seek and save those who are lost. — Luke 19:10

> Love is patient and kind. Love is not jealous or boastful or proud or rude. It does not demand its own way. It is not irritable, and it keeps no record of being wronged. — 1 Corinthians 13:4–5

July 21

I WAS SO REMINDED TODAY OF OUR NEED FOR COMMUNITY. The Scriptures emphasize how we cannot navigate life well in isolation (**Ecclesiastes 4:9–10**). As Christ followers we should pray for sensitivity to the needs of those around us. This could look like initiating a coffee date or sending a message of encouragement to someone who keeps coming to your mind. We never know the difference it can make to someone just for them to discover someone is thinking or praying for them (**1 Peter 3:8**). We should heed the Holy Spirit's prompting to engage and realize it is an act of obedience. The other day I was driving and felt pricked to reach out to a friend I hadn't seen in a while. She responded immediately with how much she needed my contact in that particular moment, revealing she was feeling very alone that day. She mentioned my message made her feel seen by God and helped reorient her mind (**1 Thessalonians 5:11**). He is truly the good shepherd who sees our needs and provides the right solution at the right time in the right way. May we be people who *come together and celebrate His goodness.*

> Two people are better off than one, for they can help each other succeed. If one person falls, the other can reach out and help. But someone who falls alone is in real trouble. — Ecclesiastes 4:9–10

> Finally, all of you should be of one mind. Sympathize with each other. Love each other as brothers and sisters. Be tenderhearted, and keep a humble attitude. — 1 Peter 3:8

> So encourage each other and build each other up, just as you are already doing. — 1 Thessalonians 5:11

> Give thanks to the Lord, for he is good! His faithful love endures forever. — Psalm 107:1

July 22

I HAVE ALWAYS LOVED THE IMAGERY OF GOD as our shepherd. Psalm 23 encompasses various roles that a shepherd has with his flock, which certainly mirrors the way our heavenly Father cares for us. In our humanity there can be blurred lines between needs and wants, but there is great rest found in knowing our needs are provided for (**Psalm 23:1**). Peace is always the best indicator as to whether or not we are heading in the right path. He leads us with steadiness and calm (**Psalm 23:2–3**). He provides a strong sense of comfort even through the most difficult water (**Psalm 23:4**). The Lord prepares a place for David and anoints his head with oil, symbolizing David as His honored guest (**Psalm 23:5**). God's goodness and love will follow us all the days of our lives, and this love is forevermore (**Psalm 23:6**). This psalm is so rich and these are all promises we can embrace and celebrate. When we *pause, reflect, and soak in the goodness of God*, we are able to be the royal priesthood He called us out of darkness to experience. He is where our satisfaction is found.

> *The Lord is my shepherd; I have all that I need. He lets me rest in green meadows; he leads me beside peaceful streams. He renews my strength. He guides me along right paths, bringing honor to his name. Even when I walk through the darkest valley, I will not be afraid, for you are close beside me. Your rod and your staff protect and comfort me. You prepare a feast for me in the presence of my enemies. You honor me by anointing my head with oil. My cup overflows with blessings. Surely your goodness and unfailing love will pursue me all the days of my life, and I will live in the house of the Lord forever. — Psalm 23*

July 23

THE COMPLEXITY OF OUR HUMAN RELATIONSHIPS IS, to say the least, an exhaustive topic. If we are observant, we constantly hear people discussing their struggles or victories with others or commenting on what someone else is doing (**Matthew 7:3**). We seem to be experts on finding solutions to problems that are not our own. I love that our heavenly Father will often graciously redirect us to help us stay in our lane and leave others' heart change to Him (**Proverbs 21:1**). When we aren't attempting to manage or control one another, it's amazing how we are freed up to love well as God intended (**Romans 12:8**). We waste so much precious time in the grips of division over things that one day we are likely to consider trivial. Oftentimes the most difficult relationships in our families are the ones we grow from the most. It's not hard to care for those who are easy to love, but as we exercise our spiritual dependence on God to love in the more difficult scenarios, that is where the love of Christ shines the brightest (**John 13:35**). We should all *be thankful for the love* that is poured out on us when we are the ones who are hard to love.

> And why worry about a speck in your friend's eye when you have a log in your own? — Matthew 7:3

> The king's heart is like a stream of water directed by the Lord; he guides it wherever he pleases. — Proverbs 21:1

> If your gift is to encourage others, be encouraging. If it is giving, give generously. If God has given you leadership ability, take the responsibility seriously. And if you have a gift for showing kindness to others, do it gladly. — Romans 12:8

> Your love for one another will prove to the world that you are my disciples. — John 13:35

July 24

HAVE YOU EVER HAD A CONVERSATION WITH SOMEONE and thought to yourself, "Where did that come from?" or "I can't remember exactly what I said"? This can occur when we make ourselves available for the Holy Spirit to speak through us (**Matthew 10:20**). We need to be inviting the Holy Spirit to move us out of the way and to invade our words and thoughts. I will often pray for God to open my ears and heart to the promptings from the Spirit at all times, including when I have a preconceived notion of how a conversation will go (**Proverbs 4:20–22**). So often the most precious communication skill is to listen well. Listening to someone and caring for them well go hand in hand. When we react too quickly we can make a mess of things, whereas pausing and being led by the Spirit is more beneficial for everyone (**James 1:19**) When we *wait, pray, and invite God in*, our conversations are more fruitful, our motives are more pure, and God's purpose and plans reign in the atmosphere of humility and trust.

> *For it is not you who will be speaking—it will be the Spirit of your Father speaking through you. — Matthew 10:20*

> *My child, pay attention to what I say. Listen carefully to my words. Don't lose sight of them. Let them penetrate deep into your heart, for they bring life to those who find them, and healing to their whole body. — Proverbs 4:20–22*

> *Understand this, my dear brothers and sisters: You must all be quick to listen, slow to speak, and slow to get angry. — James 1:19*

> *Commit everything you do to the Lord. Trust him, and he will help you. — Psalm 37:5*

July 25

HOW MANY TIMES HAVE WE HEARD THE PHRASE, "I feel like there is something more"? Or sometimes we say, "I feel like I should be doing more." Oftentimes it's not doing more, it's simply doing differently (**Psalm 31:15**). Anytime we are sensing a lack in our soul, we can approach God with a posture of willingness and humility. When we are seeking God and surrendering our days to Him for His purposes, our spirits will feel full and satisfied even in challenging scenarios. Simply placing ourselves under God's authority and direction brings peace and security, not to mention the sense of accomplishment we feel, not because of what we have done but out of our desire to be on mission with Him (**Romans 12:1**). We were made for more than we realize. We were created to love and be loved by God in personal ways. We were made to build each other up and encourage one another in God's plans and purposes. We were created to get out of our comfort zones and make a difference in this world (**2 Corinthians 5:20**). He is not only the Lord of our lives, He is the Lord of our days and schedules. *Surrender your time to the One who* can make the most of it.

> My future is in your hands. Rescue me from those who hunt me down relentlessly. — Psalm 31:15

> And so, dear brothers and sisters, I plead with you to give your bodies to God because of all he has done for you. Let them be a living and holy sacrifice—the kind he will find acceptable. This is truly the way to worship him. — Romans 12:1

> "So we are Christ's ambassadors; God is making his appeal through us. We speak for Christ when we plead, 'Come back to God!'" — 2 Corinthians 5:20

> Make the most of every opportunity in these evil days. — Ephesians 5:16

July 26

A SPECIAL FRIEND OF MINE SHARED WITH ME HOW SHE WAS INVITED into a family situation she deemed uncomfortable. She did not want to attend, but she felt the Holy Spirit prompting her to go (**Psalm 34:18**). She was reluctant to return to a place of wounding, but God wanted to show her it was okay because He was with her, giving her strength to endure; and proving Himself faithful in that—she was glad she went (**Psalm 56:3–4**). Since we were created for utter dependence and reliance on God, we can be brave entering unknown territories with the confidence of not being alone. My sweet friend shared with me how God had been pursuing her, inviting her to be in His presence more by turning off the radio and TV and listening for His voice (**Psalm 62:5**). Drawing close to the heart of God involves learning to be vulnerable with Him, sharing our hearts and emotions. Even though He already knows our heart, He longs to be invited in where He can strengthen us from the inside out, equipping us to have courage because *we know our Father is with us.*

> The Lord is close to the brokenhearted; he rescues those whose spirits are crushed. — Psalm 34:18

> But when I am afraid, I will put my trust in you. I praise God for what he has promised. I trust in God, so why should I be afraid? What can mere mortals do to me? — Psalm 56:3-4

> Let all that I am wait quietly before God, for my hope is in him. — Psalm 62:5

> For God has not given us a spirit of fear and timidity, but of power, love, and self-discipline. —2 Timothy 1:7

July 27

I HAVE ALWAYS EMBRACED THE IMAGERY OF BEING AN AMBASSADOR FOR CHRIST. As Christ followers, we are called to this role by God, and this particular calling will look different depending on the environment you may find yourself in. Christ will give opportunities to reflect His character, and fulfilling this commission with an expectant heart leads to satisfaction for our souls (**2 Corinthians 5:20**). The special characteristics of an ambassador are those *we must rely on the Holy Spirit* to demonstrate through us. They mirror the fruits of the Spirit, such as patience, honesty, humility, and genuine love for one another (**Galatians 5:22–23**). We all live in more of a spiritual environment than we realize, where there is always a battle taking place. We can and should live in a way that emulates our spot on His victorious team with love and gratitude in our hearts (**1 Corinthians 15:57**). We don't need to be dismayed with our world's state of chaos. We can know whose we are and where we are going. Living out well our role as ambassadors, makes a watching world curious about the secure hope of Christ and eternity with Him.

> So we are Christ's ambassadors; God is making his appeal through us. We speak for Christ when we plead, 'Come back to God!' — 2 Corinthians 5:20

> But the Holy Spirit produces this kind of fruit in our lives: love, joy, peace, patience, kindness, goodness, faithfulness, gentleness, and self-control. There is no law against these things! — Galatians 5:22–23

> But thank God! He gives us victory over sin and death through our Lord Jesus Christ. — 1 Corinthians 15:57

> Faith shows the reality of what we hope for; it is the evidence of things we cannot see. — Hebrews 11:1

July 28

AS GOD MOVES WITH POWER IN OUR LIVES, we get the privilege of testifying of His goodness (**Acts 20:24**). Along with representing Christ well by our actions, we get the opportunity to speak life and hope into others, sharing and celebrating how He has worked in our own lives. There is nothing as moving as hearing the way Christ captivated and transformed a lost soul (**Hebrews 4:12**). Being transformed from the inside out motivates and empowers our role as ambassadors in His Kingdom. The same way Christ has worked in your heart is the way He wants to move in another. We need to seek opportunities to spur one another toward change. One of the spiritual enemy's favorite lies is that change is impossible, but we who have been changed are living proof anything is possible with God and a surrendered heart (**Deuteronomy 30:6**). *We need to pray Christ would be magnified* in and through our actions, words, and unapologetic devotion to Him above all else (**John 8:29**). Imagine how it pleases our heavenly Father to see His children living out loud in word and action, glorifying His name for all He is and all He has done. Amen!

> But my life is worth nothing to me unless I use it for
> finishing the work assigned me by the Lord Jesus—the work of telling others
> the Good News about the wonderful grace of God. — Acts 20:24

> For the word of God is alive and powerful. It is sharper
> than the sharpest two-edged sword, cutting between
> soul and spirit, between joint and marrow. It exposes our innermost
> thoughts and desires. — Hebrews 4:12

> The Lord your God will change your heart and the
> hearts of all your descendants, so that you will love him
> with all your heart and soul and so you may live!
> — Deuteronomy 30:6

> And the one who sent me is with me—he has not deserted me. For I always do
> what pleases him. — John 8:29

July 29

YESTERDAY I WAS STRUCK WITH EMOTION ON MY WAY TO A CHURCH service as I remembered the moment God interrupted my self-absorbed life to reorient me to Himself **(Proverbs 19:21)**. My recollection of that day seemed to come out of nowhere, but in true divine fashion, it fell right in line with the message I was about to hear, for the pastor shared his own story of redemption and how God continues to bend and mold him. It never ceases to amaze me how God orchestrates our eyes and ears to His activity **(Revelation 3:20)**. He is constantly inviting us to move towards the desires of His heart and focusing our attention to His eternal mission. As we respond to His call on our lives through faith and surrender, the worries of this present world are minimized while the cross and all it represents grow larger **(Colossians 3:2–3)**. Our heavenly Father so often is reaching for us, ready to reveal Himself and all His plans. The question is, *are we listening, and how will we respond to His call?*

> You can make many plans, but the Lord's purpose will prevail.
> — Proverbs 19:21

> Look! I stand at the door and knock. If you hear my voice and open the door, I will come in, and we will share a meal together as friends. — Revelation 3:20

> Think about the things of heaven, not the things of earth. For you died to this life, and your real life is hidden with Christ in God. — Colossians 3:2–3

> And now he has made all of this plain to us by the appearing of Christ Jesus, our Savior. He broke the power of death and illuminated the way to life and immortality through the Good News. — 2 Timothy 1:10

July 30

THE RELATIONSHIPS WE GET TO EXPERIENCE WITH OTHERS can and should be one of our most valued gifts (**Proverbs 17:17**). We all have had friendships in our lives that were a place of comfort and joy. On the other hand, relationships can breed conflict or unrest that may lead to disappointment and division. God provides clear direction from the Scriptures about the purest way to conflict resolution (**Matthew 18:15**). We should prayerfully go to our brother or sister in Christ with the intention of restoration. So often we prematurely bring in a third party before addressing the matter with those directly involved. When it comes to dealing with conflict, *we should continuously pray*, "Father, help me to be led by your Spirit, not my flesh." If we sense our flesh taking over, that is our cue to be quiet and reorient ourselves back to Jesus before moving forward (**Proverbs 15:1**). While there are certainly relationships that are only in our lives for a season, there are others that can be sustained and reconciled as we love and care for them in a way that honors and pleases God.

A friend is always loyal, and a brother is born to help in time of need. — Proverbs 17:17

If another believer sins against you, go privately and point out the offense. If the other person listens and confesses it, you have won that person back. — Matthew 18:15

A gentle answer deflects anger, but harsh words make tempers flare. — Proverbs 15:1

Instead, be kind to each other, tenderhearted, forgiving one another, just as God through Christ has forgiven you. — Ephesians 4:32

July 31

UNFORTUNATELY, ALMOST ALL OF US SUFFER SOME SORT OF EMOTIONAL WOUNDING early in our lives. We are raised by imperfect people in an imperfect world, where even the best of parents will fall short in some ways (**Romans 3:23**). The earlier we can learn to seek emotional support from Jesus, the more spiritually, emotionally, and even physically healthy we will be. Allowing Jesus to be our emotional support brings a two-fold benefit. First of all, it alleviates the temptation to rely too heavily on human relationships to meet our needs where only Jesus can (**Philippians 4:19**). Our heavenly Father invites us into His presence, and as we respond to His prompting, He fills us with satisfaction, joy, and strength to live out the purpose we were created for. Secondly, as we go to Him first, He reorients the way we see our situations, bringing our minds in line with His activity instead of our own agenda (**Isaiah 55:8–9**). Finally, and maybe most importantly, He enables us to see others through the lens of His grace. A mere ounce of *Christlike love can radically change the way we view* someone. We all need Jesus in such a powerful way.

> For everyone has sinned; we all fall short of God's glorious standard. — Romans 3:23

> And this same God who takes care of me will supply all your needs from his glorious riches, which have been given to us in Christ Jesus. — Philippians 4:19

> "'My thoughts are nothing like your thoughts,' says the Lord. 'And my ways are far beyond anything you could imagine. For just as the heavens are higher than the earth, so my ways are higher than your ways and my thoughts higher than your thoughts.'" — Isaiah 55:8–9

> All of them ate the same spiritual food, and all of them drank the same spiritual water. For they drank from the spiritual rock that traveled with them, and that rock was Christ. — 1 Corinthians 10:3–4

August 1

I HAD THE PLEASURE OF TALKING WITH A GROUP OF WOMEN who shared how they are intentionally seeking Jesus to be their emotional support. The more we dive deeper into our relationship with Him, the more access we allow His influence (**Philippians 4:6–7**). Jesus cares deeply about our emotions and feelings. He simply loves us too much to leave us on our own with them. We need to allow Him to invade our thought life, for our thoughts lay the groundwork for our attitudes and behavior. The more we think on things of eternal value, the less room we allow for things counterproductive to spiritual, emotional, and physical well-being. Fall is just around the corner, so this is a great time to create new habits for improved health. *Begin the day asking the Lord to help you* have an expectant heart and focus on what is positive (**Proverbs 17:22**). Try to avoid conversations where people just seem to be complaining with no solution in sight (**1 Corinthians 10:10**). Take a late evening walk listening to praise music or praying to wind down from the day (**Isaiah 40:31**). It's beneficial to mix things up so we don't get stagnant in any area of our health and well-being. Becoming too set in our ways creates resistance to new opportunities.

> *A cheerful heart is good medicine, but a broken spirit saps a person's strength.*
> *— Proverbs 17:22*

> *And don't grumble as some of them did, and then were destroyed by the angel of death. —1 Corinthians 10:10*

> *But those who trust in the Lord will find new strength. They will soar high on wings like eagles. They will run and not grow weary. They will walk and not faint. — Isaiah 40:31*

> *There is a wide-open door for a great work here, although many oppose me.*
> *— 1 Corinthians 16:9*

I WOKE UP THIS MORNING WITH THE WORSHIP SONG, "O Praise the Name of the Lord our God" on my heart, and I was immediately reminded of how true it is that God inhabits the praises of His people (**Psalm 22:3**). A lady walked into the gym this morning with a t-shirt on that repeated "Thank you, God" several times, and there was a light in her that was unmistakably reflecting Jesus (**John 8:12**). Possessing that attitude of gratitude is indicative of a genuine heart for Christ, all He is, and all He's done. It is a gratitude not set on having our own way or great circumstances, but one of thankfulness for the cross and all it represents, and a Savior willing to take on our sin and shame to save a lost world from ultimate death and destruction (**Matthew 1:21**). Unfortunately, our human nature tends to drift toward what we don't have, but we can *intentionally celebrate every day* all that is available to us as followers of Christ: our salvation, our redemption, and the opportunity to shine for Him day-in and day-out, rejoicing in who He is and how He cares for us completely.

> *Yet you are holy, enthroned on the praises of Israel.*
> *— Psalm 22:3*

> *"Jesus spoke to the people once more and said, 'I am the light of the world. If you follow me, you won't have to walk in darkness, because you will have the light that leads to life.'" — John 8:12*

> *And she will have a son, and you are to name him Jesus, for he will save his people from their sins.*
> *— Matthew 1:21*

> *Never! Can a mother forget her nursing child? Can she feel no love for the child she has borne? But even if that were possible, I would not forget you! — Isaiah 49:15*

I HAD THE PRIVILEGE OF ATTENDING THE SWEETEST CHURCH SERVICE where the speaker focused on sitting at the feet of Jesus (**Luke 7:37**). The speaker painted a beautiful picture of how important it was for this woman to get to Jesus, sit at His feet, and even wash His feet with the contents of her alabaster jar and her hair. My husband made a comment about the speaker, noticing the light of Christ in her eyes and her love for the Lord. This attribute was obvious in her because she too knows the importance and unmatched benefit of sitting at the feet of Jesus. The story Mary and Martha also emphasizes Mary desiring and realizing the beauty of simply sitting at Jesus' feet (**Luke 10:41–42**). How often are we invited into His presence by that still, small voice and we choose a lesser option of some sort of distraction (**Hebrews 4:16**)? As we make the wise decision to *say yes to the opportunity to intimately meet with our Savior,* we are always changed for the better. We need His touch desperately, and the more aware we are of that need, the more we will respond in awe at the opportunity to fellowship with Christ. Nobody ever regrets marinating in His presence.

> *When a certain immoral woman from that city heard he was eating there, she brought a beautiful alabaster jar filled with expensive perfume.* — Luke 7:37

> *"But the Lord said to her, 'My dear Martha, you are worried and upset over all these details! There is only one thing worth being concerned about. Mary has discovered it, and it will not be taken away from her.'"* — Luke 10:41–42

> *So let us come boldly to the throne of our gracious God. There we will receive his mercy, and we will find grace to help us when we need it most.* — Hebrews 4:16

> *"Then Jesus said, 'Come to me, all of you who are weary and carry heavy burdens, and I will give you rest.'"* — Matthew 11:28

August 4

As humans, we are prone to a universal delusion that we have to be in control, believing control makes us powerful. As with many things, when we live God's way, the opposite is true (**Galatians 2:2**). Making the wise decision to die to an old way of life and embrace new life in Christ begins the journey of utter surrender, trust, and reliance on God (**Romans 6:13**). One of the most beautiful transformations in the life of a believer is embracing the reality that God is in control, and as we seek Him with humility, we are empowered. Our power, our effectiveness, and success in all areas are only because of Him (**Philipppians 4:13**). We will always come to a breaking point when we draw from our own strength. The illusion of control breeds anxiety, stress, and ultimately disappointment, whereas resting in God's hands produces peace, energy, and gratification. The culture seems to push the lie that we are more powerful than we are, while the Scriptures consistently remind us how powerful God is and that *He is always where our help is found*. On our own we are prideful and powerless, but with Christ we are made new, humbled, and empowered.

> I went there because God revealed to me that I should go. While I was there I met privately with those considered to be leaders of the church and shared with them the message I had been preaching to the Gentiles. I wanted to make sure that we were in agreement, for fear that all my efforts had been wasted and I was running the race for nothing. — Galatians 2:2

> Do not let any part of your body become an instrument of evil to serve sin. Instead, give yourselves completely to God, for you were dead, but now you have new life. So use your whole body as an instrument to do what is right for the glory of God. — Romans 6:13

> For I can do everything through Christ, who gives me strength. — Philippians 4:13

> But you will receive power when the Holy Spirit comes upon you. And you will be my witnesses, telling people about me everywhere—in Jerusalem, throughout Judea, in Samaria, and to the ends of the earth. — Acts 1:8

August 5

We had a beautiful message at church on the value of the last season of our lives here on earth. This side of heaven, God gives us the gift of time, and the opportunity to invest it wisely or unwisely is up to us (**Psalm 90:12**). One of my favorite things about the years going by is that my experience and history with Jesus deepens and grows. I love how I see that my personal relationship with and my reliance on God is by far the most critical and valuable part of my life (**Mark 12:29–30**). The more immersed we are in our zeal for Jesus, the more we organically share that with others without even realizing it. The most important gesture of love towards anyone is prayer, but words of encouragement are also critical (**Romans 15:5**). No matter what anyone may be going through, pointing them towards Jesus is always appropriate. We do this not only by words but by the way we choose to live and love. The sooner we *begin intentionally lifting others up and loving them well*, the better quality of life we will experience while being confident we are investing our gift of time well.

> *Teach us to realize the brevity of life, so that we may grow in wisdom.*
> *— Psalm 90:12*

> *Jesus replied, 'The most important commandment is this: "Listen, O Israel! The Lord our God is the one and only Lord. And you must love the Lord your God with all your heart, all your soul, all your mind, and all your strength."'*
> *— Mark 12:29–30*

> *May God, who gives this patience and encouragement, help you live in complete harmony with each other, as is fitting for followers of Christ Jesus. — Romans 15:5*

> *We pleaded with you, encouraged you, and urged you to live your lives in a way that God would consider worthy. For he called you to share in his Kingdom and glory. — 1 Thessalonians 2:12*

August 6

THERE IS AN OLD GOSPEL SONG I HAD THE PLEASURE OF HEARING recently called "Two Coats." The song emphasizes the significance of trading your old coat with the remnants of your old life for a new coat symbolizing new life in Christ (**2 Corinthians 5:17–18**). Oftentimes we yearn for a closer walk with God and the ability to discern His guidance while we are unwilling to walk away from the very things that drive a wedge in our spirit (**Romans 12:2**). There is a bridge between our old life and abundant life in Christ, but we have to make the decision to cross it. No other human, nor even God, can make the strides of obedience that will position us closer and deeper into the heart of God. This is the most important journey any of us will ever make, and the freedom, joy, and quality of life waiting for us on the other side are extraordinary (**Romans 6:23**). We have eternity to look forward to, but joy this side of heaven is about being who God has called us to be, doing what He has called us to do, and leaning into His arms more every day so He can empower us as only He can. *We need God and we need others.* We were not meant to cross that bridge alone.

> *This means that anyone who belongs to Christ has become a new person. The old life is gone; a new life has begun! And all of this is a gift from God, who brought us back to himself through Christ. And God has given us this task of reconciling people to him.* — 2 Corinthians 5:17-18

> *Don't copy the behavior and customs of this world, but let God transform you into a new person by changing the way you think. Then you will learn to know God's will for you, which is good and pleasing and perfect.*
> — Romans 12:2

> *For the wages of sin is death, but the free gift of God is eternal life through Christ Jesus our Lord.* — Romans 6:23

> *Once you had no identity as a people; now you are God's people. Once you received no mercy; now you have received God's mercy.*
> — 1 Peter 2:10

We can all have confidence in knowing God is always at work in and around us, but there are times when He gives us the blessing of a front row seat to His transformative power in a way that feels tangibly supernatural (**Psalm 19:1**). Upon arriving at a special meeting with a friend, where I knew there would be a hard conversation, I had five messages in a row of people praying over our time. The peace and expectancy I held in my heart for our time together was surreal (**Ephesians 3:20**). On certain occasions, God will equip us to comfort, love, and support one another in ways that it's simply an honor to be a part of. The experience of sensing the Holy Spirit desiring a child of God to feel safe and loved in a unique way is a reminder of how our heavenly Father is so rich in grace and mercy (**2 Corinthians 1:4**). When we are led by the Spirit to care for others, *our role is to be obedient to that call*. The way they respond and the outcome of our time together is not in our control. That's all God. The gift of seeing the love of Christ invade someone's heart in a way that begins a process of healing and freedom is one of the most beautiful images this side of heaven. Glory be to God for answered prayers and His faithfulness.

> The heavens proclaim the glory of God. The skies display his craftsmanship.
> —Psalm 19:1

> Now all glory to God, who is able, through his mighty power at work within us, to accomplish infinitely more than we might ask or think. — Ephesians 3:20

> He comforts us in all our troubles so that we can comfort others. When they are troubled, we will be able to give them the same comfort God has given us.
> — 2 Corinthians 1:4

> He is the Rock; his deeds are perfect. Everything he does is just and fair. He is a faithful God who does no wrong; how just and upright he is!
> — Deuteronomy 32:4

August 8

I WAS REMINDED TODAY OF THE IMPORTANCE OF EACH OF US RUNNING the race that God has laid out for us and of remaining open-handed regarding what God has in store (**2 Timothy 4:7**). We have to remember the reality that God has woven the fabric of our lives together in such a way that every day and every second counts. Even the days that don't seem eventful to us at all have significance to God (**Isaiah 45:15**). Oftentimes we can get distracted by our own agendas to the degree we lose sight of allowing God to dictate our daily activities and priorities. It is important that we plan, but *we must remember to bring the Lord into the initial planning,* asking Him to be in charge as we listen and obey (**Proverbs 16:3**). We could actually avoid some failures and disappointments by seeking His will initially instead of being our own master planner. We can tend to believe we have way more wisdom than we actually do and not place ourselves below the One Almighty God of the Universe who has the power to help us run our race and finish well. He is the author and finisher of our faith.

> *I have fought the good fight, I have finished the race, and I have remained faithful.* — 2 Timothy 4:7

> *Truly, O God of Israel, our Savior, you work in mysterious ways.* — Isaiah 45:15

> *Commit your actions to the Lord, and your plans will succeed.* — Proverbs 16:3

> *We do this by keeping our eyes on Jesus, the champion who initiates and perfects our faith. Because of the joy awaiting him, he endured the cross, disregarding its shame. Now he is seated in the place of honor beside God's throne.* — Hebrews 12:2

August 9

ANYTHING GOOD IN ANY OF US IS ONLY BECAUSE OF GOD. He uniquely fashioned every one of us on purpose, for a purpose (**Psalm 139:13–16**). It is beyond fascinating to think in our mother's womb there were plans and paths He had in mind for us. During a popular sports or entertainment event, there is always a different heart posture coming from the ones who in their victory give God the glory (**James 1:17**). When we realize our gifts, talents, and the very air we breathe are all God's, it creates the spirit of humility that is organically full of gratitude and does not boast of self-sufficiency. I will often say out loud, "Father, everything is from you, in you, and for you." These are important truths to remind ourselves of (**Colossians 1:15–16**). We should regularly and eagerly give God all the glory due His name regarding every area of our lives, remembering that He is in every area and genuinely wants us to acknowledge Him and His goodness. This mindset keeps us from self-promoting and self-righteousness. As we *humble ourselves*, knowing all we are is because of Him, we can live in unhindered devotion as we should.

> You made all the delicate, inner parts of my body and knit me together in my mother's womb. Thank you for making me so wonderfully complex! Your workmanship is marvelous—how well I know it. You watched me as I was being formed in utter seclusion, as I was woven together in the dark of the womb. You saw me before I was born. Every day of my life was recorded in your book. Every moment was laid out before a single day had passed. —Psalm 139:13–16

> Whatever is good and perfect is a gift coming down to us from God our Father, who created all the lights in the heavens. He never changes or casts a shifting shadow. — James 1:17

> Christ is the visible image of the invisible God. He existed before anything was created and is supreme over all creation, for through him God created everything in the heavenly realms and on earth. He made the things we can see and the things we can't see—such as thrones, kingdoms, rulers, and authorities in the unseen world. Everything was created through him and for him. — Colossians 1:15–16

> I am saying this for your benefit, not to place restrictions on you. I want you to do whatever will help you serve the Lord best, with as few distractions as possible. — 1 Corinthians 7:35

August 10

OUR DEVOTION TO GOD SHINES THROUGH OUR LIVES IN SEVERAL WAYS. Living a lifestyle of devotion is multifaceted and comes with desire, intentionality, and a pure heart for the Lord (**Deuteronomy 4:29**). Devotion is birthed through determination, perseverance, and gratitude. It is also something our heavenly Father is most deserving of (**1 Kings 8:61**). Since He has sacrificially loved and rescued us, we can in return honor Him by the way we love Him and His children, remain steadfast in loyalty to Him, and *enthusiastically share His hope* as he gives us opportunity (**Romans 12:11**). My daughter shared an interaction she had with a lady who had somewhat deconstructed her faith. My daughter engaged with the woman by admiring some pictures she was drawing, and shared with the woman that she was a Christ follower. They had a great interaction because my daughter showed interest in the woman's artwork. Who knows what seeds were planted in that interaction, but my daughter's devotion to Jesus was on full display in a way that was warm and inviting. Our love and zeal for the Lord is contagious, and He prepares the way for us to shine for Him.

> *But from there you will search again for the Lord your God. And if you search for him with all your heart and soul, you will find him.*
> — Deuteronomy 4:29

> *And may you be completely faithful to the Lord our God. May you always obey his decrees and commands, just as you are doing today.*
> — 1 Kings 8:61

> *Never be lazy, but work hard and serve the Lord enthusiastically.* — Romans 12:11

> *In the same way, let your good deeds shine out for all to see, so that everyone will praise your heavenly Father.* — Matthew 5:16

When I think of four powerful spiritual muscles we need to regularly exercise, I think of belief, surrender, obedience, and humility (**Philippians 2:12–13**). These are characteristics of our faith walk that lead us toward the satisfying abundant life we all desire. Everything truly begins with what we believe, which is never dictated by feelings but by the absolute truth found in the Scriptures (**Psalm 19:7**). Surrender is the action responding to the authority of He who is all-knowing and sovereign (**Ephesians 1:11**). Obedience to the direction we receive from the Holy Spirit leads to freedom and the peace found in staying under the umbrella of God's will (**Proverbs 13:13**). The beauty and warmth of a humble heart makes us radiant with love. *We need humility in every relationship* we experience. Being humble opposes the human tendency for self-sufficiency and pride. The more conscious we are to remain humble, the more we will organically remind ourselves of our need for God. Strengthening these spiritual muscles empowers us to be brave, bold witnesses for the One who has given us salvation and life.

> *Dear friends, you always followed my instructions when I was with you. And now that I am away, it is even more important. Work hard to show the results of your salvation, obeying God with deep reverence and fear. For God is working in you, giving you the desire and the power to do what pleases him.*
> — Philippians 2:12–13

> *The instructions of the Lord are perfect, reviving the soul. The decrees of the Lord are trustworthy, making wise the simple.* — Psalm 19:7

> *Furthermore, because we are united with Christ, we have received an inheritance from God, for he chose us in advance, and he makes everything work out according to his plan.* — Ephesians 1:11

> *People who despise advice are asking for trouble; those who respect a command will succeed.* — Proverbs 13:13

> *For this is how God loved the world: He gave his one and only Son, so that everyone who believes in him will not perish but have eternal life.* — John 3:16

August 12

THE HOLY SPIRIT HAS BROUGHT THE MEDITATION IN MY HEART all day of the gift of God's mercies being new every morning (**Lamentations 3:22–23**) The idea of new mercies contains a wealth of blessings for us. The mercy of God's love, forgiveness, and compassion begins new every day, bringing a fresh start full of gratitude for His kindness (**Psalm 107:1**). Our life with God is an adventure in that we never know what each day will hold. Beginning the day with a thankful heart positions us to be alert to God's activity and allows us to notice small gifts, such as an unexpected conversation or something beautiful in nature that may capture our attention (**Colossians 4:2**). As we *acknowledge and embrace God's mercies* for us, we are motivated to show mercy for others in a way that reflects and spreads Christ's love and hope (**Luke 6:36**). A healthy, Christlike perspective is the result of deciding to lean in to the fresh mercy of God every morning, expecting that He will move and reveal Himself.

> *The faithful love of the Lord never ends! His mercies never cease. Great is his faithfulness; his mercies begin afresh each morning.* — Lamentations 3:22–23

> *Give thanks to the Lord, for he is good! His faithful love endures forever.* — Psalm 107:1

> *Devote yourselves to prayer with an alert mind and a thankful heart.* — Colossians 4:2

> *You must be compassionate, just as your Father is compassionate.* — Luke 6:36

> *But from there you will search again for the Lord your God. And if you search for him with all your heart and soul, you will find him.* — Deuteronomy 4:29

August 13

Responding to the invitation from the Holy Spirit to pause and meet with God never disappoints (**Mark 1:35**) We are certainly way too busy as a culture, and we create undue stress and pressure on ourselves, striving to accomplish things we were not called to do. Jesus can radically change the trajectory of our day in just a few moments of quality time with Him (**Matthew 8:3**). A touch from Jesus has the ability to get our flesh out of the way so we can be Spirit-led. The culture is frantic and worried, while followers of Christ can be peaceful and confident in the knowledge that it is God who orders our steps (**Proverbs 16:9**). How gracious of God to draw us into His presence to realize how much we need Him, when we are so easily distracted. The more we *allow Jesus to reorient our hearts* and minds, the more we will crave the stability of His provision. He is there to meet our needs before we are even aware of them. Our good shepherd, Father, and friend is worthy of our time.

> *Before daybreak the next morning, Jesus got up and went out to an isolated place to pray.* — Mark 1:35

> *Jesus reached out and touched him. 'I am willing,' he said. 'Be healed!' And instantly the leprosy disappeared.* — Matthew 8:3

> *We can make our plans, but the Lord determines our steps.* — Proverbs 16:9

> *I will praise you every day; yes, I will praise you forever.* — Psalm 145:2

August 14

TRUSTING GOD WITH THE OUTCOMES OF SITUATIONS IS DEFINITELY a faith hurdle. I think of it in terms of a hurdle because in order to grow in this area, we are required to jump (**Luke 1:37**). When God directs you to be involved in a piece of the work He is doing in someone's heart, that doesn't mean the outcome is your responsibility. We can have peace knowing we did our part, but how that person responds is out of our hands (**Galatians 6:1–2**). I often find that the harder conversations God invites me into are areas of struggle that I have also experienced. I love that God gives us these kinds of opportunities so we can testify to what He has done in our own lives, encouraging our brother or sister in Christ. He can do the same for them (**2 Corinthians 1:3–4**). The old cliché you can lead a horse to water but you can't make him drink is certainly true. However, *we need to engage in the opportunities God gives us* to be a bridge to Him, trusting that when we do our part, He has already done His.

> For the word of God will never fail.
> — Luke 1:37

> Dear brothers and sisters, if another believer is overcome by some sin, you who are godly should gently and humbly help that person back onto the right path. And be careful not to fall into the same temptation yourself. Share each other's burdens, and in this way obey the law of Christ. — Galatians 6:1–2

> All praise to God, the Father of our Lord Jesus Christ. God is our merciful Father and the source of all comfort. He comforts us in all our troubles so that we can comfort others. When they are troubled, we will be able to give them the same comfort God has given us.
> — 2 Corinthians 1:3–4

> You go before me and follow me. You place your hand of blessing on my head.
> — Psalm 139:5

August 15

One of the most inviting attributes of a Christ follower is joy. Joy is an emotion of delight, satisfaction, and pleasure. Knowing we are children of God, fully known and fully loved, is more than enough to experience joy regularly, regardless of circumstances (**Philippians 4:4–5**). The joy we hold in our hearts as God's image bearers is unmovable. We can walk away from a heated interaction with a loved one without our joy being stolen because it's not others who provide joy (**Psalm 118:6–7**). Our joy is also meant to be an encouragement to others experiencing a hard time. If someone comes to us with an issue and we immediately join their downward spiral, it can fuel their despair. We need to *show empathy* in a way that is hopeful (**Ephesians 4:32**). A good heart-check question is, "Is my life marked by joy?" And if it is, celebrate that, knowing it's a daily choice. And if it's not, be intentional with prayer and reflection, realizing the difference that clothing ourselves in joy can make to us and others.

> *Always be full of joy in the Lord. I say it again—rejoice! Let everyone see that you are considerate in all you do. Remember, the Lord is coming soon.*
> *— Philippians 4:4-5*

> *The Lord is for me, so I will have no fear. What can mere people do to me? Yes, the Lord is for me; he will help me. I will look in triumph at those who hate me.*
> *— Psalm 118:6-7*

> *Instead, be kind to each other, tenderhearted, forgiving one another, just as God through Christ has forgiven you. — Ephesians 4:32*

> *Dear brothers and sisters, when troubles of any kind come your way, consider it an opportunity for great joy. For you know that when your faith is tested, your endurance has a chance to grow. — James 1:2-3*

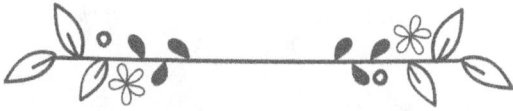

August 16

When I reflect on where and when I've seen God build spiritual and emotional strength in my life or the lives of others, it's in the broken places. So often we need to experience the brokenness to be put back together (**Isaiah 61:3**). The way God weaves courage, stability, and freedom through hard things is gracious and life-giving (**Isaiah 40:29**). Individuals who have experienced the most hardships in life are naturally more appreciative of opportunities to do life differently. If we will allow the Holy Spirit to be our guide, we will notice how our heavenly Father is regularly revealing Himself and the purposes and plans available to us (**Ephesians 2:10**). We truly are God's workmanship, and all of our experiences are taken into consideration in His grand design. No choice we make is a surprise to God, and He uses our mistakes, victories, and brokenness in ways beyond our comprehension (**Romans 8:28**). We can *be fully confident, as we seek His strength*, that He will equip us to live out the purposes and plans He has decided long ago, and He uses every part of who we are, even the broken pieces He puts back together.

> *To all who mourn in Israel, he will give a crown of beauty for ashes, a joyous blessing instead of mourning, festive praise instead of despair. In their righteousness, they will be like great oaks that the Lord has planted for his own glory.* — Isaiah 61:3

> *He gives power to the weak and strength to the powerless.* — Isaiah 40:29

> *For we are God's masterpiece. He has created us anew in Christ Jesus, so we can do the good things he planned for us long ago.* — Ephesians 2:10

> *And we know that God causes everything to work together for the good of those who love God and are called according to his purpose for them.* — Romans 8:28

August 17

I heard a wise woman once say that God builds bridges, not fences. So much of how we are a witness for God is how we love others, especially those who may not agree with us or share the same faith (**Matthew 9:3**). As believers, we would love for everyone to invite Jesus into their hearts, but the reality is some will and some will not. The way we love others cannot be based on when or whether they accept Christ (**1 John 4:7**). We need to *engage and love others as the Holy Spirit prompts us*. God works in such wonderfully mysterious ways. He may lay someone on your heart to be in prayer for that you have only seen from a distance, and then years later you have an opportunity to meet and begin a relationship with that person (**Isaiah 14:24**). A supernatural love can be birthed in your heart for someone you don't even know yet, just by being obedient in prayer. God is truly a waymaker, drawing us into a relationship with Himself and others.

> "But some of the teachers of religious law said to themselves, 'That's blasphemy! Does he think he's God?'" — Matthew 9:3

> Dear friends, let us continue to love one another, for love comes from God. Anyone who loves is a child of God and knows God. — 1 John 4:7

> "The Lord of Heaven's Armies has sworn this oath: 'It will all happen as I have planned. It will be as I have decided.'" — Isaiah 14:24

> So now I am giving you a new commandment: Love each other. Just as I have loved you, you should love each other. — John 13:34

August 18

One of the many things I love about the Scriptures is the boldness and power it holds (**Psalm 119:11**). When we learn, study, and cling to God's Word in a way that it fills our hearts, it truly strengthens every fiber of our being. When the Holy Spirit illuminates a story or word from the Bible, it brings revelation to our emotions or circumstances (**1 Corinthians 2:7**). Spending precious time with God in His Word is one of the most common ways He speaks and shares His wisdom and truth. Believing the value of aligning our hearts with God's will motivate us to dive deeper and not be satisfied with surface level understanding (**2 Timothy 3:16–17**). The wisdom and adventure in Scripture is unending, which means this side of heaven we will never stop benefiting from its insight. God created us to *be image bearers so we could be extensions of His love* to the world, and also for us to rest, being confident in His sovereignty, knowing that all is well in His hands. Clinging to His Word enables us to be the salt and light we are intended to be.

> I have hidden your word in my heart, that I might not sin against you. — Psalm 119:11

> No, the wisdom we speak of is the mystery of God—his plan that was previously hidden, even though he made it for our ultimate glory before the world began. — 1 Corinthians 2:7

> All Scripture is inspired by God and is useful to teach us what is true and to make us realize what is wrong in our lives. It corrects us when we are wrong and teaches us to do what is right. God uses it to prepare and equip his people to do every good work. — 2 Timothy 3:16–17

> You are the salt of the earth . . . You are the light of the world—like a city on a hilltop that cannot be hidden. — Matthew 5:13–14

It has always amazed me how keenly aware God is not only of our weaknesses but of specific scenarios of temptations for us (**1 Corinthians 10:13**). I can clearly remember times in my life when I made bad decisions and the ways of escape God provided that I pridefully ignored. In order for us to walk in victory amidst temptation, we have to be proactive. This can look like being mindful of atmospheres that are not spiritually healthy for us and our obedience to God's direction (**Proverbs 4:26–27**). It's critical that we *spend time cultivating and nurturing our love relationship with God*, because our love for Him must begin to outweigh the desire to gratify our flesh. The time to say no to a temptation is before it's even presented. Making up your mind ahead of time what you will or will not do will help you not to give in to temptation. Walking in the freedom that we are no longer slaves to what we used to do is possible and liberating because of God's gift of regeneration, redirection, and, most importantly, restoration to Himself and all He has in store for your new life in Him.

> *The temptations in your life are no different from what others experience. And God is faithful. He will not allow the temptation to be more than you can stand. When you are tempted, he will show you a way out so that you can endure.* — 1 Corinthians 10:13

> *Mark out a straight path for your feet; stay on the safe path. Don't get sidetracked; keep your feet from following evil.* — Proverbs 4:26–27

> *So you must live as God's obedient children. Don't slip back into your old ways of living to satisfy your own desires. You didn't know any better then.*
> — 1 Peter 1:14

August 20

WHEN I THINK OF THE ABOUNDING GRACE IN THE WAY GOD WORKS in our lives, it fills my heart with gratitude and awe. He is continually reorienting us back to Himself with intentionality and creativity (**Colossians 1:19–20**). When I think of Adam and Eve in the garden, I always reflect on the beautiful truth that God wanted to be in fellowship with them, sharing the glory of His creation. He loves us so much that He made a way for us to have regular fellowship with Him through the cross and gave us the Holy Spirit to dwell inside of us (**2 Corinthians 13:14**). As we acknowledge Him, inviting Him to walk with us and talk with us daily, that peace that surpasses all understanding creates a hedge of protection around us like an armor of love (**Philippians 4:7**). So often we spend our energy resisting God and striving to be strong and in charge on our own strength, leading to exhaustion or anxiety. *Pray today to take advantage of the fellowship with God available to you, inviting Him to reorient your heart and mind back to Him.*

> *For God in all his fullness was pleased to live in Christ, and through him God reconciled everything to himself. He made peace with everything in heaven and on earth by means of Christ's blood on the cross.* — Colossians 1:19–20

> *May the grace of the Lord Jesus Christ, the love of God, and the fellowship of the Holy Spirit be with you all.* — 2 Corinthians 13:14

> *Then you will experience God's peace, which exceeds anything we can understand. His peace will guard your hearts and minds as you live in Christ Jesus.* — Philippians 4:7

> *Search for the Lord and for his strength; continually seek him.* — 1 Chronicles 16:11

August 21

THERE ARE SO MANY TIMES IN THE SCRIPTURES WHERE THE LORD is encouraging us to keep our eyes on Him, trusting His ways and His timing (**Psalm 16:8–9**). This is such a gracious directive from our Father, who is so aware of our tendency to fear and doubt, challenging us to trust God with the practical things in life (**Matthew 6:33**). Some translations of **Hebrews 12:2** talk about "fixing our eyes on Jesus," which suggests that our seeking has to be intentional and proactive because it doesn't come naturally. Our human nature wants to control, manipulate, and manage; whereas, our spirit is called to seek, trust, and rest in Him, not in our feelings or circumstances. He has the power to keep us in perfect peace amidst the most chaotic scenarios, and when we allow Him to help us navigate the chaos, He becomes larger in our life as the chaos becomes smaller, losing its power (**Isaiah 26:3**). What a beautiful safe space God provides for us if we will simply *embrace the reality of His sovereign care.*

> *I know the Lord is always with me. I will not be shaken, for he is right beside me. No wonder my heart is glad, and I rejoice. My body rests in safety.*
> *— Psalm 16:8–9*

> *Seek the Kingdom of God above all else, and live righteously, and he will give you everything you need. — Matthew 6:33*

> *We do this by keeping our eyes on Jesus, the champion who initiates and perfects our faith. Because of the joy awaiting him, he endured the cross, disregarding its shame. Now he is seated in the place of honor beside God's throne.*
> *— Hebrews 12:2*

> *You will keep in perfect peace all who trust in you, all whose thoughts are fixed on you! — Isaiah 26:3*

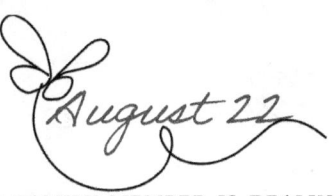

August 22

When a friend or family member is dealing with something difficult and wants to talk about it, I've often found that, if you ask them enough questions, they come to their own answers (**John 16:13–15**). A sweet friend of mine was struggling with why she felt distant from the Lord, and during our time together she realized she was not spending enough time in His Word. One of the many benefits of marinating in Scripture is the nearness to God that's activated as we explore His word (**Psalm 119:10**). A huge part of seeking peace and direction from God is found in the stories and wisdom of the Bible, and all too often people who say they believe and desire a closer walk with God neglect the primary resource where these desires are met (**Hebrews 4:16**). We all need to *work this spiritual discipline into our daily routine.* His Word holds so much power that a little goes a long way, and there is certainly an abundance of studies, apps, and resources to meet all of our learning styles and preferences. Take time to do it and you will experience God.

> *"When the Spirit of truth comes, he will guide you into all truth. He will not speak on his own but will tell you what he has heard. He will tell you about the future. He will bring me glory by telling you whatever he receives from me. All that belongs to the Father is mine; this is why I said, 'The Spirit will tell you whatever he receives from me.'"*
> — John 16:13–15

> *I have tried hard to find you—don't let me wander from your commands.* — Psalm 119:10

> *So let us come boldly to the throne of our gracious God. There we will receive his mercy, and we will find grace to help us when we need it most.*
> — Hebrews 4:16

> *Come close to God, and God will come close to you. Wash your hands, you sinners; purify your hearts, for your loyalty is divided between God and the world.* — James 4:8

August 23

TODAY IS MY WEDDING ANNIVERSARY, AND I CANNOT HELP BUT THINK of how God has so graciously cared for my heart and general well-being over the years (**Psalm 139:23–24**). I have always longed to be a wife and mother, so much so that I repeatedly took selecting a spouse into my own hands. How often do we decide what we are going to do and ask God to bless it, instead of seeking Him on the front end (**Proverbs 16:9**)? When I finally surrendered my search to God, realizing that He, and only He, knew who would be best for me, He revealed the love story He wrote for me (**Isaiah 48:17**). My husband and I have such opposing strengths, and I genuinely could not imagine one without the other. God is all-knowing, all-wise, and, most importantly, all-loving. His plans for us have purpose and meaning way beyond what our finite minds can imagine. The more we *move toward Him in faith and surrender*, the more we can look back and see His almighty provision.

> Search me, O God, and know my heart; test me and know my anxious thoughts. Point out anything in me that offends you, and lead me along the path of everlasting life. — Psalm 139:23–24

> We can make our plans, but the Lord determines our steps. — Proverbs 16:9

> "This is what the Lord says— your Redeemer, the Holy One of Israel: 'I am the Lord your God, who teaches you what is good for you and leads me along the paths you should follow.'" — Isaiah 48:17

> And this same God who takes care of me will supply all your needs from his glorious riches, which have been given to us in Christ Jesus. — Philippians 4:19

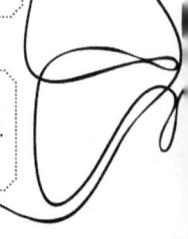

August 24

Today as I was leaving the gym, my son walked in with one of his friends, and it just filled my heart with gratitude for the great friendships my children have in their lives (**1 Thessalonians 5:11**). When we seek God's guidance in drawing ourselves and those we love towards healthy connections, He leads us to good ones and away from the ones we don't need. If it warms my heart to see my children with life-giving friendships, how much more must it be pleasing to God for us to engage in healthy community (**Psalm 133:1**). One of Satan's favorite tactics is isolation, and he will do anything he can to cause division and strife among God's people. Isolation can lead to depression, whereas community keeps us accountable and known (**1 Peter 4:8–10**). The people God gives us access to are not a coincidence. He will lead us towards relationships where we have the opportunity to complement each other with various gifts and strengths. Genuine friends will both *encourage us and speak truth in love*, helping us notice blind spots we may not notice. We need to be intentionally investing in the God-given gift of relationships.

> So encourage each other and build each other up, just as you are already doing. — 1 Thessalonians 5:11

> How wonderful and pleasant it is when brothers live together in harmony! — Psalm 133:1

> Most important of all, continue to show deep love for each other, for love covers a multitude of sins. Cheerfully share your home with those who need a meal or a place to stay. God has given each of you a gift from his great variety of spiritual gifts. Use them well to serve one another. — 1 Peter 4:8–10

> Two people are better off than one, for they can help each other succeed. — Ecclesiastes 4:9

August 25

A SWEET FRIEND OF MINE TEXTED ME BEFORE CHURCH THIS MORNING asking for prayer, communicating she was experiencing a heaviness of heart she could not identify. After praying for her, I texted her **Psalm 139:23–24** and continued to pray God would reveal what was going on. I also prayed that a sense of gratitude would wash over her throughout the day (**Psalm 118:24**). It never ceases to amaze me how cultivating a spirit of gratitude can reorient our hearts. The first and last words on our lips *every day should revolve around gratitude for God and His goodness.* This is not a gratitude contingent on circumstances or feelings, but a gratitude of knowing God is good and has made a way for us to persevere, hope, and thrive in and through anything that comes our way (**Colossians 2:6–7**). The good things or blessings of this life are simply extras on top of the joy and peace found in our life-giving relationship with Jesus. When our vitality is found in the intimacy we share with Christ, our hearts can overflow with gratitude for the satisfaction that never disappoints.

> *Search me, O God, and know my heart; test me and know my anxious thoughts. Point out anything in me that offends you, and lead me along the path of everlasting life.* — Psalm 139:23–24

> *This is the day the Lord has made. We will rejoice and be glad in it.* — Psalm 118:24

> *And now, just as you accepted Christ Jesus as your Lord, you must continue to follow him. Let your roots grow down into him, and let your lives be built on him. Then your faith will grow strong in the truth you were taught, and you will overflow with thankfulness.* — Colossians 2:6–7

> *Now all glory to God, who is able, through his mighty power at work within us, to accomplish infinitely more than we might ask or think.* — Ephesians 3:20

Every so often a circumstance will arise that gives us an opportunity to reflect on how God has pruned us in a specific area (**John 15:2**). This may look like the realization that you are no longer fazed by a disruption that would have once aggravated you because you've learned to be more open-handed with your time. In areas where our grip is too tight, God creatively helps us loosen it as we trust Him more with our circumstances and schedules (**Psalm 90:12**). I reflect often on the reality that we tend to give ourselves too much power and God not enough. He is Lord of all. So certainly He is Lord over our time. As we *notice how God has reoriented our hearts*, we should celebrate that movement, rejoicing that He cares enough about us to be constantly molding us to become more like Him and running the race He has mapped out for us daily. Our refining looks like us letting go of hindrances and attitudes that can derail the purposes and plans God has for our days.

> *He cuts off every branch of mine that doesn't produce fruit, and he prunes the branches that do bear fruit so they will produce even more.* — John 15:2

> *Teach us to realize the brevity of life, so that we may grow in wisdom.* — Psalm 90:12

> *Therefore, since we are surrounded by such a huge crowd of witnesses to the life of faith, let us strip off every weight that slows us down, especially the sin that so easily trips us up. And let us run with endurance the race God has set before us. We do this by keeping our eyes on Jesus, the champion who initiates and perfects our faith. Because of the joy awaiting him, he endured the cross, disregarding its shame. Now he is seated in the place of honor beside God's throne.* — Hebrews 12:1-2

August 27

I love how God will graciously give us glimpses of how seeds we've planted have grown. A while back I was meeting with a special friend, and the Holy Spirit prompted me to discuss the importance of willingness, wisdom, and words (**John 16:13**). I was specifically encouraging her to pray for willingness to be open-handed with God, wisdom for interactions, and using her words to encourage and love well. We met again and she shared how she had put those things into practice and the blessings she has already experienced (**Proverbs 2:15**). God will use others as vessels to speak into our lives, and as we listen and put those suggestions into practice we can experience lasting change (**Proverbs 1:5–6**). Clearly, we all must be prayerful of who we seek out for wise counsel, and *we should always line suggestions up with scripture*, but as we take action on creating new habits we reap the reward. The gift of sharing life with others and literally seeing God's movement in one another's lives is awe-inspiring. Christ-centered relationships are always life-giving, and witnessing the way the Holy Spirit pours into our individual hearts is indescribable.

> *When the Spirit of truth comes, he will guide you into all truth. He will not speak on his own but will tell you what he has heard. He will tell you about the future.* —John 16:13

> *Their actions are crooked, and their ways are wrong.* — Proverbs 2:15

> *Let the wise listen to these proverbs and become even wiser. Let those with understanding receive guidance by exploring the meaning in these proverbs and parables, the words of the wise and their riddles.* — Proverbs 1:5–6

> *Yet I have never used any of these rights. And I am not writing this to suggest that I want to start now. In fact, I would rather die than lose my right to boast about preaching without charge.* — 1 Corinthians 9:15

The unfortunate reality of the vast number of people who struggle with their mental and emotional health is unbelievable and so sad (**2 Corinthians 10:3-5**). We are all involved in not only an overarching spiritual battle but also an internal conflict in our own hearts and minds. Depression and anxiety are all too common for both unbelievers and followers of Christ (**Psalm 9:9**). There are many scriptures we can cling to assuring us of the Lord's presence, as so often during mental anguish He seems distant. One of the most critical choices we make every day is whether we will listen to our flesh or our spirit. Our flesh is motivated by feelings while *our spirit is held up by Truth* (**Psalm 9:10**). Reminding ourselves out loud that God has not abandoned us is in itself an act of faith. As we preach this truth to ourselves over and over, so often our emotions will follow. We can read the Psalms and know the battle of the mind is not a new issue. We can also know our God is with us, for us, and has already won the battle.

> *You, dear children, are from God and have overcome them, because the one who is in you is greater than the one who is in the world. — 1 John 4:4 (NIV)*

> *We are human, but we don't wage war as humans do. We use God's mighty weapons, not worldly weapons, to knock down the strongholds of human reasoning and to destroy false arguments. We destroy every proud obstacle that keeps people from knowing God. We capture their rebellious thoughts and teach them to obey Christ. — 2 Corinthians 10:3-5*

> *The Lord is a shelter for the oppressed, a refuge in times of trouble. Those who know your name trust in you, for you, O Lord, do not abandon those who search for you. — Psalm 9:9-10*

August 29

WITH MY WAKING BREATH THIS MORNING THE FIRST WORDS out of my mouth were, "Father, I'm thankful I can rest in your sovereignty today." This is a powerful truth that we all need to be reminded of often (**Romans 8:28**). Navigating our lives through the lens *He is working everything for good* helps us to resist coming undone as we witness situations around us seeming unmanageable. Just like one of my wisest friends saying, "Christ did not go to the cross for you to manage your sin," I like to remind myself God did not place people in my life for me to manage, but to love (**Galatians 5:22-28**). So often our flesh urges us to orchestrate or manipulate; whereas, our spirit can be cultivated to lean into seeking God and trusting Him for outcomes. Freedom follows believing that God is working everything for His good, in light of the fact that only He ultimately knows *what good is* (**Psalm 145:7**). We benefit from the release of control more than we can imagine as *we surrender our will to His daily,* and learn to seek and abide in His capable hands.

> Oh, the depth of the riches of the wisdom and knowledge of God! How unsearchable his judgments, and his paths beyond tracing out! — Romans 11:33 (NIV)

> And we know that God causes everything to work together for the good of those who love God and are called according to his purpose for them. — Romans 8:28

> Everyone will share the story of your wonderful goodness;
> they will sing with joy about your righteousness. — Psalm 145:7

August 30

Years ago a special friend of mine gave me a bracelet with the words of **John 1:1** engraved on the front of it. I recall looking at those words and, although I had seen them many times before, the richness of this Scripture was illuminated in my heart. This verse reminds us that Jesus was with God since the beginning in that He is God and the plan was already in motion for Jesus' redemptive work (**Ephesians 1:4–5**). One of the many beautiful attributes of God's Word is how it speaks to every heart a little differently based on heart posture, circumstances, and timing. This Scripture has always emphasized to me how God and His Word go hand-in-hand, meaning one is not void of the other. Oftentimes I have seen people recognize they are feeling distant from God and connecting the dots, yet they have neglected reading His words. There are no words worthy of describing the magnificent gift of the Scriptures and how His presence is there to be found as we *realize the significance of reading His Word.*

> *In the beginning the Word already existed. The Word was with God, and the Word was God. — John 1:1*

> *Even before he made the world, God loved us and chose us in Christ to be holy and without fault in his eyes. God decided in advance to adopt us into his own family by bringing us to himself through Jesus Christ. This is what he wanted to do, and it gave him great pleasure. — Ephesians 1:4-5*

> *But you must remain faithful to the things you have been taught. You know they are true, for you know you can trust those who taught you. You have been taught the holy Scriptures from childhood, and they have given you the wisdom to receive the salvation that comes by trusting in Christ Jesus. All Scripture is inspired by God and is useful to teach us what is true and to make us realize what is wrong in our lives. It corrects us when we are wrong and teaches us to do what is right. God uses it to prepare and equip his people to do every good work. — 2 Timothy 3:14-17*

August 31

Isn't it ironic that so much of what we stress and worry about are things completely out of our control? We experience emotional havoc due to decisions and choices other people make (**Philippians 2:13**). Our human nature desires to control, whereas when we allow God to empower us, He actually helps us to "stay in our lane." We all have areas of concern and areas of responsibility. When these lines become blurred, it leads to anxiety. When those around us are struggling, the best thing we can do for ourselves and others is to remain faithful to what God is calling us to do (**James 1:12**). Oftentimes we can get distracted by all the chaos happening around us to the point we neglect the most helpful thing we can do, which is nurture and maintain our own spiritual health (**Ephesians 6:10**). When others are suffering, instead of trying to manage and fix them, we would do better to remain focused on God and sensitive to how He is leading us to love them well (**Isaiah 41:10**). *Only God can change people.* He will strengthen us to love, encourage, pray, and be a vessel, but God does the heavy lifting, not us.

> For God is working in you, giving you the desire and the power to do what pleases him. — Philippians 2:13

> God blesses those who patiently endure testing and temptation. Afterward they will receive the crown of life that God has promised to those who love him. — James 1:12

> A final word: Be strong in the Lord and in his mighty power. — Ephesians 6:10

> Don't be afraid, for I am with you. Don't be discouraged, for I am your God. I will strengthen you and help you. I will hold you up with my victorious right hand. — Isaiah 41:10

September 1

SEPTEMBER IS THE PERFECT TIME TO CHALLENGE OURSELVES with new habits. Summer is over and a sense of structure naturally sets in (**Proverbs 4:20–22**). Even the most carefree of us need guidelines and direction. The Scriptures provide wisdom for all three areas of wellness: spirit, mind, and body. Since we all have different needs, I would encourage praying about creative ways to take wellness to the next level (**Proverbs 17:22**). Spiritually speaking, think of an area that needs attention. Maybe it's experiencing joy or hope. These attributes do wonders for spiritual vitality. Wherever you detect a deficit, learn and meditate on a Scripture that will breathe life into your weakness (**Proverbs 3:7–8**). For a better state of mind, let go of any habits or attitudes that are no longer in line with who God is calling you to be. Letting go of one negative thing can reap great rewards. Take care of the body God gave you through better nutrition, more rest, or a new activity. Only you know the things coming to your mind that would be beneficial. Taking care of ourselves is an act of worship. *Pray and enjoy the results of necessary changes.*

> *My child, pay attention to what I say. Listen carefully to my words. Don't lose sight of them. Let them penetrate deep into your heart, for they bring life to those who find them, and healing to their whole body.* — Proverbs 4:20–22

> *A cheerful heart is good medicine, but a broken spirit saps a person's strength.* —Proverbs 17:22

> *Don't be impressed with your own wisdom. Instead, fear the Lord and turn away from evil. Then you will have healing for your body and strength for your bones.*
> — Proverbs 3:7–8

> *So whether you eat or drink, or whatever you do, do it all for the glory of God.*
> — 1 Corinthians 10:31

September 2

ONE OF THE MOST DISTINCTIVE ATTRIBUTES OF BEING A CHRIST FOLLOWER IS how we receive and demonstrate sacrificial love (**Ephesians 5:2**). As humans, our hearts and minds will not completely understand the vastness of God's love for us, but we can take the time to meditate on the Scriptures that so beautifully describe it (**Romans 5:5**). Inviting and allowing God's redemptive work in our heart provides a personal experience that reaches beyond Sunday school teaching or surface knowledge. As we *engage in the restoration process with God*, it gives us eyes to see others through the lens of God's story in their life (**Titus 2:14**). This lens helps us to love sacrificially without judgment, knowing their story isn't over yet and neither is ours (**Philippians 1:6**). As we nurture the idea of sacrificial love as a whole, we create an atmosphere where His supernatural river of grace marks the way we love God, others, and even ourselves.

> *Live a life filled with love, following the example of Christ. He loved us and offered himself as a sacrifice for us, a pleasing aroma to God.* — Ephesians 5:2

> *And this hope will not lead to disappointment. For we know how dearly God loves us, because he has given us the Holy Spirit to fill our hearts with his love.* — Romans 5:5

> *He gave his life to free us from every kind of sin, to cleanse us, and to make us his very own people, totally committed to doing good deeds.* — Titus 2:14

> *And I am certain that God, who began the good work within you, will continue his work until it is finally finished on the day when Christ Jesus returns.* — Philippians 1:6

> *Do not seek revenge or bear a grudge against a fellow Israelite, but love your neighbor as yourself. I am the Lord.* — Leviticus 19:18

September 3

THIS PAST SUNDAY, OUR PASTOR ASKED ONE OF THE MOST IMPORTANT QUESTIONS for us to ponder: "Are you putting yourself in a position to be a part of God's redemptive work for His Kingdom?" There are clearly different ways to view this idea, but it made me think of discipling others and being discipled (**Matthew 28:18–20**). In other words, are we pouring into others and simultaneously allowing others to pour into us? God's redemptive work begins in the hearts of His people (**Ephesians 1:4**). We cannot live holy lives on our own, and just as kingdoms used to crumble as a result of autonomous leaders, so can ministries, churches, and families. We all need leadership, encouragement, and accountability (**Hebrews 13:17**). So often people will shy away from discipleship or serving opportunities because they feel too young in their faith, but we have to remember *wherever we are, there is God* and He will honor our vulnerability and use it to grow our faith and meet a need. God doesn't need us, but He graciously uses us to carry out His purpose. (**Ephesians 2:10**). We all need God, and others, to carry out His divine mission.

> "Jesus came and told his disciples, 'I have been given all authority in heaven and on earth. Therefore, go and make disciples of all the nations, baptizing them in the name of the Father and the Son and the Holy Spirit. Teach these new disciples to obey all the commands I have given you. And be sure of this: I am with you always, even to the end of the age.'" — Matthew 28:18–20

> Even before he made the world, God loved us and chose us in Christ to be holy and without fault in his eyes. — Ephesians 1:4

> Obey your spiritual leaders, and do what they say. Their work is to watch over your souls, and they are accountable to God. Give them reason to do this with joy and not with sorrow. That would certainly not be for your benefit.
> — Hebrews 13:17

> For we are God's masterpiece. He has created us anew in Christ Jesus, so we can do the good things he planned for us long ago.
> — Ephesians 2:10

September 4

THERE WAS A WORSHIP SONG REQUEST AT CHURCH LAST NIGHT for the song entitled, "I Was Made for More." I have referenced the words to this song before, and it always brings an enthusiastic response when we sing its powerful lyrics (**Jeremiah 1:5**). If we are going to walk in our God-given Holy Spirit confidence, it is vital we *acknowledge our identity in Christ* daily (**Psalm 139:16**). This is an area for men and women alike that cannot be overlooked or minimized. Over the years, I have unfortunately witnessed women verbalizing negative self-talk, and I will often say, "You are talking about God's creation, and He says you are valued, loved, and fought for" (**Isaiah 64:8**). Some people will even label negative self-talk as humility, and that is definitely not biblical humility. We can daily turn to our Creator and be reminded of the masterpiece He had in mind as He breathed us into existence (**Ephesians 2:10**). This is not a worldly arrogance, but an act of worship, a declaration that *I know who I am because I know my Father in heaven, and He created and defines all that I am.*

> *I knew you before I formed you in your mother's womb. Before you were born I set you apart and appointed you as my prophet to the nations.*
> — Jeremiah 1:5

> *You saw me before I was born. Every day of my life was recorded in your book. Every moment was laid out before a single day had passed.* — Psalm 139:16

> *And yet, O Lord, you are our Father. We are the clay, and you are the potter. We all are formed by your hand.* — Isaiah 64:8

> *For we are God's masterpiece. He has created us anew in Christ Jesus, so we can do the good things he planned for us long ago.*
> — Ephesians 2:10

September 5

IT NEVER CEASES TO AMAZE ME WHEN I LOOK BACK ON MY LIFE and see how God intentionally and patiently brought me from death to life (**Ephesians 1:7–8**). Yesterday I had the pleasure of being with my siblings to celebrate my brother's birthday. As a result of my colorful past, paired with how passionate I am about Jesus today, I've set myself up for statements like, "Do you remember that girl?" (**2 Corinthians 5:17**). My family loves me dearly, but being the baby of the family naturally brings some razzing. The reality is that they have been witness to me becoming a new creation. When God came for me, He came with power and clarity that my life was going to change and that He had plans for me that did not match my current choices (**Galatians 2:20**). We all have some kind of rescue story, some more dramatic than others but equally strong. When we *invite Jesus to be our Savior and Lord of our life*, He brings us out of darkness into His everlasting light (**2 Corinthians 4:6**). His gracious, restorative power in our lives is an example of what can happen when a loving, powerful God rescues a broken, in-need-of-a-Savior child of His.

> He is so rich in kindness and grace that he purchased our freedom with the blood of his Son and forgave our sins. He has showered his kindness on us, along with all wisdom and understanding.
> — Ephesians 1:7–8

> This means that anyone who belongs to Christ has become a new person. The old life is gone; a new life has begun! — 2 Corinthians 5:17

> My old self has been crucified with Christ. It is no longer I who live, but Christ lives in me. So I live in this earthly body by trusting in the Son of God, who loved me and gave himself for me.
> — Galatians 2:20

> For God, who said, 'Let there be light in the darkness,' has made this light shine in our hearts so we could know the glory of God that is seen in the face of Jesus Christ. — 2 Corinthians 4:6

September 6

Today a faithful friend and I were discussing trusting God's timing in a situation, and I jokingly made the comment, "After walking with the Lord for nearly 30 years, I am finally more accepting of His timing and trusting in His wisdom" (**Psalm 90:12**). *Embracing His ways and timing is a daily choice*, but as we mature in our faith, it does thankfully become a little easier and more natural. God's faithfulness over the years reminds us how we've had to trust Him through seasons of pain or suffering and how He has proven to be worthy of our reliance (**Hebrews 1:1**). There is a supernatural confidence that fuels our spiritual muscles as we learn more and more the magnitude of His care for us (**2 Corinthians 3:4–5**). Trusting and accepting God's sovereignty is the best anti-anxiety help. I realize the epidemic of anxiety, depression, and stress of our culture and am appreciative of science and doctors with resources, but we are wise to remember our spirit, mind, and body connection. Everything originates from our spirit and is in the capable hands of our Creator.

> Teach us to realize the brevity of life, so that we may grow in wisdom. — Psalm 90:12

> Long ago God spoke many times and in many ways to our ancestors through the prophets. — Hebrews 1:1

> We are confident of all this because of our great trust in God through Christ. It is not that we think we are qualified to do anything on our own. Our qualification comes from God.
> — 2 Corinthians 3:4–5

> My hands have made both heaven and earth; they and everything in them are mine. I, the Lord, have spoken! I will bless those who have humble and contrite hearts, who tremble at my word.
> — Isaiah 66:2

September 7

WE ALL REACT SLIGHTLY DIFFERENTLY TO A "PLAN OF THE DAY" THAT GOES SIDEWAYS. Oftentimes our plans can get rearranged for a reason way bigger than we realize (**Job 42:2**). Some plans I had today were canceled, and it was definitely something I was looking forward to, but the Holy Spirit led me to believe God had somewhere else in mind I needed to be (**Ephesians 6:18**). Immediately there was an expectancy of what God had in store. So praying for sensitivity and obedience was next. Clearly, we are human and can read situations wrongly, but if in fact God was giving me an opportunity to be there for someone I wanted to be alert (**1 John 3:22–23**). It turned out I was able to spend some time with a special friend who needed some love and prayer. I left our interaction reflecting on God's goodness and how He saw her and cared for her in that moment. There was strong confirmation of the importance of our time together, and what an encouragement it was for both of us. May we be people who *allow God full access* to our time and schedules.

I know that you can do anything, and no one can stop you. — Job 42:2

Pray in the Spirit at all times and on every occasion. Stay alert and be persistent in your prayers for all believers everywhere. — Ephesians 6:18

And we will receive from him whatever we ask because we obey him and do the things that please him. And this is his commandment: We must believe in the name of his Son, Jesus Christ, and love one another, just as he commanded us. — 1 John 3:22-23

You can make many plans, but the Lord's purpose will prevail. — Proverbs 19:21

September 8

TODAY AT CHURCH, THE CONGREGATION WAS CHALLENGED WITH THE QUESTION, "Are you willing to be used by God?" Most believers would automatically reply "of course" to this question, but what we really need to consider is, are we posturing ourselves to be used by God (**2 Timothy 2:21**)? Immediately three ideas came to mind as I reflected on the pastor's question. First, to be used by God, we ourselves need to be seeking Him and cultivating our hearts for service. We are never equipped by our own wisdom, but *we do need to be led by the Spirit* (**James 3:17**). Secondly, we make room in our lives to sow into people and situations outside of ourselves. So often we pack our schedules too full and, therefore, have no margin (**Mark 10:45**). Finally, we find the courage to get out of our comfort zones, to be vulnerable, and to meet a need. The value of stepping out into God-given opportunities to share His love and hope is one of the best investments of His love, and hope is one of the best investments of our time here on this earth (**Psalm 31:15**). He is the giver of our time and our lives. We should be His hands and feet, being thankful for the chance to do so.

> *If you keep yourself pure, you will be a special utensil for honorable use. Your life will be clean, and you will be ready for the Master to use you for every good work.* — 2 Timothy 2:21

> *But the wisdom from above is first of all pure. It is also peace loving, gentle at all times, and willing to yield to others. It is full of mercy and the fruit of good deeds. It shows no favoritism and is always sincere.* — James 3:17

> *For even the Son of Man came not to be served but to serve others and to give his life as a ransom for many.* —Mark 10:45

> *My future is in your hands. Rescue me from those who hunt me down relentlessly.* — Psalm 31:15

September 9

IT'S GRADUATION DAY FOR ONE OF THE MINISTRIES GOD HAS GIVEN ME the honor and privilege to be involved with. My favorite part of loving on these women in this season is witnessing God breathing His fresh breath of love, life, and hope into what could have been destruction (**Ezekiel 37:1–3**). Our heavenly Father says dry bones that represent spiritual poverty can be resurrected and brought back to life by His power and plan (**Psalm 51:12**). The way in which God pursues us in His perfect timing, weaving the tapestry of our lives in a way of rescue and redemption is clearly supernatural. My constant prayer for these ladies and everyone is that there would be a love for Jesus ignited in their hearts with a passion that runs so deep they would never be the same. *Embracing, seeking, and chasing after Jesus* in all He wants to do in and through our lives brings purpose, vibrancy, and hope to an otherwise corrupt world. Thanks be to God, the cross and His everlasting love for His children.

> *"The Lord took hold of me, and I was carried away by the Spirit of the Lord to a valley filled with bones. He led me all around among the bones that covered the valley floor. They were scattered everywhere across the ground and were completely dried out. Then he asked me, 'Son of man, can these bones become living people again?' 'O Sovereign Lord,' I replied, 'you alone know the answer to that.'"*
> — Ezekiel 37:1–3

> *Restore to me the joy of your salvation, and make me willing to obey you.*
> — Psalm 51:12

> *For through Him we both have access to the Father by one Spirit. Consequently, you are no longer foreigners and aliens, but fellow citizens with God's people and members of God's household.*
> —Ephesians 2:18-19 (NIV)

September 10

Although it is true that, as a follower of Christ, our lives should be marked by joy, this does not mean we won't have days that seem more melancholy or less cheerful (**Matthew 11:28**). We are human and feel the burdens and heaviness of life, but the good news is we are not intended to shoulder that alone. Sometimes our hearts can feel heavy and we don't even know why. I have always found such comfort in the reality that my heavenly Father knows my heart better than I do, which means He knows exactly how to care for me (**Jeremiah 17:10**). The all-knowing, all-wise nature of God allows us to rest in His presence and trust He can guide us into revelation of what's going on. The truth is that feeling downcast can be the result of many things, such as fatigue, worry, or even just being too busy. If we are feeling overwhelmed, bothered, or easily frustrated, we are wise to *get quiet, get with God, and allow Him to revitalize* our hearts and minds as only He can. Focusing on God always leads to peace.

> "Then Jesus said, 'Come to me, all of you who are weary and carry heavy burdens, and I will give you rest.'" — Matthew 11:28

> "But I, the Lord, search all hearts and examine secret motives. I give all people their due rewards, according to what their actions deserve." —Jeremiah 17:10

> And Jesus answered and said to her, "Martha, Martha you are troubled about many things. But one thing is needed, and Mary has chosen that good part which will not be taken away from her." — Luke 10:41-42 (NKJV)

> You will keep in perfect peace all who trust in you, all whose thoughts are fixed on you! —Isaiah 26:3

September 11

The idea of hope is mentioned in the Scriptures around 130 times. Whenever God illuminates a word repeatedly, it's something the Lord wants us to keep on the forefront of our minds (**Psalm 62:5**). Our culture attempts to convince us to find our hope in our success, our relationships, possessions, or even beauty, but the Scriptures encourage us again and again that our hope is in God alone (**Psalm 42:1**). God may bless us with incredible earthly gifts as far as loyal friends, family, or talents and resources, but all of these can and will disappoint us in some way. God desperately wants His children to realize *He is the only lifeline* that is eternal and unchanging (**Psalm 102:27**). If you're wondering what you put your hope in, think of things that irritate you when they don't go according to plan or when your feelings get easily wounded by a certain person. So often we put our hope in things that will ultimately fall short of our expectations or are temporary. May we be people who realize where our ultimate hope is found and learn to rest securely in this precious gift.

Let all that I am wait quietly before God, for my hope is in him. — Psalm 62:5

As the deer longs for streams of water, so I long for you, O God. — Psalm 42:1

But you are always the same; you will live forever. — Psalm 102:27

These trials will show that your faith is genuine. It is being tested as fire tests and purifies gold—though your faith is far more precious than mere gold. So when your faith remains strong through many trials, it will bring you much praise and glory and honor on the day when Jesus Christ is revealed to the whole world. — 1 Peter 1:7

 September 12

THERE IS AN UNFORTUNATE COMMON DENOMINATOR WE SEE IN REBELLION and bad behavior resulting from unaddressed pain. Although God is with us in suffering and will always bring a silver lining, if we are not walking with God, we handle hurt with hurt (**Isaiah 30:1**). So often when others seem to be mean or difficult to deal with, there are circumstances in their background that have been ignored, dismissed, minimized, or forgotten. The beautiful reality is that God meets us where we are and desires to regenerate our souls if we will allow it (**Psalm 34:18**). Regeneration is the supernatural work of the Holy Spirit, but oftentimes it takes extremely difficult seasons for us to realize how desperately we need God's rescue (**Psalm 71:20**). When we notice ourselves or others acting out in one way or another, we would be wise to *move towards Christ instead of running away*. His miraculous outstretched arms are ready to reach for, deliver, and love us back to life no matter how messy the scenario. He is waiting, willing, and able. We only need to realize He is the answer.

> "'What sorrow awaits my rebellious children,' says the Lord. 'You make plans that are contrary to mine. You make alliances not directed by my Spirit, thus piling up your sins.'" — Isaiah 30:1

> The Lord is close to the brokenhearted; he rescues those whose spirits are crushed. — Psalm 34:18

> You have allowed me to suffer much hardship, but you will restore me to life again and lift me up from the depths of the earth. — Psalm 71:20

> "Jesus looked at them intently and said, 'Humanly speaking, it is impossible. But with God everything is possible.'" — Matthew 19:26

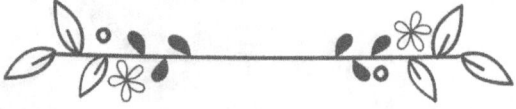

September 13

Today I have been overwhelmed with gratitude for the way God works within the context of community. God created us to be relational and live interdependently, yielding ourselves to accountability, encouragement, and support (**1 Thessalonians 5:11**). While I was meeting with a sweet friend of mine today who has been through a catastrophic ordeal, I was overwhelmed by the way God has sustained her through the means of people, medical care, and practical needs being completely met, down to specific details (**Philippians 4:19**). What stood out above all was how her countenance radiated joy and peace as she acknowledged the ways others have been and continue to be there for her and how she has already been witness to some of the blessings God has provided in the midst of this suffering (**Romans 8:17**). We all experience some type of suffering throughout our stay on this earth, and it is often in those times that we get to see the mighty workings of God's hand up close and personal. *He will provide* people around us, solutions to the problems, and, most importantly, the strength our spirits need to endure and overcome.

So encourage each other and build each other up, just as you are already doing. — 1 Thessalonians 5:11

And this same God who takes care of me will supply all your needs from his glorious riches, which have been given to us in Christ Jesus. — Philippians 4:19

And since we are his children, we are his heirs. In fact, together with Christ we are heirs of God's glory. But if we are to share his glory, we must also share his suffering. — Romans 8:17

For I can do everything through Christ, who gives me strength. — Philippians 4:13

September 14

Cultivating a strong confidence in the Lord is not something that happens overnight, but as we learn to rest in that confidence it is truly life-altering (**Psalm 18:2**). The foundation for this kind of confidence is trust and hope. So often it seems easier to trust God with big things such as salvation, but difficult to trust Him with day-to-day life (**Proverbs 3:5–6**). God also is at work reorienting our minds, teaching us that our hope cannot be in the things of this world but only in Him (**Romans 12:2**). The more we turn to Him first when we're struggling the more opportunity He has to show Himself as our trustworthy refuge (**Psalm 62:8**). What can it practically look like to run to Him for shelter? It may look like going to His word and welcoming the Holy Spirit to illuminate His word to your heart, learning to be completely honest and vulnerable with your thoughts and feelings, venting to Him instead of a friend or family member. Oftentimes for me it looks like solitude, turning off the noise of others, radio or TV, being silent and attentively listening for His voice of authority, love, and guidance. *He is our source, refuge and hope.*

> The Lord is my rock, my fortress, and my savior; my God is my rock, in whom I find protection. He is my shield, the power that saves me, and my place of safety. — Psalm 18:2

> Trust in the Lord with all your heart; do not depend on your own understanding. Seek his will in all you do, and he will show you which path to take. — Proverbs 3:5–6

> Don't copy the behavior and customs of this world, but let God transform you into a new person by changing the way you think. Then you will learn to know God's will for you, which is good and pleasing and perfect. — Romans 12:2

> O my people, trust in him at all times. Pour out your heart to him, for God is our refuge. — Psalm 62:8

> The Lord is my light and my salvation—so why should I be afraid? The Lord is my fortress, protecting me from danger, so why should I tremble? — Psalm 27:1

September 15

TODAY I HAVE BEEN REMINDED OF HOW CHOICES WE MAKE HAVE A LASTING impact way beyond ourselves (**Deuteronomy 30:19**). I have been witness to both a miracle and a tragedy. We celebrated the miracle of baptism at church. The radiant joy in the person who publicly declared their faith, in their family, and in the pastor was profound. The joy in the congregation of brothers and sisters in Christ was tangible (**Psalm 32:11**). We celebrated my husband's 52nd birthday, and we gave thanks for his salvation and for our children's faith, spiritual growth, and impact on their community (**Deuteronomy 6:6–7**). At the same time, tragedy has struck a sweet family with rippling effects that will certainly take time to heal (**Galatians 6:7–8**). The silver lining of suffering is that our hope is not in this world, and although circumstances can be bad, *we serve a good God* who brings beauty from ashes and whose mercies are new every morning (**Malachi 4:2**). New days bring new opportunities to love God, love others, and choose well.

> *Today I have given you the choice between life and death, between blessings and curses. Now I call on heaven and earth to witness the choice you make. Oh, that you would choose life, so that you and your descendants might live! — Deuteronomy 30:19*

> *So rejoice in the Lord and be glad, all you who obey him! Shout for joy, all you whose hearts are pure! — Psalm 32:11*

> *And you must commit yourselves wholeheartedly to these commands that I am giving you today. Repeat them again and again to your children. Talk about them when you are at home and when you are on the road, when you are going to bed and when you are getting up. — Deuteronomy 6:6–7*

> *Don't be misled—you cannot mock the justice of God. You will always harvest what you plant. Those who live only to satisfy their own sinful nature will harvest decay and death from that sinful nature. But those who live to please the Spirit will harvest everlasting life from the Spirit. — Galatians 6:7–8*

> *But for you who fear my name, the Sun of Righteousness will rise with healing in his wings. And you will go free, leaping with joy like calves let out to pasture. —Malachi 4:2*

September 16

THE OLD WORSHIP SONG "THIS ONE IS WITH ME" has been playing over and over in my heart today. Its lyrics are a beautiful image of how Jesus makes a way for us to be in union with our Father in heaven (**John 14:6**). The singer dreams of seeing Jesus petition the Father and affirm that His death on the cross covers the singer, who can now be welcomed into heaven (**John 10:28–29**). Jesus' care for and nurture of our hearts is illuminated in the chorus as the beautiful melody plays. It is important that we *become acquainted with the personal touch of Jesus* and what He chose to do on our behalf all those years ago at Calvary (**Colossians 1:13–14**). There is a heart posture of humility and gratitude that is birthed out of intentionally connecting with that moment in history— the moment that changed everything and has not lost momentum since. The most powerful event in history was orchestrated and executed on our behalf because that's how profound God's love is for His children. May the lives we live reflect our gratitude.

> *"Jesus told him, 'I am the way, the truth, and the life. No one can come to the Father except through me.'" — John 14:6*

> *"I give them eternal life, and they will never perish. No one can snatch them away from me, for my Father has given them to me, and he is more powerful than anyone else. No one can snatch them from the Father's hand." — John 10:28–29*

> *For he has rescued us from the kingdom of darkness and transferred us into the Kingdom of his dear Son, who purchased our freedom and forgave our sins. — Colossians 1:13–14*

> *I will sing of the Lord's unfailing love forever! Young and old will hear of your faithfulness. — Psalm 89:1*

September 17

I RECENTLY WITNESSED AN ENCOUNTER BETWEEN MOMS OF TEENAGERS in which one was completely exasperated, clearly trying to control beyond healthy measure (**Philippians 4:6**). Both women are believers and, like most mothers, have well-intended hope for their children, but it was evident one of them was struggling to trust God and His timing. We all desire the people we love—especially our children—to follow Christ, but if/when that happens is up to their response to Christ's invitation, nothing else (**Revelation 3:20**). I have experienced these feelings of angst concerning a child, and the Lord kept tapping me on the shoulder, reminding me to "stay in my lane," because He's got this. As I embraced my role of mother instead of Holy Spirit, I experienced immense, ongoing freedom that moved me from a posture of angst, to peace and hope. That freedom helped me trust God and accept the reality that my child's salvation is not where my hope is found. *Proverbs 22:6 (NKJV) says, "Train a child up in the way he should go, and when he is old he will not depart from it,"* but this Scripture is a proverb, not a promise. All we can do is nurture our own faith and *be a source of stability and compassion for our loved ones,* trusting God to do His part and praying for them to accept His offer.

> Don't worry about anything; instead, pray about everything. Tell God what you need, and thank him for all he has done.
> — Philippians 4:6

> Look! I stand at the door and knock. If you hear my voice and open the door, I will come in, and we will share a meal together as friends. — Revelation 3:20

> I will give them hearts that recognize me as the Lord. They will be my people, and I will be their God, for they will return to me wholeheartedly.
> — Jeremiah 24:7

September 18

THE WAY GOD WEAVES RELATIONSHIPS INTO OUR LIVES FOR OUR GOOD and His glory is such a clear reminder of what an intentional and personal God He is (**Mark 10:9**). God reveals these connections in many ways. It could be neighbors, people in your church small group, or even a random stranger you are immediately drawn to (**1 John 4:7**). Since God is the One who wired us, He knows how and when we are going to click with others; He even sets the stage for our connection. Oftentimes He will lead us to others who have experienced similar circumstances so we can encourage one another that we are not alone in our struggles (**Colossians 3:14**). We are wise to be sensitive to that supernatural pull towards certain people, realizing that this new connection could benefit both parties. God holds close to His heart the value of relationships and, since we were created in His image, so should we. Isolation is an enemy of our soul, and we should never let it take root in our lives. *Prayerfully seek* the solid life-giving friendships God has provided and love each other well.

> "... let no one split apart what God has joined together." — Mark 10:9

> *Dear friends, let us continue to love one another, for love comes from God. Anyone who loves is a child of God and knows God.* —1 John 4:7

> *Above all, clothe yourselves with love, which binds us all together in perfect harmony.* — Colossians 3:14

> *Most important of all, continue to show deep love for each other, for love covers a multitude of sins.* — 1 Peter 4:8

September 19

THE DUALITY OF LIFE SEEMS MUCH MORE APPARENT ON SOME DAYS over others. Today was one of those days because I attended a beautiful burial service for a young mom who lost her battle with addiction on this earth (**Psalm 30:5**). When a person transitions from here to their eternal home, immense sadness and joy can share the same moment. There is sadness when we feel a life was cut short, but the reality is we are not on our own time table (**Ecclesiastes 3:11**). As I was standing at the service grieving for the family, the fresh wind and the chirping of the birds displayed the calming peace of God in the air. I always marvel at the wonder of our heavenly home, and the longer we walk with God, the more we yearn for it. There is such great joy and anticipation resting on the reality that we will be restored to fellowship with our loved ones, heroes of the faith, and hopefully people we ourselves have encouraged towards Christ (**John 14:1–3**) The greatest reunion will be when we come face-to-face with Jesus. Imagine looking into the glorious image of the One who made a way for eternal life, who transforms every part of our being, and who reached for us knowing we needed a Savior. *There is nothing greater than the love of Christ* and we should spend our earthly time worshiping Him with our devotion and love.

> For his anger lasts only a moment, but his favor lasts a lifetime! Weeping may last through the night, but joy comes with the morning. — Psalm 30:5

> Yet God has made everything beautiful for its own time. He has planted eternity in the human heart, but even so, people cannot see the whole scope of God's work from beginning to end. — Ecclesiastes 3:11

> Don't let your hearts be troubled. Trust in God, and trust also in me. There is more than enough room in my Father's home. If this were not so, would I have told you that I am going to prepare a place for you? When everything is ready, I will come and get you, so that you will always be with me where I am. — John 14:1–3

September 20

How many times have we heard the phrase, "It's not so much what they said but how they said it"? This idea highlights the importance of our tone of voice when we are communicating (**Colossians 4:6**). Our words are so important, but just as important is the way we say them. The delivery of a message greatly determines how someone receives what we are saying. If our heart posture is warm and inviting, our words will reflect peace and love, and will create a safe place (**Proverbs 15:1**). If our tone of voice is harsh and rude, it immediately puts the hearer on the defensive; they will feel the need to protect themselves. With the world of technology we live in, sometimes it seems as though the art of communication has been lost, leaving conversations feeling stale or awkward. We need to be intentional about talking face-to-face as much as we can. Even a phone conversation is more personal than a text. The tone of voice is lost in a text, which means the heart of the sender isn't clear (**Proverbs 25:15**). A great way for us to ensure soft speech is to have a soft heart. We should *ask ourselves*, "Does this sound like the way Jesus would communicate?" God cares greatly about our words and also how we say them.

> Let your conversation be gracious and attractive so that you will have the right response for everyone. — Colossians 4:6

> A gentle answer deflects anger, but harsh words make tempers flare. — Proverbs 15:1

> Patience can persuade a prince, and soft speech can break bones. — Proverbs 25:15

September 21

THE OTHER DAY AT THE GYM A FELLOW BELIEVER WALKED UP AS IF TO TELL ME something super exciting while I was on the treadmill (**Psalm 9:1**). The joy was so obvious I ended up talking to the person walking beside me about answered prayers and God working in our lives. When we are looking to see where God is working we will experience Him continually in new and exciting ways (**Jeremiah 29:12–13**). This is another reason we need to be in community, sharing life with other believers, so we can testify of the goodness we are witnessing (**1 Thessalonians 5:11**). The zeal of these conversations piques others' curiosity that may not know God up close and personal, giving us an opportunity to share our faith with someone new (**1 Peter 3:15**). Oftentimes I will *encourage others to pray*, "God, give me an opportunity to reflect your love, grace, and kindness to someone today." This is a prayer I regularly pray, and God shows up in the coolest ways (**Psalm 27:13**). We tend to be hyper aware of all that is wrong on a daily basis, but the goodness of God is everywhere and needs to be acknowledged and celebrated.

I will praise you, Lord, with all my heart; I will tell of all the marvelous things you have done. — Psalm 9:1

In those days when you pray, I will listen. If you look for me wholeheartedly, you will find me. — Jeremiah 29:12–13

So encourage each other and build each other up, just as you are already doing. — 1 Thessalonians 5:11

Instead, you must worship Christ as Lord of your life. And if someone asks about your hope as a believer, always be ready to explain it. — 1 Peter 3:15

Yet I am confident I will see the Lord's goodness while I am here in the land of the living. — Psalm 27:13

September 22

When we are able to fix our thoughts and focus on heavenly things, as opposed to the cares of this world, that is when the peace that surpasses all understanding occurs (**Philippians 4:7**). Jesus needs to be the first object of our affection so the other aspects of our lives will be governed by the Holy Spirit, not by our flesh. So often in the Scriptures, we see Jesus encouraging people to leave behind lesser things to follow Him, the Giver of all things (**Luke 14:33**). God knows when we place other things before our faith, we create idols in our lives. This may look like family, hobbies, education, or careers. Although these things are certainly not bad, if they are not placed under the authority of Christ, they can slowly take priority (**Exodus 20:3**). God cares about every part of who we are and is available to help us navigate all areas as we seek His guidance. He knows our areas of weakness and our blind spots; therefore, the Holy Spirit can lead us away from what might get us off course (**Psalm 32:8**). *Being intentional to keep Christ on the throne of our hearts* will help us keep all else in proper perspective.

> Then you will experience God's peace, which exceeds anything we can understand. His peace will guard your hearts and minds as you live in Christ Jesus.
> — Philippians 4:7

> So you cannot become my disciple without giving up everything you own. — Luke 14:33

> You must not have any other god but me.
> — Exodus 20:3

> "The Lord says, 'I will guide you along the best pathway for your life. I will advise you and watch over you.'" — Psalm 32:8

> Instead, you must worship Christ as Lord of your life. And if someone asks about your hope as a believer, always be ready to explain it.
> — 1 Peter 3:15

September 23

A QUESTION OFTEN ASKED AFTER A TRAGEDY IS, "What good can come out of this?" This is a legitimate, fair concern, but the truth we can stand on is that no matter how hopeless a situation appears, God will bring good from it some way, somehow (**Romans 8:28**). Oftentimes when we see no light at the end of the tunnel, God has already started the process of healing and restoration (**Proverbs 3:5**). The more eternally minded we become, the less dramatic the highs and lows of life on this earth will be. There is a great peace in realizing we can't forecast or understand what God is going to do; we can rest in knowing He will act (**Psalm 46:10**). What does it look like for us to move beyond fear or resentment and move towards rest in a sovereign God who is all-knowing, all-loving, and completely good? We have to begin by getting ahead of our feelings and preach truth to ourselves immediately. We have to *be anchored in the assurance of God's wisdom* and the realization that He is God and we are not (**Psalm 24:1**). We can rest in the eternal hope provided by our heavenly Father.

> And we know that God causes everything to work together for the good of those who love God and are called according to his purpose for them. — Romans 8:28

> Trust in the Lord with all your heart; do not depend on your own understanding.
> — Proverbs 3:5

> Be still, and know that I am God! I will be honored by every nation. I will be honored throughout the world. — Psalm 46:10

> The earth is the Lord's, and everything in it. The world and all its people belong to him. — Psalm 24:1

September 24

ONE OF THE MISCONCEPTIONS I HAVE WITNESSED ABOUT FOLLOWERS OF CHRIST IS the belief that some people are holier to God than others. You may hear people say things like, "She has a direct line to God," or "God is particularly fond of him," when the reality is we all have a direct line to God and He is particularly fond of all of us, even in the midst of the messes we make (**Romans 3:23**). Another unfortunate myth is, "He might do it for her, but not for me." These ideologies make it seem like there is a corporate ladder we have to climb spiritually, when the beautiful reality is that God is not a respecter of persons, and He values us all through the sacrificial lens of the cross (**Romans 2:11**). The difference in our individual relationships with God is that we respond to Him differently. A vital question for us to ask ourselves is, "What am I doing with the opportunities God has put in front of me?" (**Ephesians 5:16**). We can evaluate things such as how we are spending most of our time and energy. No matter where we find ourselves spiritually, we can *wake up in the morning and choose to move towards God that day.* He is waiting to reveal Himself in new ways and teach you how much He loves you right now.

> *For everyone has sinned; we all fall short of God's glorious standard.* — Romans 3:23

> *For God does not show favoritism.* — Romans 2:11

> *Make the most of every opportunity in these evil days.* — Ephesians 5:16

> *Ask me and I will tell you remarkable secrets you do not know about things to come.* — Jeremiah 33:3

September 25

LAST NIGHT AT CHURCH, ONE OF OUR PASTORS MENTIONED "incremental movement" that is the tempo of our faith journey (**Psalm 31:14–15**). During my time working through a study with a group of women, I encouraged them to pause and celebrate how far they have come even though they weren't finished yet. The truth is, as long as we have breath and are living on this planet, we are not finished yet. Even as we sense the way God is working in and through our lives, we can be keenly aware there is still work to be done (**Philippians 1:6**). The spiritual movement we experience should be acknowledged and celebrated. Embracing this kind of heart posture provides joy that will fuel future growth. The idea that we are God's handiwork and masterpiece paints the picture of Him being present with us, observing the many facets of our lives and smoothing or softening rough edges He sees (**Ephesians 2:10**). The question we can ask ourselves is, *"Am I allowing God to incrementally mold me into who He created me to be? Am I being clay in my Potter's hands?"*

> *But I am trusting you, O Lord, saying, 'You are my God!' My future is in your hands. Rescue me from those who hunt me down relentlessly. — Psalm 31:14–15*

> *And I am certain that God, who began the good work within you, will continue his work until it is finally finished on the day when Christ Jesus returns. — Philippians 1:6*

> *For we are God's masterpiece. He has created us anew in Christ Jesus, so we can do the good things he planned for us long ago. — Ephesians 2:10*

> *O Israel, can I not do to you as this potter has done to his clay? As the clay is in the potter's hand, so are you in my hand. — Jeremiah 18:6*

September 26

A SPECIAL FRIEND OF MINE WAS SHARING WITH ME ABOUT HER time at a transitional house for ladies, where she helped them make prayer cards. She is one of my crafty, creative friends, and I thought to myself, "What a beautiful investment of time that was" (**Ecclesiastes 12:1**). Using our gift of time wisely, loving others well, and engaging in relationships is one of the great ways we can worship God. My friend has a passion for crafting, and she discovered the beauty of loving others through her gift. Every part of who we are can be used for our good and God's glory (**Romans 12:6**). When people question what their purpose is, a great place to start is thinking about your areas of interest, curiosity, and passion. God wired us in certain ways for reasons way beyond ourselves. Using our precious time to exercise our strengths, grow in our weaknesses, and spur one another on are all great investments of energy. We will find what we are looking for. It may take effort and moving out of our comfort zones, but if we *seek God* and look for life-building opportunities, He will lead us where we need to go.

> "Don't let the excitement of youth cause you to forget your Creator. Honor him in your youth before you grow old and say, 'Life is not pleasant anymore.'" — Ecclesiastes 12:1

> In his grace, God has given us different gifts for doing certain things well. So if God has given you the ability to prophesy, speak out with as much faith as God has given you. — Romans 12:6

> The Lord will guide you continually, giving you water when you are dry and restoring your strength. You will be like a well-watered garden, like an ever-flowing spring. — Isaiah 58:11

September 27

SITUATIONS AND CIRCUMSTANCES IN OUR LIVES INCLUDE BOTH JOY AND pain. Our experiences shape and mold us in unique ways (**Romans 5:3–4**). Oftentimes it is difficult for us to separate what God causes from what He allows. The reality is that God does not allow any of our experiences to be wasted, and He will use even the most unfortunate events to move us towards our purpose (**Isaiah 43:18–19**). We are wise to attempt viewing our seasons through the lens of healing and hope. Despite how bleak things can look, God's purpose and plan will one day trump the pain. Although it's counterintuitive to focus on the good God could bring from a difficult time, the more we practice this hopeful perspective, the more natural it becomes. God is so much bigger than our messes, and we can count on His goodness (**Nahum 1:7**). It should bring us such comfort knowing *we serve a sovereign God who is* fully aware and never caught off guard (**Psalm 121:4**). I love the image of ultimate protection and love we can find in His arms, giving us confidence that He will use our experiences, good or bad, to move us forward in our purpose and closer to Him.

> *We can rejoice, too, when we run into problems and trials, for we know that they help us develop endurance. And endurance develops strength of character, and character strengthens our confident hope of salvation.*
> *— Romans 5:3-4*

> *But forget all that—it is nothing compared to what I am going to do. For I am about to do something new. See, I have already begun! Do you not see it? I will make a pathway through the wilderness. I will create rivers in the dry wasteland.*
> *— Isaiah 43:18–19*

> *The Lord is good, a strong refuge when trouble comes. He is close to those who trust in him. — Nahum 1:7*

> *Indeed, he who watches over Israel never slumbers or sleeps. — Psalm 121:4*

> *In his kindness God called you to share in his eternal glory by means of Christ Jesus. So after you have suffered a little while, he will restore, support, and strengthen you, and he will place you on a firm foundation. — 1 Peter 5:10*

September 28

We had a terrible storm hit our area the past couple of days, and I reached out to a dear friend of mine who is in her eighties to make sure she was okay. She assured me she was more than okay and blessed (**Psalm 46:1-3**). She joyfully said she woke up with an old hymn playing in her head called "I Know the Master." I loved hearing the holy-spirit confidence in her voice as she described how she had been witnessing God's goodness lately in various ways (**Psalm 66:16**). There is nothing more compelling than listening to someone who has clearly spent time in the presence of Jesus share their peace-filled, encouraged spirit. There is a special sparkle in the wise words of a mature follower of Jesus who has experienced His faithfulness again and again throughout the years (**Psalm 40:10**). So often as people get older in their years they emphasize what they have found to be the important things in life, which are usually faith, family, and wise investments of time. We need to *seek out and pay attention to the wisdom of our elders*. Being in relationship with them is a two-way blessing. They enjoy the love and we can learn from the ways God has worked in and through their lives.

> *Come and listen, all you who fear God, and I will tell you what he did for me.*
> *— Psalm 66:16*

> *I have not kept the good news of your justice hidden in my heart; I have talked about your faithfulness and saving power. I have told everyone in the great assembly of your unfailing love and faithfulness. — Psalm 40:10*

> *Only be careful, and watch yourselves closely so that you do not forget the things your eyes have seen or let them fade from your heart as long as you live. Teach them to your children and to their children after them.*
> *— Deuteronomy 4:9 (NIV)*

September 29

We live in a culture where lots of people would consider themselves Christians. It's so interesting to see people's varying degrees of passion in relation to this title (**Ephesians 5:18**). It is God's desire for His children to be filled with the Holy Spirit; unfortunately, so often believers miss out on this sweet spot of their faith. I like to think of being Spirit-filled as us living out the abundant, eternal life Christ went to the cross for us to experience (**John 10:10**). Having a mundane Christian life might look like going through the motions of religious activity with little or no transformative heart change. This type of believer doesn't bear much fruit, and some would question whether they have really had an encounter with Christ (**Revelations 3:15–16**). Spirit-filled believers ooze a magnetic aroma of Christ in a way that empowers them and blesses those around them. We can *pray and ask God to ignite a passion* and hunger for Him that lights up our spirit wherever we go. This is the difference we were intended to make.

> *"Don't be drunk with wine, because that will ruin your life. Instead, be filled with the Holy Spirit . . ." — Ephesians 5:18*

> *The thief's purpose is to steal and kill and destroy. My purpose is to give them a rich and satisfying life. — John 10:10*

> *I know all the things you do, that you are neither hot nor cold. I wish that you were one or the other! But since you are like lukewarm water, neither hot nor cold, I will spit you out of my mouth! — Revelations 3:15–16*

> *May your Kingdom come soon. May your will be done on earth, as it is in heaven. — Matthew 6:10*

September 30

OUR AREA AND MANY OTHERS HAVE WEATHERED A DESTRUCTIVE HURRICANE over the past couple of days, leaving millions without power and hundreds of fatalities (**John 16:33**). These unfortunate circumstances are a breeding ground for those infamous questions, such as, "Why would God allow this?" But as with all other bad scenarios, we can be confident God will bring silver linings and blessings (**Genesis 50:20**). Two things that have already been seen amidst the turmoil is people coming together to help one another in creative ways (**2 Corinthians 1:3–4**). Our church has sent people out in teams, checking on the needs of our members and our housing community, providing hot meals, bringing fellowship and encouragement. People are realizing what a blessed society we live in, and when things return to normal, there will be a renewed sense of gratitude that will carry a sweet aroma of thankfulness (**1 Thessalonians 5:16–18**). Above all, there is the deep reflection that our hope is not found in having our modern-day conveniences, which can easily be taken away. *Our hope is found in the Rock of our salvation*, who remains forever and ever. Amen.

> *I have told you all this so that you may have peace in me. Here on earth you will have many trials and sorrows. But take heart, because I have overcome the world.* — John 16:33

> *You intended to harm me, but God intended it all for good. He brought me to this position so I could save the lives of many people.* — Genesis 50:20

> *All praise to God, the Father of our Lord Jesus Christ. God is our merciful Father and the source of all comfort. He comforts us in all our troubles so that we can comfort others. When they are troubled, we will be able to give them the same comfort God has given us.*
> — 2 Corinthians 1:3–4

> *Always be joyful. Never stop praying. Be thankful in all circumstances, for this is God's will for you who belong to Christ Jesus.*
> — 1 Thessalonians 5:16–18

October 1

During a challenging workout class at the gym this morning, the instructor repeatedly made reference to getting out of your comfort zone (**2 Timothy 1:7**). She moved on to emphasize how growth and improvement only occur as we challenge ourselves in new ways. While this is definitely true with physical exercise, the same is true spiritually and emotionally. The beginning of the month is always a great time to examine, reflect, and reboot (**Isaiah 43:18-19**). This type of transition may call for outside input in addition to prayer. Ask those who know you best for areas they see in your life that seem to be a struggle. If there is no one you would ask this of, that's a place to make a change. We all need accountability and friends who know us well enough to speak truth in love (**Proverbs 27:17**). Take some time to *prayerfully choose one change* spiritually, emotionally, and physically to challenge yourself with this month. Write those three goals down and look at them every morning this month. May God continue to strengthen us all to live out our potential in Christ.

For I can do everything through Christ who gives me strength.— Philippians 4:13

For God has not given us a spirit of fear and timidity, but of power, love, and self-discipline. — 2 Timothy 1:7

But forget all that— it is nothing compared to what I am going to do. For I am about to do something new. See, I have already begun! Do you not see it? — Isaiah 43:18-19

As iron sharpens iron, so a friend sharpens a friend. — Proverbs 27:17

October 2

THIS MORNING AT THE GYM I WAS SUPER EXCITED to run into an old friend. I noticed immediately the change in her countenance from years before. She seemed brighter and lighter (**Romans 15:13**). There were clearly positive changes that had occurred and she began telling me how she had removed some toxicity in her life. Toxicity can show up in different forms in our lives. It can be people, habits, television, music, or even our thought life (**Ecclesiastes 3:6**). We all experience different seasons in our lives, and some things, even relationships, are beneficial only temporarily. God often uses our relationships to teach us lessons and help us mature emotionally and spiritually. It's important that we continue to seek God's guidance on what is good and what is not (**1 Corinthians 15:33**). We were created to be dependent on God's direction in every area of our lives, and if we're feeling unsettled about whether something or someone is good for us, it's probably not. We can *rest in the security of God's peace* to lead us on steady ground for our good and His glory.

> Direct my footsteps according to your word. Let no sin rule over me.
> — Psalm 119:133

> I pray that God, the source of hope, will fill you completely with joy and peace because you trust in him. Then you will overflow with confident hope through the power of the Holy Spirit. — Romans 15:13

> A time to search and a time to quit searching. A time to keep and a time to throw away. — Ecclesiastes 3:6

> Don't be fooled by those who say such things, for "bad company corrupts good character."
> — 1 Corinthians 15:33

October 3

During a rich conversation with a friend today, she was sharing how God was leading her to yield and surrender to the Holy Spirit (**Galatians 5:22-23**). The concept of yielding emphasizes pausing and thoughtfully considering the next move. So often our immediate reactions are driven by our flesh or human nature as opposed to the peaceful flow of the spirit (**Galatians 5:16**). I often mention the spiritual empowerment which accompanies starting your day with Jesus.

When we come to Him early, surrendering our words, actions, and even emotions, we sensitize our ability to be spirit led throughout the day. Acknowledging our need for God to interrupt our natural reactions, and inviting Him to navigate our responses, is so valuable. The scriptures often mention how, as followers of Christ, we are image bearers which means we should *be mindful of reflecting His goodness*, especially to those who do not know him (**Genesis 1:26**). If there are things that frustrate you regularly or areas where you are easily offended, these could be places to examine the yielding process. We are all clay in our potter's hands, and as we allow it, He will continue to mold us into His image.

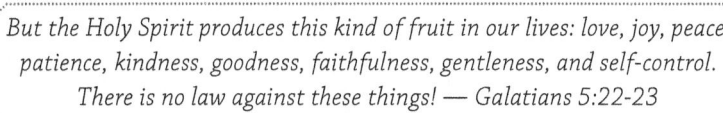

> But the Holy Spirit produces this kind of fruit in our lives: love, joy, peace, patience, kindness, goodness, faithfulness, gentleness, and self-control. There is no law against these things! — Galatians 5:22-23

> So I say, let the Holy Spirit guide your lives. Then you won't be doing what your sinful nature craves. — Galatians 5:16

> Then God said, "Let us make human beings in our image, to be like us. They will reign over the fish in the sea, the birds in the sky, the livestock, all the wild animals on the earth, and the small animals that scurry along the ground." — Genesis 1:26

October 4

Today I had the honor of spending several hours with a young lady who I have seen the Lord restore her life (piece by piece) back together (**Jeremiah 30:17**). For her, this has looked like freedom from a crippling addiction, reconciliation of relationships, and a plan in place for her and her children to experience a Christ-centered life (**John 8:36**). This restoration is available as God, in His lovingkindness, extends His hand of rescue and it is met with a humble heart desiring change. We can find ourselves so off-track that God has to reorient every part of our lives back to Him. The beauty of His supernatural power comes in taking back what our spiritual enemy attempted to steal (**John 10:10**). There is victory in the arms of Jesus, and we have the choice to live in that resurrection power daily. My heart was so encouraged knowing that her choice to live life differently would be a game changer for generations to come in her family. There is no distance far enough that He will not give us the opportunity to return to Him this side of heaven. He can bring healing and restoration to the worst messes. It is up to us to *surrender and join His plan* of freedom, hope, and victory.

> "I will give you back your health and heal your wounds," says the Lord. "For you are called an outcast—'Jerusalem for whom no one cares.'"
> — Jeremiah 30:17

> So if the Son sets you free, you are truly free.
> — John 8:36

> The thief's purpose is to steal and kill and destroy. My purpose is to give them a rich and satisfying life.
> — John 10:10

October 5

My sweet, feisty mama's birthday is today, and in my mind she is lighting up heaven the same way she lit up any room she entered here on earth. The spiritual strength that has grown in my life has roots that were encouraged by her unique way of looking at life (**Proverbs 31:26**). She watered the seeds of faith, hope, and love in practical ways, proven by her acceptance of circumstances as they were (**Hebrews 4:13**). When we are *truly trusting that God knows* what He is doing, we lose the tendency to fret over not understanding. She lived in a way of believing if God wanted her to be aware of something He would make that known. If not, she wasn't going to worry about it (**Philippians 4:6-7**). She knew our hope wasn't in this world, which means we would suffer here but not in heaven. I cherish knowing she is in her eternal home and that I will see her again (**John 16:22**). Her love was not about conditions or expectations. She paid attention to others knowing there was something special about everyone, celebrating uniqueness by God's design. The beautiful benefit of having loved ones in heaven is you think of it way more often.

> Since then, you have been raised with Christ, set your hearts on things above, where Christ is seated at the right hand of God.— Colossians 3:1 (NIV)

> When she speaks, her words are wise, and she gives instructions with kindness. —Proverbs 31:26

> Nothing in all creation is hidden from God. Everything is naked and exposed before his eyes, and he is the one to whom we are accountable. —Hebrews 4:13

> Don't worry about anything; instead, pray about everything. Tell God what you need, and thank him for all he has done. Then you will experience God's peace, which exceeds anything we can understand. His peace will guard your hearts and minds as you live in Christ Jesus. —Phil. 4:6-7

> So you have sorrow now, but I will see you again; then you will rejoice, and no one can rob you of that joy. — John 16:22

October 6

I HAVE BEEN SO REMINDED TODAY OF HOW LITTLE THINGS make big differences. When we surrender our time and energy to God, we invite the Holy Spirit's promptings during the day (**Romans 8:14**). This morning before church I thought of an old friend and felt I should reach out and check on her. She immediately responded with how special that made her feel and how it brightened her day (**Ephesians 4:30**). Oftentimes when we think of someone we should reach out or pray for them. No matter how differently we are wired we all like to know we are thought about or prayed for. With the world of technology we live in, just a short face-to-face visit with a friend can rejuvenate your spirit and increase connectivity (**Hebrews 10:26**). Running into another friend from the past at the store today brought to mind fun times we shared and how God allows our paths to intersect every once in a while. Relationships during our lifetime provide an opportunity for love, fellowship, and encouragement along with long-suffering, forgiveness, and loyalty. We should *heed the Holy Spirit's promptings* to live, love, and be faithful friends.

> *A friend loves at all times, and a brother is born for a time of adversity.*
> *— Proverbs 17:17(NIV)*

> *For all who are led by the Spirit of God are children of God.*
> *— Romans 8:14*

> *And do not bring sorrow to God's Holy Spirit by the way you live. Remember, he has identified you as his own, guaranteeing that you will be saved on the day of redemption. — Ephesians 4:30*

> *Dear friends, if we deliberately continue sinning after we have received knowledge of the truth, there is no longer any sacrifice that will cover these sins. — Hebrews 10:26*

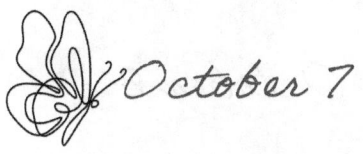
October 7

IN THE AREA WHERE WE LIVE WE ARE SLOWLY BUT SURELY getting pieced back together after a terrible hurricane. There are locations not too far from us who were hit much worse than we were, and the frailty of this world has become glaringly obvious (**1 Corinthians 15:19**). Our preacher made the observation yesterday that we, as creatures, can be captivated more by the things created than by the creator Himself (**Exodus 20:3**). Clearly, having all your modern conveniences stripped away can help reorient our hearts, but how can that be shifted into a lifestyle change? (**Matthew 6:33**) We would be wise to remember that all is from Him, to Him, through Him, and ultimately for Him. As we *learn to acknowledge His Lordship in every area* of our lives we are less likely to compartmentalize things as if He has nothing to do with it. When we invite His authority, He can reshape our perspective, or heart posture, in regards to our priorities. As we mature in our faith, learning to set our minds more on the things above, we are more satisfied in His presence and less devastated over the temporary trials here on earth.

You make known to me the path of life; you will fill me with joy in Your presence, with eternal pleasures at Your right hand. — Psalm 16:11

And if our hope in Christ is only for this life, we are more to be pitied than anyone in the world. — 1 Corinthians 15:19

You must not have any other god but me. — Exodus 20:3

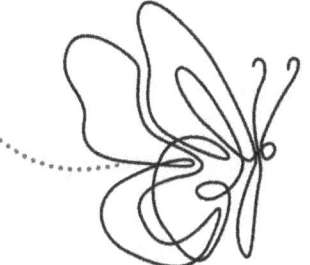

Seek the Kingdom of God above all else, and live righteously, and he will give you everything you need. — Matthew 6:33

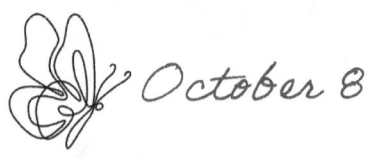

October 8

I HAD THE BLESSING YESTERDAY TO HAVE WHAT I CALL "a breath of fresh air" meeting with a special friend. She was so eager to share with me how she had been experiencing God in a whole new way recently (**Psalm 103:2**). She had invited and allowed the Holy Spirit to transform her heart posture. Prior to this shift she was operating from fear and control; whereas, now she was acting out of love, and trusting God (**Proverbs 3:5-6**). The freedom and peace she was experiencing was radiating from her words and smile. There was a holy-spirit confidence that was literally palpable. The atmosphere in her spirit was at rest with what God had in store for her in contrast to desperation for what she thought she needed to be fulfilled (**Isaiah 55:8-9**). She had begun *an openhanded dialogue with God*, being vulnerable, sharing her hopes and desires, but acknowledging He knows not only what she needs in her life but when she needs it. The bottom line of her renewed joy was that God had His rightful place on the throne of her heart. He was Lord over all in a way He had not been before. Her mindset and heart posture had been transformed by His goodness and her obedience.

> *Do not conform to the pattern of this world, but be transformed by the renewing of your mind. Then you will be able to test and approve what God's will is–His good, pleasing and perfect will. — Romans 12:2 (NIV)*

> *Let all that I am praise the Lord; may I never forget the good things he does for me. — Psalm 103:2*

> *Trust in the Lord with all your heart; do not depend on your own understanding. Seek his will in all you do, and he will show you which path to take. — Proverbs 3:5-6*

> *"My thoughts are nothing like your thoughts," says the Lord. "And my ways are far beyond anything you could imagine. For just as the heavens are higher than the earth, so my ways are higher than your ways and my thoughts higher than your thoughts. — Isaiah 55:8-9*

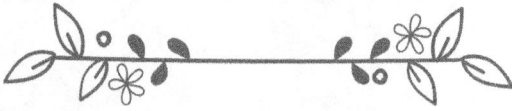

October 9

SO OFTEN IT TAKES A LONG TIME FOR US TO REALIZE how God's design and boundaries for situations or relationships are to protect our well=being, not to confine us. We have the free will to choose to align with His design or attempt to navigate scenarios our own way (**Proverbs 14:12**). Unfortunately, our human nature has the tendency to justify things to satisfy our worldly desires, but when we find ourselves justifying something, it's usually because we know what we are doing is contrary to the way God is leading us (**Isaiah 55:8-9**). When we rationalize, it usually leads to compromise. Compromise creates cracks in our foundation of being rooted in truth (**Hebrews 3:14**). Perseverance in holding on tightly to God's ways is not always easy or popular, but in the end it's well worth it (**Romans 8:23**). If and when we compromise, we can allow unwanted shame and guilt that remove clarity from God's guidance. Following the Spirit's leading produces peace that opens our ears and hearts to see and hear God more clearly (**Psalm 85:8**). God's boundaries protect us from unnecessary suffering and hardship. Obedience invites holy-spirit empowerment that absolutely nothing can stand against. *Walking in the spirit equips* us to deny risky compromise.

There is a path before each person that seems right, but it ends in death. — Proverbs 14:12

"My thoughts are nothing like your thoughts," says the Lord. "And my ways are far beyond anything you could imagine. For just as the heavens are higher than the earth, so my ways are higher than your ways and my thoughts higher than your thoughts." — Isaiah 55:8-9

For if we are faithful to the end, trusting God just as firmly as when we first believed, we will share in all that belongs to Christ. — Hebrews 3:14

And we believers also groan, even though we have the Holy Spirit within us as a foretaste of future glory, for we long for our bodies to be released from sin and suffering. We, too, wait with eager hope for the day when God will give us our full rights as his adopted children, including the new bodies he has promised us. — Romans 8:23

I listen carefully to what God the Lord is saying, for he speaks peace to his faithful people. But let them not return to their foolish ways. — Psalm 85:8

So I say, let the Holy Spirit guide your lives. Then you won't be doing what your sinful nature craves. — Galatians 5:16

October 10

Today I noticed a good friend of mine had a new book in her hand. She looked super excited about it, and I saw the title, "Humility." (**Proverbs 11:2**). Honestly, I admired her humility displayed by choosing to read the book, but also what a critical piece of our faith humility is. Pride finds itself at the root of so many of our issues and certainly presents itself in different forms. Although being humble is very counter-culture, a humble spirit is very inviting and results in freedom (**1 Peter 5:5**). Inviting others into our thoughts, actions, and lifestyle builds meaningful relationships that make differences in our lives and others'. This looks like observing when others seem to do certain things well, meeting up to pick their brain on this or that, and seeking out others who may have had similar experiences. There is always freedom when we are obedient. The scriptures lead us to *seek wise counsel* (**Proverbs 1:5**). God always honors our dependence on Him and knows when we are seeking His will above all else (**2 Chronicles 7:14**). Self-reliance and self-sufficiency lead to pride, usually ending with anxiety and stress. Navigating life from a humble heart produces expectancy, faith, and surrender. Therein lies a posture of rest and confidence in God, not ourselves.

> Pride leads to disgrace, but with humility comes wisdom. — Proverbs 11:2

> In the same way, you who are younger must accept the authority of the elders. And all of you, dress yourselves in humility as you relate to one another, for "God opposes the proud but gives grace to the humble." — 1 Peter 5:5

> Let the wise listen to these proverbs and become even wiser. Let those with understanding receive guidance. — Proverbs 1:5

> Then if my people who are called by my name will humble themselves and pray and seek my face and turn from their wicked ways, I will hear from heaven and will forgive their sins and restore their land. — 2 Chronicles 7:14

> Humble yourselves before the Lord and He will lift you up. — James 4:10 (NIV)

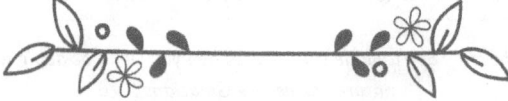

October 11

A WISE FRIEND OF MINE UTTERED A PHRASE THE OTHER DAY that caught my attention and continues to pop up in my thoughts. She said, "re-surrendering the process," and it perfectly described something I had been wrestling with in my heart (**Proverbs 16:3**). This idea brought to my mind being openhanded with what the Lord is calling you to over the seasons (**Psalm 96:7-9**). We all tend to be creatures of habit in one way or another, even how we serve God. He created us with different strengths, and naturally we settle into roles regarding our aptitudes. In the same way, we don't want to be complacent in our relationship with the Lord or others. We should be sensitive to not find ourselves complacent in serving (**Ecclesiastes 3:11**). There is certainly a time and season for everything, and God is the creator of new opportunities. Any time we are willing to *step out in faith and do something different* there is the assurance of growth and a new chance to rely on God in different ways. He will move us in and out of comfort zones when we surrender our time, talents, and abilities to the One who knows where and how we could be benefitting His work in ourselves and others.

Commit your actions to the Lord, and your plans will succeed. — Proverbs 16:3

O nations of the world, recognize the Lord; recognize that the Lord is glorious and strong. Give to the Lord the glory he deserves! Bring your offering and come into his courts. Worship the Lord in all his holy splendor. Let all the earth tremble before him. — Psalm 96:7-9

Yet God has made everything beautiful for its own time. He has planted eternity in the human heart, but even so, people cannot see the whole scope of God's work from beginning to end. — Ecclesiastes 3:11

October 12

THROUGHOUT MY YEARS OF BEING INVOLVED WITH DIFFERENT MINISTRIES, I've always been sensitive to people who seem to slip through the cracks (**Matthew 18:12-14**). We may often hear people say things like, "if someone wants help, they will ask for it," or, "God helps those who help themselves." While we can't minimize the value of doing our part, sometimes there is a level of brokenness that makes it difficult to reach out for help.

As followers of Christ we should *be prayerful to notice and connect people in ways they may not think of themselves* (**Matthew 28:19-20**). Part of all our calling is to go out into the world, love others, and encourage them towards Christ. In order to notice those around us, we have to be sensitive to the Spirit's leading and not be so "in our own world" that we neglect to see, really see, those around us. Connectivity is key, and it's difficult to connect others if we ourselves are not part of the local body (**Galatians 5:13**). Inviting others to church is always a good idea, but making sure they are cared for and welcomed when they get there is equally as important. One of my most cherished characteristics within my relationship with God is knowing I am seen, valued, and cared for. May we be people who mirror this attribute of our Father's heart for others.

> *If a man has a hundred sheep and one of them wanders away, what will he do? Won't he leave the ninety-nine others on the hills and go out to search for the one that is lost? And if he finds it, I tell you the truth, he will rejoice over it more than over the ninety-nine that didn't wander away! In the same way, it is not my heavenly Father's will that even one of these little ones should perish. — Matthew 18:12-14*

> *Therefore, go and make disciples of all the nations, baptizing them in the name of the Father and the Son and the Holy Spirit. Teach these new disciples to obey all the commands I have given you. And be sure of this: I am with you always, even to the end of the age. — Matthew 28:19-20*

> *For you have been called to live in freedom, my brothers and sisters. But don't use your freedom to satisfy your sinful nature. Instead, use your freedom to serve one another in love. — Galatians 5:13*

October 13

During a visit to the hospital today I was so reminded of the fragility of our earthly bodies and how our health can turn on a dime (**2 Corinthians 4:7**). As I prayed with my cousin I was visiting, the Holy Spirit led my words to the emphasis of our hope being so much beyond what we are experiencing here and now. The more chaotic the world becomes, along with loved ones going to be with the Lord, it creates an anticipation and eagerness to arrive in our eternal home (**Hebrews 12:28**). The hope of our unshakeable Kingdom of Heaven should support our desire to run the race God has set before us here on earth. The blessings we receive—a marriage, children, or success—pale in comparison to the privilege of being adopted into God's family (**Ephesians 1:5**). When we have the desire to experience God every day, He will show up. Cultivating eyes to see Him is an endeavor worth pursuing. The light of Christ will illuminate our hearts and minds, but what we choose to focus on can determine how bright that light shines. There is no amount of suffering or despair that God will not walk us through. As we *call on His name* and lean into His strength, He delivers us from our trials and provides the eternal hope of what's to come.

> We now have this light shining in our hearts, but we ourselves are like fragile clay jars containing this great treasure. This makes it clear that our great power is from God, not from ourselves.
> — 2 Corinthians 4:7

> Since we are receiving a Kingdom that is unshakable, let us be thankful and please God by worshiping him with holy fear and awe. — Hebrews 12:28

> Since, then, you have been raised with Christ, set your hearts on things above, where Christ is seated at the right hand of God. — Colossians 3:1

> God decided in advance to adopt us into his own family by bringing us to himself through Jesus Christ. This is what he wanted to do, and it gave him great pleasure. — Ephesians 1:5

October 14

I HAD THE SWEET OPPORTUNITY TO ENGAGE WITH SOME AWESOME WOMEN today who are all moving deeper in their relationship with God. I asked them the question, *What does it look like to experience satisfaction in Jesus?* and I loved the variety of answers (**Psalm 16:11**). Finding contentment and satisfaction in Jesus has a lot to do with cultivating joy in His presence. One lady mentioned this grandiose type encounter with some very clear direction from the Holy Spirit. Another mentioned reading His word and finding comfort in His promises, while another mentioned being surrounded by sisters in Christ today having a God-centered discussion (**Exodus 33:14**). The reality is that we can all sense His presence in different ways. We can look at several of our heroes of our faith and discover how God dealt with all of them uniquely, such as Moses, David, and Saul who became Paul. Learning to *rest in His presence*, allowing Him to become our safe place, can be monumental in the growth of our faith. He longs to provide shelter for us and be the first place we run (**Psalm 91:4**). The beauty in all of this is how unchanging, everlasting, and compassionate God's love is for us. He is the God who always sees, always listens, and never disappoints.

> *You will show me the way of life, granting me the joy of your presence and the pleasures of living with you forever.* — Psalm 16:11

> *The Lord replied, "I will personally go with you, Moses, and I will give you rest—everything will be fine for you."* — Exodus 33:14

> *He will cover you with his feathers. He will shelter you with his wings. His faithful promises are your armor and protection.* — Psalm 91:4

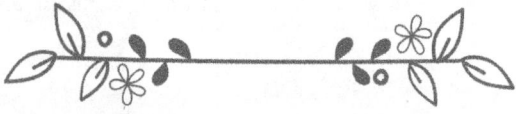

October 15

How many times have we heard others say, or said ourselves, "I need to get out of my head." Our minds can be a battlefield where Satan regularly wages war on our peace (**Philippians 4:8**). The daily challenge we all face is to set our minds on truth and allow our imaginations to be captivated by those things producing hope, faith, and goodness. Technology has wreaked havoc with the constant influx of information we don't need (**Proverbs 4:23**). We all open ourselves up for data or facts that have absolutely nothing to do with us or things the Holy Spirit may be pointing us towards. These useless distractions create detours from the purposes and plans God may be inviting us into. The only way for us to live counter-culturally is to be intentional to turn off the noise and prioritize having margin in our lives to *seek and hear from God* (**Exodus 25:8**). Learning to be held, resting in His presence is an attribute of our faith that can provide more strength and peace than we could ever imagine. One of the best ways to not be swept away by the cares of this world is to be so preoccupied with Jesus that all else shrinks in importance. This looks like re-surrendering our hearts and minds daily, dwelling in His presence where our joy is found.

> *And now, dear brothers and sisters, one final thing. Fix your thoughts on what is true, and honorable, and right, and pure, and lovely, and admirable. Think about things that are excellent and worthy of praise.* — Philippians 4:8

> *Guard your heart above all else, for it determines the course of your life.* — Proverbs 4:23

> *Have the people of Israel build me a holy sanctuary so I can live among them.* — Exodus 25:8

October 16

Oftentimes we yearn to experience our sweet spot with God, meaning we want to live in peace and sense the guidance of the Holy Spirit, but we neglect to live out the clear directions God has provided (**Philippians 4:9**). There is so much division in our world right now, whether surrounding politics, religion, or simply opinions. The scriptures actually point to ways we can love each other well in the midst of our differences (**Galatians 5:22**). When we act out the fruits of the Spirit during our interactions with others, anger and animosity don't come as quickly. Some people wake up looking for a fight, but we are responsible for how we respond. When frustration or anger are met with kindness and self-control, it is de-escalating. I have witnessed the fruit resulting from resetting our heart posture every morning. When we pray to be led by our Spirit as opposed to our flesh, there is a humility that says, "I can't do this on my own, God, and I am aware of my need for you to help me navigate situations and people."

When we *simply seek God*, acknowledging our desperate need of a shepherd, He is there to guide us by still waters, allowing us to experience that peace that surpasses all understanding. We know this, but need to live it out.

> Keep putting into practice all you learned and received from me—everything you heard from me and saw me doing. Then the God of peace will be with you. — Philippians 4:9

> You will keep in perfect peace those whose minds are steadfast, because they trust in you.
> — Isaiah 26:3 (NIV)

> But the Holy Spirit produces this kind of fruit in our lives: love, joy, peace, patience, kindness, goodness, faithfulness. — Galatians 5:22

October 17

I was able to experience the blessing today of spending time with a special birthday girl who turned 56 years old, celebrating her first sober birthday in 29 years. She had the wonder and awe of a young girl enjoying the birthday extravaganza of her dreams (**Psalm 139:14**). She was bursting at the seams to share with anyone who would listen how God Himself had rescued her, delivered her, and set her on solid ground with a straight path (**Proverbs 4:11**). Witnessing her joy, enthusiasm and gratitude to be held by God and transformed, was simply inspiring and beautiful (**2 Corinthians 5:17**) Her exact words were, "I will never go back to the way I was." And even though I've seen many relapses in my day, I would be surprised if she did. She has opened her heart for the Spirit of God to rewire life as she knew it. The key thing she said that made my heart smile the most was, "God has to be the center of my life." (**Matthew 6:33**) Embracing and living out the truth of acknowledging Him as Lord and King over all that we are creates an environment where we live with purpose, love in truth, and *run the race marked out before us.*

Thank you for making me so wonderfully complex! Your workmanship is marvelous— how well I know it. —Psalm 139:14

I will teach you wisdom's ways and lead you in straight paths.— Proverbs 4:11

This means that anyone who belongs to Christ has become a new person. The old life is gone; a new life has begun! — 2 Corinthians 5:17

Seek the Kingdom of God above all else, and live righteously, and he will give you everything you need. — Matthew 6:33

October 18

DURING A QUALITY TIME OF CONVERSATION WITH TWO DIFFERENT people at two different places today, I was reminded of the critical value of connection we all need in our lives (**Romans 12:4-5**). As I was listening to these two radically distinct scenarios occurring in these ladies' lives, the first step of the solution was exactly the same: encourage each of them to choose a church body and begin allowing roots to grow (**Genesis 2:18**). There seems to be an epidemic of church hoppers in our culture. The reality is there are a plethora of churches and denominations to choose from, and although it's difficult to choose, the decision needs to be made (**Acts 2:42**). While it can be awkward inserting ourselves into new situations and to begin sharing life, it's unarguably one of the key components to spiritual satisfaction and growth. We desperately need others, and they need us. I've often thought how satisfying it is to Satan that Christians can nitpick each other, theology, and church so much to where they end up floundering and being unsettled. We should *seek God*, find a place, get planted, and thrive.

> Just as our bodies have many parts and each part has a special function, so it is with Christ's body. We are many parts of one body, and we all belong to each other. —Romans 12:4-5

> Then the Lord God said, "It is not good for the man to be alone. I will make a helper who is just right for him."
> — Genesis 2:18

> All the believers devoted themselves to the apostles' teaching, and to fellowship, and to sharing in meals (including the Lord's Supper), and to prayer.
> — Acts 2:42

October 19

For some reason when I woke up this morning I had some uninvited thoughts run through my head that I did not want to carry. Before I was willing to let my feet touch the floor I prayed God would help me to reorient my heart and mind (**Philippians 4:8**). After feeling revitalized by the scripture the Holy Spirit brought to mind, I spent some time appreciating the power of scripture and the importance of keeping His Word fresh in our hearts. We may never understand how and when intrusive thoughts pop into our heads, but the reality is how we respond to them is what matters (**2 Corinthians 10:5**). We can exercise control over our thought life, and the tone of a thought can make it clear whether it is for our good or meant for harm. Even if the Spirit of God is throwing us caution or conviction, it is in love as opposed to a tone of condemnation or shame (**Romans 8:1**) As we *stay connected to Jesus* we can discern what is of God and what is not. We also are empowered with His infallible Word which is our offensive, indestructible weapon that nothing can stand against!

> *And now, dear brothers and sisters, one final thing. Fix your thoughts on what is true, and honorable, and right, and pure, and lovely, and admirable. Think about things that are excellent and worthy of praise.*
> *— Philippians 4:8*

> *We destroy every proud obstacle that keeps people from knowing God. We capture their rebellious thoughts and teach them to obey Christ. — 2 Corin. 10:5*

> *So now there is no condemnation for those who belong to Christ Jesus.*
> *— Romans 8:1*

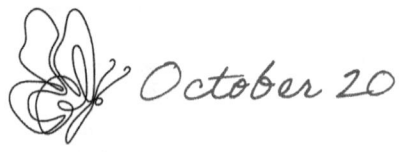

October 20

WE ARE CURRENTLY LIVING IN AN EXTREMELY hostile political environment. I have friends who are stressed about the upcoming selection of our president, and political tension is certainly high. Our pastor did a beautiful job today challenging our congregation to focus more on Jesus' kingdom than the kingdoms of this world (**John 18:36**). When followers of Christ act equally as combative as non-believers, it doesn't reflect an abiding trust in Christ. We, as Christians, can rest securely in the mighty hands of God despite who the president is (**John 16:33**). There are ways we can keep our eyes on Jesus and experience peace through the tension. The best way to handle awkward confrontational interactions is to be prayed up beforehand. We never know who God is going to give us the opportunity to engage with on any given day. So surrendering all your conversations early in the day is a great strategy. Being combative in our interactions is hardly ever fruitful (**Ephesians 4:15**). Our goals, no matter what the condition of the world might be in any particular season, should be peace, love, hope, and unwavering stability because we are standing on the solid ground of the gospel. May we *represent Christ well* and draw others to the eternal Kingdom of Jesus.

> Jesus answered, "My Kingdom is not an earthly kingdom. If it were, my followers would fight to keep me from being handed over to the Jewish leaders. But my Kingdom is not of this world."
> — John 18:36

> I have told you all this so that you may have peace in me. Here on earth you will have many trials and sorrows. But take heart, because I have overcome the world.
> — John 16:33

> Instead, we will speak the truth in love, growing in every way more and more like Christ, who is the head of his body, the church.
> — Ephesians 4:15

October 21

IT HAS OFTEN BEEN SAID WE TEND TO BE THE HARDEST ON THOSE who are the closest to us. We are commanded in the scriptures to love one another, but so often we can be more gracious to a stranger than our own family (**Romans 12:10**). I am certainly prone to be extremely kind to a cashier with an attitude because I wonder if they're having a bad day, but may not be as immediately forgiving to my husband. When we have a relationship history with people there can be lingering pockets of pain that need God's touch in order for us to love well (**1 Peter 4:8**). We are wise to be intentional in praying for a forgiving heart in that the more we can love like Jesus, the more it benefits us and our loved ones. Loving well is medicine for our souls. Love is the backbone of our faith, and learning to love difficult people reaps great rewards spiritually and emotionally (**Colossians 3:14**). No one has more compassion for our pain than our Father in Heaven. He sees it all, knows it all, and has already made a way for healing and wholeness. We have the freedom and power through Christ to *love unconditionally* even through the most difficult seasons.

> *But to you who are listening I say: Love your enemies, do good to those who hate you. Bless those who curse you, pray for those who mistreat you.*
> *— Luke 6:27-28 (NIV)*

> *Most important of all, continue to show deep love for each other, for love covers a multitude of sins. —1 Peter 4:8*

> *Love each other with genuine affection, and take delight in honoring each other. — Romans 12:10*

> *Above all, clothe yourselves with love, which binds us all together in perfect harmony. — Colossians 3:14*

October 22

As I woke up this morning, the value of creating space for God to minister to our souls came to my mind. For me personally this looks like me setting myself up to wake up before the rest of my household by going to bed earlier (**Psalm 5:3**). There has just always been something sacred about those early morning hours. We can clearly connect with God anytime, anywhere, but the value of being quiet and still in His presence, maybe with soft worship music in the background, is inviting His presence in an intimate way (**Ecclesiastes 3:7**). I inherently love to talk, so I *prayerfully seek the Holy Spirit's guidance* for wisdom as to when to shut my mouth, as well as open it. God has taught me the beauty of restraint, which has benefited all of my relationships immensely (**Proverbs 10:19**). The more familiar or comfortable we become with God the easier it is to sit still in His presence, being satisfied in the powerful stillness of His existence. When we practice not being hurried with God, His heart posture can radiate into our other interactions and activities for the day. May we be people who simply cherish the satisfaction of being still in His presence.

> *Listen to my voice in the morning, Lord. Each morning I bring my requests to you and wait expectantly.* — Psalm 5:3

> *A time to tear and a time to mend. A time to be quiet and a time to speak.* —Ecclesiastes 3:7

> *Too much talk leads to sin. Be sensible and keep your mouth shut.* —Proverbs 10:19

> *"He got up, rebuked the wind and said to the waves, 'Quiet! Be Still.' Then the wind died down and it was completely calm."* — Mark 4:39 (NIV)

October 23

I woke up this morning thinking about the strength that's found in having an undivided heart towards Jesus (**Psalm 86:11**). This type of heart posture looks like Jesus is first and foremost in your life and everything else is considered secondary to your allegiance to Him (**Hebrews 12:23**). Cultivating a devotion to Jesus that is solid and sustaining doesn't occur overnight, but making the choice to move towards Him daily makes it a reality. *A lifestyle surrendered to God* is actually less complicated in that we don't have to resolve issues or conflicts based on our own understanding, thoughts or feelings. We do not need to copy our culture, or fear what others may think, because we are leaning on absolute truth and love to guide our decisions and actions (**Romans 12:2**). The freedom and confidence that accompanies being all in with Jesus is unmatched. The eternal security we experience in the arms of our Savior is capable of giving us the strength and resilience we need this side of heaven.

> *Teach me your ways, O Lord, that I may live according to your truth! Grant me purity of heart, so that I may honor you.* —Psalm 86:11

> *You have come to the assembly of God's firstborn children, whose names are written in heaven. You have come to God himself, who is the judge over all things. You have come to the spirits of the righteous ones in heaven who have now been made perfect.* — Hebrews 12:23

> *For I can do everything through Christ, who gives me strength.* — Philippians 4:13

> *Don't copy the behavior and customs of this world, but let God transform you into a new person by changing the way you think. Then you will learn to know God's will for you, which is good and pleasing and perfect.* — Romans 12:2

October 24

ONE OF MY FAVORITE WAYS TO INVEST MY TIME IS spending quality time with people whose lives have been touched and transformed by God's relentless pursuit (**1 Samuel 10:2**). Although one-on-one conversation is valuable, getting a group of believers in one space and listening to story after story of God's restoration is almost angelic. The reality is if one person begins to acknowledge and praise God's activity it is contagious. Surrounding ourselves with the right people in the right environment is life-altering (**1 Corinthians 15:33**). It is important to pay attention to how we feel when we've been engaging with different people. If you leave an event or get-together feeling alone or discouraged, those are probably not your people. In contrast, leaving a room feeling lifted up and inspired is encouraging. We are commanded in the scriptures to spur one another on and to support one another in prayer (**Hebrews 10:24**). If we ever feel prompted to share what God is doing in and through our hearts, we shouldn't shy away from the opportunity. We never know when *our God story is exactly what someone needs* to hear.

> *When you leave me today, you will see two men beside Rachel's tomb at Zelzah, on the border of Benjamin. They will tell you that the donkeys have been found and that your father has stopped worrying about them and is now worried about you. He is asking, 'Have you seen my son?'* — 1 Samuel 10:2

> *Don't be fooled by those who say such things, for "bad company corrupts good character."* — 1 Corinthians 15:33

> *Let us think of ways to motivate one another to acts of love and good works.* — Hebrews 10:24

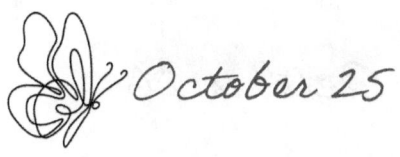

October 25

One of the most precious overarching ideas I personally cling to (and encourage others to do the same) is that our God is the God who sees us. There are many descriptive names for God in the scriptures, but "El Roi" has always had such an intimate undertone (**Genesis 16:13**). We are all desperate for intimacy, and as we learn and experience how present, as well as perfect, God's love is for us we can thrive and blossom (**Ephesians 3:18-19**). When we allow this supernatural personal love to be woven into our entire being, it creates an armor of identity so powerful it cannot be broken. This armor equips us to navigate relationships, as well as circumstances, from a posture of wholeness, being fully aware that God is not only aware of what's taking place, but is also aware of our spiritual and emotional condition (**Psalm 139:1**). The reality that our Heavenly Father knows everything there is to know about us should provide great comfort and confidence for us. *We should often pray* phrases like, "God, I am continually in awe of your love and provision over me," just to remind ourselves He is always aware, He is always there, and our best interests are always in His heart.

> "'For I know the plans I have for you,' declares the Lord, 'plans to prosper you and not to harm you, plans to give you hope and a future.'" — Jeremiah 29:11

> Thereafter, Hagar used another name to refer to the Lord, who had spoken to her. She said, "You are the God who sees me." She also said, "Have I truly seen the One who sees me?" — Genesis 16:13

> And may you have the power to understand, as all God's people should, how wide, how long, how high, and how deep his love is. May you experience the love of Christ, though it is too great to understand fully. Then you will be made complete with all the fullness of life and power that comes from God.
> — Ephesians 3:18-19

> O Lord, you have examined my heart and know everything about me.
> —Psalm 139:1

October 26

THERE ARE SEVERAL PEOPLE WE LEARN ABOUT IN THE SCRIPTURES which fall into the category of being heroes of our faith. Paul has always seemed to stand out amongst these heroes in the way his life was radically changed in an instant, even resulting in his name change from Saul to Paul (**Philemon 1:15-16**). He possessed a passion to point others toward Christ through his own experiences, as well as emphasizing God's sincere love for them (**Ephesians 3:16, Romans 5:8**). Paul received, embraced, and lived out the new way God showed him to live. His admirable examples of contentment during adversity, faith amidst despair, and strong conviction to never compromise what he knew to be true of God was revolutionary (**1 Corinthians 15:27**). One of the most powerful attributes of Paul's character was his humility and acknowledgment that anything good within him was created, motivated, and powered by God, and not in and of himself (**2 Corinthians 12:9-10**). Paul's confidence and perseverance are qualities we can imitate as we *daily surrender and acknowledge the Lordship of Christ.* Paul's zeal fueled his motivation to encourage others by word and deed to live out their salvation with passion and hope.

> *It seems you lost Onesimus for a little while so that you could have him back forever. He is no longer like a slave to you. He is more than a slave, for he is a beloved brother, especially to me. Now he will mean much more to you, both as a man and as a brother in the Lord.*
> —Philemon 1:15-16

> *I pray that from his glorious, unlimited resources he will empower you with inner strength through his Spirit.* — Ephesians 3:16

> *But God showed his great love for us by sending Christ to die for us while we were still sinners.* — Romans 5:8

> *For the Scriptures say, "God has put all things under his authority." (Of course, when it says "all things are under his authority," that does not include God himself, who gave Christ his authority.)* — 1 Corin. 15:27

> *Each time he said, "My grace is all you need. My power works best in weakness." So now I am glad to boast about my weaknesses, so that the power of Christ can work through me. That's why I take pleasure in my weaknesses, and in the insults, hardships, persecutions, and troubles that I suffer for Christ. For when I am weak, then I am strong.* — 2 Corin. 12:9-10

October 27

So much of our faith is rooted in the depth at which we are trusting God (**Jeremiah 17:7-8**). There is immense value in identifying spiritual markers in our lives where we find ourselves in the midst of uncertainties and God shows up in ways that were undeniably Him (**Ephesians 1:11**). I love imagining the twists and turns that one day we will realize were all part of God's will for our lives. The steps of faith we walk lead us to actively rest in His sovereignty. A key component of faith is the confidence that God is always at work in and around us. This knowledge makes life's mysteries secure and purposeful even in our lack of understanding (**Romans 8:18**). This heart posture of trust can lead us to *pray with expectancy*, waiting for Him to reveal His activity. Witnessing His transformative work in and around us creates an atmosphere of hope and resolve (**Joshua 1:9**). We all have the tendency to backslide in the unwavering trust in God we desire whenever we doubt or feel discouraged, but the magnificent reality is He is always only a prayer away from reorienting us back with secure footing and a firm place to stand.

> But blessed are those who trust in the Lord and have made the Lord their hope and confidence. They are like trees planted along a riverbank, with roots that reach deep into the water. Such trees are not bothered by the heat or worried by long months of drought. Their leaves stay green, and they never stop producing fruit. — Jeremiah 17:7-8

> Furthermore, because we are united with Christ, we have received an inheritance from God, for he chose us in advance, and he makes everything work out according to his plan. — Ephesians 1:11

> Yet what we suffer now is nothing compared to the glory he will reveal to us later. — Romans 8:18

> This is my command—be strong and courageous! Do not be afraid or discouraged. For the Lord your God is with you wherever you go. —Joshua 1:9

October 28

ONE OF MY FAVORITE SCENARIOS IS WHEN THE HOLY SPIRIT points out something we have known forever but sheds new light for us to notice (**John 14:25-26**). A revelation occurred to me this morning that Jesus did not worry about His time to go to the cross drawing near. We know He experienced a very emotional time in the garden of Gethsemane, but this seems to be the only documented time of distress (**Matthew 26:37-38**). I think of how much time we waste agonizing over events that often, don't even come to pass. Yet, clearly, Jesus knew for a fact He would experience the cross but was always present and focusing on what God set before Him that day. I believe the strength and peace He possessed hinged on the truth He knew regarding what was coming: Eternity. We, as Christ followers, have the same Eternal Home to *look forward to*—*Heaven*: our final destination (**Colossians 3:1**). We would be wise to remind ourselves the sufferings and trials we experience here on earth are just that—here on earth. These things will all pass away and our Heavenly Home is waiting.

> *I am telling you these things now while I am still with you. But when the Father sends the Advocate as my representative—that is, the Holy Spirit—he will teach you everything and will remind you of everything I have told you.*
> *— John 14:25-26*

> *He took Peter and Zebedee's two sons, James and John, and he became anguished and distressed. He told them, "My soul is crushed with grief to the point of death. Stay here and keep watch with me."*
> *— Matthew 26:37-38*

> *Since you have been raised to new life with Christ, set your sights on the realities of heaven, where Christ sits in the place of honor at God's right hand.*
> *— Colossians 3:1*

October 29

All day today I have had the beautiful phrase in my head, "good shepherd, good friend," which is a lyric to a worship song we sing at church. These words resonate so alive in my Spirit in that so often He is both our shepherd and friend simultaneously (**Psalm 23:1, John 15:14**). The Lord shows up as our shepherd in His sovereign control in all things, and His supernatural ability to guide us in the right direction, even when we don't realize it (**Ecclesiastes 11:5**). The Shepherd is always in tune with the rhythms of his flock, even their propensity to wander. God's relentless pursuit of us never ceases to amaze me, either in my life, or in the lives of those around me. I will say out loud, "Lord, thank you, that you are continually caring for me in more ways than I could ask or imagine" (**Ephesians 3:20-21**). I often feel that God himself is my best friend. He is always with me, for me, and I tend to communicate with Him all day about everything. We can always *be encouraged* that the more we practice His presence, we are creating an awareness of His nearness, and we will experience His friendship in new ways. Knowing He covers us from every angle should bring abundant joy and peace.

> The Lord is my shepherd; I have all that I need. — Psalm 23:1

> You are my friends if you do what I command. — John 15:14

> Just as you cannot understand the path of the wind or the mystery of a tiny baby growing in its mother's womb, so you cannot understand the activity of God, who does all things. — Ecclesiastes 11:5

> Now all glory to God, who is able, through his mighty power at work within us, to accomplish infinitely more than we might ask or think. Glory to him in the church and in Christ Jesus through all generations forever and ever! Amen.
> — Ephesians 3:20-21

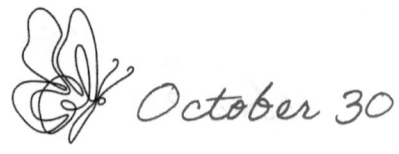
October 30

A WELL MEANING FRIEND OF MINE REACHED OUT and invited me to what seemed to be an empowerment-for-women get together which included a book launch and fellowship. Although this friend is a strong believer, for some reason I had a check in my spirit, so I began praying about it (**Colossians 2:8**). God led me to research the author of the book, and she was focused on self-empowerment, as opposed to Christ-empowerment. This is a trend we have all heard about in one way or another, but it's always a good idea to make sure our help is coming from the right source (**Proverbs 14:12**). Our strength from within lies only in Christ. He created us. He will sustain and equip us with all we will ever need. We were created to be dependent on the one true God for all of our strength, plans, and, most important, our healing (**Romans 11:36**). My sweet friend didn't even realize what was happening, and Satan is hard at work attempting to convince the culture to be their own God. His strategies sometimes change, but his goal is for destruction and a Godless world. We need to *be so connected to God* and His truth that our spiritual armor repels anything not of God.

> Don't let anyone capture you with empty philosophies and high-sounding nonsense that come from human thinking and from the spiritual powers of this world, rather than from Christ.
> — Colossians 2:8

> There is a path before each person that seems right, but it ends in death.
> —Proverbs 14:12

> For everything comes from him and exists by his power and is intended for his glory. All glory to him forever! Amen. —Romans 11:36

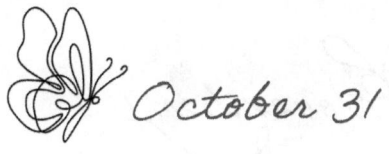
October 31

As believers, God's transformative work in our hearts doesn't stop this side of Heaven. I often sense that God's desire is for us to slow down, notice, and acknowledge all He has so brilliantly created (**Psalm 8:3-4**.) The magnificent work of His hands is everywhere, including nature, the air we breathe, and, even more valuable—His children created in His image (**Genesis 1:27**).

While encouraging an amazing group of women today, I suggested they include in their prayer time, "Father, I am thankful that I am who You say I am." Declarations to God of our place in this world, and in His family, is powerful. So often, we underestimate our value in what matters and overestimate where it's not that important (**Ephesians 3:19, Colossians 3:2**). Who we are in and because of the love of Christ, brings the fullness of life. We should get outside and notice the beauty, the wind, and whatever life-giving meditations the Spirit of God brings to our hearts. An atmosphere of awareness and gratitude can be life-changing. *Ask God for a renewed sense of wonder* for all He has created, including you.

> *When I look at the night sky and see the work of your fingers—the moon and the stars you set in place— what are mere mortals that you should think about them, human beings that you should care for them?* — Psalm 8:3-4

> *So God created human beings in his own image. In the image of God he created them; male and female he created them.* — Genesis 1:27

> *May you experience the love of Christ, though it is too great to understand fully. Then you will be made complete with all the fullness of life and power that comes from God.* — Ephesians 3:19

> *Think about the things of heaven, not the things of earth.* — Colossians 3:2

November 1

I LOVE THE BEGINNING OF THE MONTH TO PRAYERFULLY CONSIDER personal challenges, as well as spiritual, mental, and, yes, physical ones, too. It's always important to consider our motives for any new challenge, and God knows what needs attention in our lives. This is why seeking His guidance in all these areas is critical (**Psalm 37:4**).

A physical goal could include adding 10 minutes to an existing exercise routine, to incorporate more core exercises or committing to moving your body at least 30 minutes four times a week. A spiritual goal could be studying the different names God has been given in the scriptures, how they came to pass, and the ways He has revealed Himself to you in that way; names like El Roi, El Shaddai, Yahweh (**Exodus 6:2-3**). For me, personally, this month to care for myself mentally I am going to attempt to not be in a hurry by leaving earlier when I need to be somewhere. Traffic has gotten terrible in our area, and being late causes me to feel scattered. Whatever it may be for you this month—*pray, decide, and execute.*

> Commit your actions to the Lord, and your plans will succeed.
> — Proverbs 16:3

> Take delight in the Lord, and he will give you your heart's desires.
> — Psalm 37:4

> And God said to Moses, "I am Yahweh—'the Lord.' I appeared to Abraham, to Isaac, and to Jacob as El-Shaddai—'God Almighty'—but I did not reveal my name, Yahweh, to them." — Exodus 6:2-3

November 2

THIS MORNING THE HOLY SPIRIT BROUGHT TO MY MIND the question, "How can I love like Jesus today and carry myself as an image bearer?" (**John 13:34**) Immediately the *Fruits of the Spirit* popped into my head and I started examining where I may be lacking (**Galatians 5:22-23**). Two elements of these characteristics where I tend to struggle are self-control or meekness. Whenever I have a strong opinion about something *I have to continually pray*, "God, is this a situation where I need to open my mouth or close it?"

The Lord gave me two separate opportunities today that highlighted how much I need the wisdom of the Holy Spirit to love well; speaking tactfully from love and not frustration. It's so beautiful the way God illuminates how critical our dependence is on Him and we simply cannot bear spiritual fruit apart from Him (**John 15:5**). Embracing a posture of humility is always honoring to God. He delights in overshadowing our weakness with His strength. Our desire, dependence, and obedience paves the way to be more like Jesus.

> *So now I am giving you a new commandment: Love each other. Just as I have loved you, you should love each other. — John 13:34*

> *But the Holy Spirit produces this kind of fruit in our lives: love, joy, peace, patience, kindness, goodness, faithfulness, gentleness, and self-control. There is no law against these things! — Galatians 5:22-23*

> *Yes, I am the vine; you are the branches. Those who remain in me, and I in them, will produce much fruit. For apart from me you can do nothing. — John 15:5*

November 3

THIS YEAR WE HAVE YET ANOTHER PRESIDENTIAL ELECTION that the media is deeming the most important decision of our time. If we put our hope in God, we know whomever is elected is not a surprise to Him, and He is ultimately still on His throne over and above everything (**Daniel 2:20-21**). No matter the winner, He will use the next four years to reveal Himself in new ways, reminding us our allegiance needs to be to Him, and not a government party or leader (**Revelation 17:14**). Believers should take a stand on political issues, but how we stand is as important as if we stand at all.

Paul, who wrote some of the most powerful thought provoking scriptures in the Bible, stood for Christ with a Holy Spirit confidence fueled by love and not desperation (**Philippians 3:7-8**). He spoke with words rooted in experience, truth, and passion, clearly pointing anyone who would listen to the hope of Christ. There is nothing more important for us as followers of Christ than how we love others, especially during cultural tension. We need to love people where they are, regardless of if we agree. We should be prayerful, lean on our faith, love well, and trust God with the outcome.

> *I know that you can do anything, and no one can stop you.*
> *— Job 42:2*

> *He said, "Praise the name of God forever and ever, for he has all wisdom and power. He controls the course of world events; he removes kings and sets up other kings. He gives wisdom to the wise and knowledge to the scholars."*
> *— Daniel 2:20-21*

> *Together they will go to war against the Lamb, but the Lamb will defeat them because he is Lord of all lords and King of all kings. And his called and chosen and faithful ones will be with him. — Revelations 17:14*

> *I once thought these things were valuable, but now I consider them worthless because of what Christ has done. Yes, everything else is worthless when compared with the infinite value of knowing Christ Jesus my Lord. For his sake I have discarded everything else, counting it all as garbage, so that I could gain Christ. — Philippians 3:7-8*

November 4

ONE OF THE MANY ATTRIBUTES THAT I LOVE ABOUT THE SCRIPTURES IS the way in which anything and everything we have the potential to struggle with is addressed (**2 Timothy 3:16-17**). His Word as a whole provides a place of solidity, refreshment, and encouragement. While the absolute truth does provide peace, it can also illuminate areas where we need to reorient our thinking or actions. Much like holding a mirror up, the scriptures provide an accurate reflection (**Psalm 139:23-24**).

If or when our thoughts are spiraling and we feel out of sorts, the Word of God reminds us what is beneficial for us to focus on (**Philippians 4:8**). *Aligning our thoughts with what is praise-worthy* has the ability to shift our perspective on most anything. Our spiritual enemy can persistently hurl distractions our way, but sometimes our own thoughts prevent us from experiencing peace and joy (**Isaiah 26:3**). Whether we are just feeling melancholy or experiencing legitimate sadness, the scriptures are always a safe place to run to for rejuvenation and rest.

> *All Scripture is inspired by God and is useful to teach us what is true and to make us realize what is wrong in our lives. It corrects us when we are wrong and teaches us to do what is right. God uses it to prepare and equip his people to do every good work.* — 2 Timothy 3:16-17

> *Search me, O God, and know my heart; test me and know my anxious thoughts. Point out anything in me that offends you, and lead me along the path of everlasting life.* — Psalm 139:23-24

> *And now, dear brothers and sisters, one final thing. Fix your thoughts on what is true, and honorable, and right, and pure, and lovely, and admirable. Think about things that are excellent and worthy of praise.* — Philippians 4:8

> *You will keep in perfect peace all who trust in you, all whose thoughts are fixed on you!* — Isaiah 26:3

November 5

In light of today being presidential election day 2024, our church sent out a corporate prayer request based off of **1 Timothy 2:1-4**. Although this was a familiar text for me, it was very convicting in that this is a particular command I do not regularly exercise. The words from this scripture illuminated the value of praying consistently for the leaders and governing officials in our nation. Quite often I pray for leaders and elders of our church, and certainly I pray for my husband to lead our family well, but seldom on a daily basis do I think of our government. The sting in my spirit grew as I realized I don't have much faith or interest in politics, which says to me all the more reason to pray for a spiritual awakening regarding government, coupled with a clear command to pray (**Psalm 22:28**). My faith, hope, and trust lies with God. God alone has the final say concerning the world and everything in it, but until His final say comes, I am thankful for the opportunity to stand with believers around the world and country to *pray for His will to be done.*

> *I urge you, first of all, to pray for all people. Ask God to help them; intercede on their behalf, and give thanks for them. Pray this way for kings and all who are in authority so that we can live peaceful and quiet lives marked by godliness and dignity. This is good and pleases God our Savior, who wants everyone to be saved and to understand the truth.* — 1 Timothy 2:1-4

> *For royal power belongs to the Lord. He rules all the nations.* — Psalm 22:28

THE VALUE AND COMPLEXITY OF OUR RELATIONSHIPS HAS DOMINATED the meditations of my heart today (**Romans 12:10**). I was communicating with the Lord a warm gratitude for the opportunity this morning to pray with my daughter, make my son breakfast, and spend coffee time with my husband. We all have relationships in our lives that we need to nurture, whether it be family or friends (**Ephesians 4:2-3**).

As the day progressed, two separate friends of mine shared with me relational struggles they were dealing with, one with a brother and one with a friend. From the outside looking in, regarding both scenarios, it was clear how our spiritual enemy was creeping in causing division (**Ephesians 6:12**). Strong unity in relationships is a force creating spiritual and emotional stability (**Ecclesiastes 4:9**). Oftentimes trivial matters attempt to poke holes in our valued relationships, but if we are humble, vulnerable, honest, and gentle in our communication, even the conflict will make us grow closer. *God's people desperately need each other*, and we all need Christlike love to hold us together.

> Love each other with genuine affection, and take delight in honoring each other. — Romans 12:10

> Always be humble and gentle. Be patient with each other, making allowance for each other's faults because of your love. Make every effort to keep yourselves united in the Spirit, binding yourselves together with peace. — Ephesians 4:2-3

> For we are not fighting against flesh-and-blood enemies, but against evil rulers and authorities of the unseen world, against mighty powers in this dark world, and against evil spirits in the heavenly places. — Ephesians 6:12

> Two people are better off than one, for they can help each other succeed. — Ecclesiastes 4:9

November 7

I LOVE THAT THE SCRIPTURES ARE SO ALIVE IN THAT OUR SPIRITS can be transformed by the same verses in multiple ways in different seasons of life (**1 Peter 1:23**). In the beginning of my journey with God, the first wall He completely tore down and built again was my self-worth. He gently began to show me how my worth and value were found in Him alone. The absolute truth being that He created, wired, and carefully thought out every detail of who we are and the plans that would take place in our time here on earth (**Jeremiah 1:5**). **Psalm 139** has always been a life-changing word for me, but as I listened to a respected preacher teach it in a different way, I realized even more how the beautiful imagery of the Psalm had become like wallpaper lining my heart over the past three decades of my life. The security of our self-worth *being rooted only in the unshakeable God of the Universe* frees us to not be defined by accolades, accomplishments, or pain. The One who created us is the One who defines us, and His word is final.

> *And you have been given fullness in Christ, who is the head over every power and authority.* — Colossians 2:10

> *For you have been born again, but not to a life that will quickly end. Your new life will last forever because it comes from the eternal, living word of God.* — 1 Peter 1:23

> *I knew you before I formed you in your mother's womb. Before you were born I set you apart and appointed you as my prophet to the nations.* — Jeremiah 1:5

November 8

A SWEET FRIEND OF MINE WAS SCHEDULED FOR A SURGICAL PROCEDURE and requested prayer from a few ladies in our community. The day of the procedure she reached out to let us know it had been postponed due to a hospital scheduling error (**Proverbs 19:21**). Although situations like this are frustrating, God has shifted my perspective to consider these changes "divine disruptions." Thinking about this concept brought reflections of these timely disruptions in my own life and how I can look back and notice God blocking plans of mine that were not part of His plan, but mine (**Jeremiah 29:11**). We are wise to acknowledge these divine detours and *thank God that He loves us enough* to protect us from our own agenda at times. We certainly live in an instant gratification culture, but we all know the *instant* description typically applies to how quickly it fades, as well. The concept of divine disruption moves my heart to gratitude in the awareness that I worship and serve a God who pays attention to the details (**Psalm 37:23-25**). We all need the step-by-step guidance of our Creator, even abiding through the detours.

> You can make many plans, but the Lord's purpose will prevail.
> — Proverbs 19:21

> "For I know the plans I have for you," says the Lord. "They are plans for good and not for disaster, to give you a future and a hope." — Jeremiah 29:11

> The Lord directs the steps of the godly. He delights in every detail of their lives. Though they stumble, they will never fall, for the Lord holds them by the hand. Once I was young, and now I am old. Yet I have never seen the godly abandoned or their children begging for bread. — Psalm 37:23-25

November 9

I WOKE UP THIS MORNING WITH MY PATERNAL GRANDMOTHER on my mind. She has long resided in her heavenly home, but for some reason she was vividly on my mind. I realized, as the morning progressed, that I don't really have anything tangible from her as far as jewelry or an heirloom. In our human nature we crave the tangible, and my mind shifted to when Jesus explained to the disciples He was leaving, but the Holy Spirit would be with them, which was far better (**John 16:7**). The truth is tangible items can be lost, and people as we know them can leave our lives here on earth. The beautiful reality that the Spirit of the living God is alive and active in our lives is insurmountably glorious and permanent (**1 Kings 8:57**). My heart was filled with gratitude, reminding me that the same God living in me is the God of all the heroes of the faith and all of my ancestors who have gone before me to their home in Heaven. I *cherish that we serve a Savior who made a way* for us to experience eternal reunions and a hope that never fails or fades.

> *There is more than enough room in my Father's home. If this were not so, would I have told you that I am going to prepare a place for you?*
> — John 14:2

> *But in fact, it is best for you that I go away, because if I don't, the Advocate won't come. If I do go away, then I will send him to you.*
> — John 16:7

> *May the Lord our God be with us as he was with our ancestors; may he never leave us or abandon us.*
> — 1 Kings 8:57

November 10

As I was attempting to fall asleep last night my spirit was unsettled because I couldn't talk, or pray, myself out of a heart posture concerning something I knew was wrong (**Psalm 51:10**). The Holy Spirit prompted me to turn on my light and go to the Word. This was a clear reminder of how incapable I am of heart transformation apart from the scriptures. Immediately I was drawn to a clear command to wait on the Lord regarding the scenario troubling me. The peace of making the choice to lay it down and await further instruction quieted my soul for a good night's rest (**Isaiah 40:31**). My heart began to ponder the truth of the Lord's refining work during our times of waiting. This is not passive waiting where we are stagnant, but active waiting as we *allow God to purify our hearts* or orchestrate other events needing to take place (**Proverbs 16:9**). There is cumulative confidence birthed as we humble ourselves regularly, acknowledging His wisdom and our lack of it on our own.

> *Trust in the Lord with all your heart and lean not on your own understanding; in all your ways acknowledge Him, and He will make your paths straight.*
> *— Proverbs 3:5-6*

> *Create in me a clean heart, O God. Renew a loyal spirit within me.*
> *— Psalm 51:10*

> *But those who trust in the Lord will find new strength. They will soar high on wings like eagles. They will run and not grow weary. They will walk and not faint.*
> *— Isaiah 40:31*

> *We can make our plans, but the Lord determines our steps.*
> *— Proverbs 16:9*

I HAVE SIMPLY BEEN OVERWHELMED TODAY WITH THE GOODNESS OF GOD. During a conversation with some precious women who are choosing to allow God to do something new in their lives, I was in awe of His pursuit, rescue, and willingness to provide a new way of life (**1 Peter 2:9**). We were focusing not so much on the overcoming idea as we were the idea of *becoming* who God has created us to be (**Isaiah 43:7**). This was clearly a group of ladies eager for change with open eyes and hearts, desiring to not only get to know God better, but know themselves in light of their identity in Christ (**Galatians 2:20**). God's relentless pursuit of us is threefold in that He rescues us, He is with us, and He is for us. Therefore, our responsibility is only to be in agreement with His timing and decide on the commitment to be all in. God is always at work inspiring, refining, and purifying our character. May we *choose to cooperate with the One* who created us so we can fulfill every purpose and plan He had in mind.

> *For we are God's handiwork, created in Christ Jesus to do good works, which God prepared in advance for us to do.. — Ephesians 2:10 (NIV)*

> *But you are a chosen people, a royal priesthood, a holy nation, God's special possession, that you may declare the praises of him who called you out of darkness into his wonderful light. — 1 Peter 2:9 (NIV)*

> *Bring all who claim me as their God, for I have made them for my glory. It was I who created them. — Isaiah 43:7*

> *My old self has been crucified with Christ. It is no longer I who live, but Christ lives in me. So I live in this earthly body by trusting in the Son of God, who loved me and gave himself for me. — Galatians 2:20*

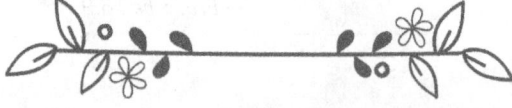

November 12

As I was folding my daughter's laundry last night, I noticed she had a cheetah print pair of pajama pants in there that were my mama's. I intentionally saved them for last to be folded because I just wanted to hold them a while. Holding them close to my heart, reflecting on how I miss her, I enjoyed the overwhelming sense that she is in Heaven waiting for me, and that my future with her is much greater than any past memory (**Isaiah 25:8**). The hope of Heaven poured over me as I thought of so many loved ones I look forward to seeing. Since our hope is not here in this life on earth, we can glance at the chaos in this world in the light of the silver lining of eternity. The mystery of what Heaven will truly be like does captivate my imagination often, but the truths I know anchor my hope in all there is to look forward to (**Luke 23:43**). My soul never loses the awe that, as believers, *we serve a mighty King* who has provided a path into eternal life that never ends and only gets closer every day.

> *For God so loved the world that He gave his one and only son, that whoever believes in Him shall not perish but have eternal life.* — John 3:16 (NIV)

> *He will swallow up death forever! The Sovereign Lord will wipe away all tears. He will remove forever all insults and mockery against his land and people. The Lord has spoken!* — Isaiah 25:8

> *And Jesus replied, "I assure you, today you will be with me in paradise."* — Luke 23:43

November 13

PRAYER IS INARGUABLY ONE OF THE MOST CRUCIAL INGREDIENTS for a vibrant faith and an intimate relationship with God (**Ephesians 6:18**). Prayer peppers my entire day in a variety of ways, which reminds me of the vital role it plays in my heart. Most days I find myself praying before my feet hit the floor simply because a very wise person encouraged that practice to me years ago and it has been so beneficial (**1 Thessalonians 5:16-18**).

In a waiting room today, as I looked around and being intentional to not default to my phone, I prayed silently for the people around me, thinking how cool it was that I don't know their story, but God does. Then I had the opportunity to pray with a dear friend of mine facing chronic illness struggles and seeing how prayer always relaxes her, giving her peace (**Matthew 18:20**). I think of Jesus and how, in His humanity, He did nothing apart from the Father. He was only about His father's business and rose early to connect with God (**Mark 1:35**). The more we *communicate with God* the more we crave His presence, peace, and stability. We should never take for granted the privilege of prayer.

> *Pray in the Spirit at all times and on every occasion. Stay alert and be persistent in your prayers for all believers everywhere.*
> — *Ephesians 6:18*

> *Always be joyful. Never stop praying. Be thankful in all circumstances, for this is God's will for you who belong to Christ Jesus.*
> — *1 Thessalonians 5:16-18*

> *For where two or three gather together as my followers, I am there among them.* — *Matthew 18:20*

> *Before daybreak the next morning, Jesus got up and went out to an isolated place to pray.* — *Mark 1:35*

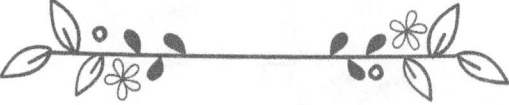

November 14

GOD CREATED US WITH SUCH A BEAUTIFUL VARIETY OF GIFTS and talents which we share and appreciate in each other (**Romans 12:6-8**). A dear friend of mine has amazing culinary skills and was willing to walk my precious daughter through a couple of made-from-scratch recipes. She and I have been friends for years and, although we don't get together too often, we have always bonded over our mutual love of the Lord and family. My daughter and I were both benefiting from her expertise regarding food and cooking, but the conversation often drifted into spiritual and relational topics (**Hebrews 10:24-25**). There is abounding wisdom for all of us in the generations before us in different areas, and we should all seek out those who have gone before us for experiential wisdom and encouragement (**Psalm 78:4**). I loved watching my daughter soak in the lessons between the lines and engaging in the God-honoring conversation. We should all have those people in our lives that we desire to sit at their feet, learning and listening. We should also *seek out those opportunities to pour into others*, possibly helping them avoid some of the pitfalls we ourselves have been through. May we all seek out and engage in intentional relationships.

> As iron sharpens iron, so one man sharpens another. — Proverbs 27:17

> In his grace, God has given us different gifts for doing certain things well. So if God has given you the ability to prophesy, speak out with as much faith as God has given you. If your gift is serving others, serve them well. If you are a teacher, teach well. If your gift is to encourage others, be encouraging. If it is giving, give generously. If God has given you leadership ability, take the responsibility seriously. And if you have a gift for showing kindness to others, do it gladly. — Romans 12:6-8

> Let us think of ways to motivate one another to acts of love and good works. And let us not neglect our meeting together, as some people do, but encourage one another, especially now that the day of his return is drawing near. — Hebrews 10:24-25

> We will not hide these truths from our children; we will tell the next generation about the glorious deeds of the Lord, about his power and his mighty wonders. — Psalm 78:4

THERE IS NO SWEETER SOUND THAN TO HEAR THAT SOMEONE'S LOVED ONE (who they have been praying for fervently) has made the decision to follow Christ (**James 5:16**). Receiving that news from a special friend over the phone today was clearly the highlight of the day. The joy and gratitude in her voice was tangible, and I couldn't help but imagine the joy it brings to our Father's heart when one of His wayward children finally says *yes* to Him (**Luke 15:7**). As we believers grow older, and more mature in our faith, we naturally become more heavenly minded. We begin longing for heaven more, and the desire to have our loved ones with us in eternity deepens (**Thessalonians 4:13-14**). This brings to mind the truth that as long as we have breath, we have the opportunity to come to Christ and we should never consider anyone we are praying for too far gone. God knows His perfect plan and timing for each of His children, but all too often we get frustrated when His timing doesn't align with ours. This is also a beautiful reminder to *never cease praying for those we love*. We just never know when the revelation of Christ will become a reality in their heart.

> *I have not stopped giving thanks for you, remembering you in my prayers.* — Ephesians 1:16

> *Confess your sins to each other and pray for each other so that you may be healed. The earnest prayer of a righteous person has great power and produces wonderful results.* — James 5:16

> *In the same way, there is more joy in heaven over one lost sinner who repents and returns to God than over ninety-nine others who are righteous and haven't strayed away!* — Luke 15:7

> *And now, dear brothers and sisters, we want you to know what will happen to the believers who have died so you will not grieve like people who have no hope. For since we believe that Jesus died and was raised to life again, we also believe that when Jesus returns, God will bring back with him the believers who have died.* — 1 Thessalonians 4:13-14

During a conversation with my sister discussing family dynamics, the reality crossed my mind that we all like relationships on our terms to some degree (**Philippians 2:3-4**). We all enjoy giving or receiving love in a way that pleases us; whereas, the scriptures emphasize others over ourselves. This heart posture can characterize our relationship with the Lord in many ways as well. We desperately want God in our lives, but oftentimes on our terms, not necessarily His. A thriving connection to God strongly depends on our submission to His will overriding our own agenda (**Matthew 6:33**). As we mature in our divine relationship with Him, we experience more and more how as we continually seek and move towards Him, the pieces of our lives' puzzles fit together just as He designed. We can become distracted by what we desire for Him to do for us even though the real blessings are a result of what He does *in and through* us (**Ephesians 2:10**). *Inviting and allowing His heart to work* in our lives creates the humility, love, and understanding we need for healthy, life-giving connections that are not self-seeking, but selfless.

> Don't be selfish; don't try to impress others. Be humble, thinking of others as better than yourselves. Don't look out only for your own interests, but take an interest in others, too. — Philippians 2:3-4

> Seek the Kingdom of God above all else, and live righteously, and he will give you everything you need. — Matthew 6:33

> For we are God's masterpiece. He has created us anew in Christ Jesus, so we can do the good things he planned for us long ago. — Ephesians 2:10

November 17

TODAY IS MY SISTER'S BIRTHDAY, AND AS I THINK ABOUT HER it's a reminder of the way God arranges and orchestrates the relationships we get to be a part of on this earth (**1 Corinthians 12:12-24**). My sweet, big sister has done everything from save me as I fearlessly jumped in a pool before I could swim, to help me with my wedding. She is gifted at everything I am not, and has always been a stable presence in my life. I've always considered her being my sister as a gift from God. We care for and love each other well with our different strengths and weaknesses.

If we think back through the fabric of our lives, we can see how God has brought people into our lives at unique times and in unique ways to serve a purpose or be an answer to prayer (**Ecclesiastes 3:1**). He brings these type of realities to fruition because He is a personal detail-oriented God who knows what we need way better than we do for ourselves (**Jeremiah 29:11**). May we all *be grateful* for the relationships He blesses us with in our lives, and even the ones He removes, being confident He is all-wise, all-knowing, and sovereign over all the details, especially relationships.

> *The earth is the Lord's, and everything in it, the world, and all who live in it.*
> — *Psalm 24:1 (NIV)*

> *For everything there is a season, a time for every activity under heaven.* — *Ecclesiastes 3:1*

> *"For I know the plans I have for you,"* says the Lord. *"They are plans for good and not for disaster, to give you a future and a hope."*
> — *Jeremiah 29:11*

November 18

The prayer, "Help me to be led by my Spirit and not my flesh" crosses my lips daily. In the same vein, I may say, *Father, move me out of the way so I can navigate life in a way that honors you.* (**James 4:10**). No matter how long we have been walking with God, the choice to surrender our will to His comes multiple times a day. Surrender is always challenging, which means we are wise to keep it on the forefront of our hearts and minds (**1 Peter 5:6**). The idea of humbling ourselves and seeking to do things God's way typically follows a long history of doing life our way, realizing our way often fails us (**Isaiah 55:8-9**). Surrender oftentimes runs parallel to taking the risk to trust God. This risk may feel unsure in the beginning, but any time we move in faith, history will prove God's got our back and the outcome is by His design (**Exodus 14:14**). Some areas may remain hard to surrender, but *the more we embrace His wisdom*, rest in His arms, and believe His way is best, the idea of surrender becomes confident peace.

> *Humble yourselves before the Lord, and he will lift you up in honor.*
> *— James 4:10*

> *So humble yourselves under the mighty power of God, and at the right time he will lift you up in honor. — 1 Peter 5:6*

> *"My thoughts are nothing like your thoughts," says the Lord. "And my ways are far beyond anything you could imagine. For just as the heavens are higher than the earth, so my ways are higher than your ways and my thoughts higher than your thoughts." — Isaiah 55:8-9*

> *The Lord himself will fight for you. Just stay calm. — Exodus 14:14*

How can we live in a way that responds with gratitude for all God is and the abundant, redemptive life He has made possible through Christ? (**Colossians 4:2**). This may look like a life characterized by prayer, devotion, surrender, and simply adoration to the holiness of God. When our imaginations are captivated by Kingdom ideas we grow to live lifestyles of worship. Worship signifies a response to God not only with music but by the way we serve, love, and navigate life with eternal focus (**2 Corinthians 4:18**). Our culture steadily creates an atmosphere of tension and pressure. This emotional poison fuels the epidemic of anxiety rampant in our world. *God offers a morning-by-morning invitation* to experience life through the lens of His love and peace (**Philippians 4:6-7**). Prayerfully asking God, "How can I worship You today with my actions, words, and thoughts," can forge a bright spot even in the midst of trials and suffering (**John 1:5**). Living a lifestyle of worship fuels a vibrant, healthy, life-giving relationship with God. Invite Him into your life as a response to all He is and helps us to be.

> *Devote yourselves to prayer with an alert mind and a thankful heart.*
> *— Colossians 4:2*

> *So we don't look at the troubles we can see now; rather, we fix our gaze on things that cannot be seen. For the things we see now will soon be gone, but the things we cannot see will last forever. — 2 Corinthians 4:18*

> *Don't worry about anything; instead, pray about everything. Tell God what you need, and thank him for all he has done. Then you will experience God's peace, which exceeds anything we can understand. His peace will guard your hearts and minds as you live in Christ Jesus. — Philippians 4:6-7*

> *The light shines in the darkness, and the darkness can never extinguish it.*
> *— John 1:5*

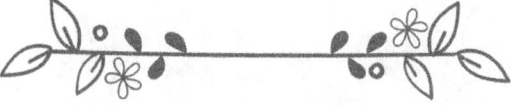

Butterflies have always been especially significant to me. The magnificent individual beauty of their shape, design, and color always reflects that God is the most brilliant artist in the universe (**Ecclesiastes 3:11**). In the same way that a caterpillar emerges as a beautiful butterfly, God transforms us from death to life with His infinite wisdom, love, and perfect timing. When we are awakened spiritually, our beautiful colors emerge in the ways of gifts, talents, and holiness only because of Christ. We become a child of God where the old is gone and the new continuously comes (**2 Corinthians 5:17**).

Anyone who is close to me is keenly aware of my obsession with butterflies. Even my mama and husband refer to me as a butterfly because I love to spread light and love to everyone around me. The desire to reflect God's love is deeply rooted in gratitude for God's rescue bringing me from death to life (**Ephesians 2:6**). When I have had the blessing to be close to a butterfly and watch it spread its wings, my heart immediately begins to thank God for allowing me to see and experience His supernatural transformations in my life and those around me (**Deuteronomy 30:6**). *He transforms our hearts* to spread our wings and become image bearers of our Lord and Savior.

> Yet God has made everything beautiful for its own time. He has planted eternity in the human heart, but even so, people cannot see the whole scope of God's work from beginning to end. — Ecclesiastes 3:11

> This means that anyone who belongs to Christ has become a new person. The old life is gone; a new life has begun! — 2 Corinthians 5:17

> For he raised us from the dead along with Christ and seated us with him in the heavenly realms because we are united with Christ Jesus. — Ephesians 2:6

> The Lord your God will change your heart and the hearts of all your descendants, so that you will love him with all your heart and soul and so you may live! — Deuteronomy 30:6

November 21

Today I was able to experience an amazing gift of listening to the way God is moving in and through the lives of a group of women learning what it looks like to truly experience God in a real and personal way (**John 10:27**). They are learning to hear God's voice and guidance in their lives through the means of His word, prayer, circumstances, and the Holy Spirit's promptings. They are learning to distinguish His direction in their lives more and more, simply because they are learning more about His character and divine love for them (**Jeremiah 33:3**). Once God, in His lovingkindness, rescues a wayward heart, that person will not find satisfaction in their old way of doing things (**Psalm 85:8**). Living out a new life in Christ looks like waking up with expectation to the activity of God that day. There is a divine shift from a self-focused life to a Christ-centered life fueled by a passion for the eternal as opposed to the temporal. Life on God's terms revolves around *faith, humility, and a desire* to spread and experience true hope and love. True dependence and life with Christ never loses His flavor and lasts forever.

> *Jesus told her, "I am the resurrection and the life. Anyone who believes in me will live, even after dying. Everyone who lives in me and believes in me will never ever die. Do you believe this, Martha?" — John 11:25-26*

> *My sheep listen to my voice; I know them, and they follow me. — John 10:27*

> *Ask me and I will tell you remarkable secrets you do not know about things to come. — Jeremiah 33:3*

> *I listen carefully to what God the Lord is saying, for he speaks peace to his faithful people. But let them not return to their foolish ways. — Psalm 85:8*

November 22

TODAY DURING A CYCLE CLASS AT THE GYM, they played a Christian worship song which was great to begin with but then she yelled out to her riders, "What's your purpose?" (**Ephesians 2:10**). Immediately I felt a whisper in my spirit that to *love well* is my purpose. I began to meditate on the scriptures that emphasize loving God with all that we are: heart, mind, soul, and strength (**Deuteronomy 6:5, Matthew 22:37**). We are clearly commanded to love others well, but this is impossible in our human nature without loving and receiving the agape love of Christ first. God has grown my spirit to be grieved if I am not showing love in a way that honors Him, but I know if I repent of my attitude and invite His divine perspective adjustment, He and only He, can reorient my heart (**Ephesians 1:18**). The truth is the love that God calls us to give can only be rooted in our devotion to Him and acknowledgment of how He loves us in spite of ourselves. He never calls us to assignments He won't equip us to carry out. The call to love well is both individual and universal. *Seek His guidance and wisdom* as to how this command applies to you today.

> When a Samaritan woman came to draw water, Jesus said to her, "Will you give me a drink?" (His disciples had gone into the town to buy food.) — John 4:7-8 (NIV)

> For we are God's masterpiece. He has created us anew in Christ Jesus, so we can do the good things he planned for us long ago. — Ephesians 2:10

> And you must love the Lord your God with all your heart, all your soul, and all your strength. — Deuteronomy 6:5

> Jesus replied, 'You must love the Lord your God with all your heart, all your soul, and all your mind.' — Matthew 22:37

> I pray that your hearts will be flooded with light so that you can understand the confident hope he has given to those he called—his holy people who are his rich and glorious inheritance. — Ephesians 1:18

November 23

This morning I had the slightly bitter and extremely sweet opportunity to take my daughter to the airport for a week-long mission trip to Costa Rica (**Matthew 28:19-20**). The bitter piece was only because she won't be here for Thanksgiving; whereas, there are a plethora of sweet spots. The mission group will be going door to door in a poverty-stricken area of Costa Rica in desperate need of clean water. Her team will be giving the families clean water filters while also sharing the Gospel of Christ (**Philippians 4:19**). The combination of meeting the practical need of clean water with the vital need of eternal life with Christ is life-altering. I cherish the truth that when our eyes are fixed on Jesus everything we need will be provided. Oftentimes, in our broken world, there are practical needs that need immediate attention, and when others experience believers being the hands and feet of Jesus, then hearts soften and are open to hear. (**Ezekiel 11:19-20**). Clearly, I'm excited that my daughter has the opportunity to spread her beautiful wings and fly, but my heart is full of gratitude for the entire team's willingness to *say yes to God's call*, seizing the assignment to share God's love and invitation to new life in Christ.

> Then he said to the crowd, "If any of you wants to be my follower, you must give up your own way, take up your cross daily, and follow me." — Luke 9:23

> Therefore, go and make disciples of all the nations, baptizing them in the name of the Father and the Son and the Holy Spirit. Teach these new disciples to obey all the commands I have given you. And be sure of this: I am with you always, even to the end of the age. — Matthew 28:19-20

> And this same God who takes care of me will supply all your needs from his glorious riches, which have been given to us in Christ Jesus. — Philippians 4:19

> And I will give them singleness of heart and put a new spirit within them. I will take away their stony, stubborn heart and give them a tender, responsive heart, so they will obey my decrees and regulations. Then they will truly be my people, and I will be their God. — Ezekiel 11:19-20

November 24

CONVERSATIONS ABOUT GRATITUDE ARE FILLING THE AIR in light of the Thanksgiving season. The message was communicated in church this morning about how we have to *choose gratitude*. The scriptures urge us to realize that a grateful heart is pleasing to God (**1 Thessalonians 5:16-18**). Discontentment is a poison that wreaks havoc on our spiritual and emotional health. So why in our human nature do we find ourselves in this state of mind so often? We tend to be entitled, constantly desiring the next thing, season of life, or whatever temporary fix we seek. This mindset basically reflects a lack of trust in God, His timing, and His ability to supply whatever we need when we need it (**Philippians 4:19**). Experiencing true contentment in any given circumstance stems from an unwavering trust and confidence in God's timing and ability to provide all we require spiritually, emotionally, and physically (**Psalm 55:22**). We are wise to daily seek satisfaction in Jesus, meaning we depend on Him, communicate with Him, and take refuge in His sovereign care of us. He is more aware than we will ever be of what is good for us and will not withhold anything we need (**Psalm 84:11**). Our hearts should overflow with gratitude in light of His constant and complete care.

> Always be joyful. Never stop praying. Be thankful in all circumstances, for this is God's will for you who belong to Christ Jesus.
> — 1 Thessalonians 5:16-18

> And this same God who takes care of me will supply all your needs from his glorious riches, which have been given to us in Christ Jesus. — Philippians 4:19

> Give your burdens to the Lord, and he will take care of you. He will not permit the godly to slip and fall. — Psalm 55:22

> For the Lord God is our sun and our shield. He gives us grace and glory. The Lord will withhold no good thing from those who do what is right.
> — Psalm 84:11

November 25

I WAS TALKING WITH A SWEET FRIEND YESTERDAY who is experiencing rough spots in a relationship and she uttered the words, "I don't want to be a box that gets checked, I want to be chosen." That phrase resonated in my heart about God. He draws us to Himself and offers us the opportunity to *choose Him* (**John 6:44**). None of us would desire a relationship where someone felt obligated to engage with us sans an authentic connection. We are wise to ask ourselves the question, "Is my relationship with God vibrant, growing, and vital in my day-to-day experience of life?" (**Psalm 139:23-24**). We can deceive ourselves going through the motions of church attendance, Bible studies, and good works, where in reality our spirits are void of the daily transformative power of God. So often we neglect to posture ourselves to embrace His outpouring of strength, wisdom, and life-altering expressions of love. He waits for us to seek all that He is and to experience life this side of heaven in a way that changes us and those around us for our good and His glory. May we not settle for stagnant Christianity.

> *I will give you a new heart and put a new spirit in you; I will remove from you your heart of stone and give you a heart of flesh.* — Ezekiel 36:26

> *For no one can come to me unless the Father who sent me draws them to me, and at the last day I will raise them up.*
> — John 6:44

> *Search me, O God, and know my heart; test me and know my anxious thoughts. Point out anything in me that offends you, and lead me along the path of everlasting life.* — Psalm 139:23-24

November 26

APPROPRIATELY ENOUGH, THE MEDITATION OF MY HEART these past few days has been centered on gratitude. During the Thanksgiving season many conversations will involve the silver lining of thankfulness (**Colossians 3:15, Colossians 4:2**). Creating an atmosphere of appreciation overshadows discontentment and negativity. Immediately after opening my eyes, most days I speak the words out loud, "Thank you, Jesus." Oftentimes I have told others it's a habit worth forming; whereas, it can serve as a reminder we always have something to be thankful for simply because of who Jesus is and what He has done for us (**Galatians 3:13**). He has made a way for us to experience reconciliation to God, restoration and healing for any suffering we may face, as well as the magnificent opportunity to experience intimacy with God on a daily basis. We have the power to choose how we will view this life and what we will focus on (**Philippians 4:8**). *Focus on what is good, life-giving and eternal.* This state of mind and posture of heart creates gratitude that is authentic, everlasting, and pleasing to the heart of God.

And let the peace that comes from Christ rule in your hearts. For as members of one body you are called to live in peace. And always be thankful. — Colossians 3:15

Devote yourselves to prayer with an alert mind and a thankful heart. — Colossians 4:2

But Christ has rescued us from the curse pronounced by the law. When he was hung on the cross, he took upon himself the curse for our wrongdoing. For it is written in the Scriptures, "Cursed is everyone who is hung on a tree." — Galatians 3:13

And now, dear brothers and sisters, one final thing. Fix your thoughts on what is true, and honorable, and right, and pure, and lovely, and admirable. Think about things that are excellent and worthy of praise. — Philippians 4:8

November 27

THE TOPIC OF FEELINGS IN OUR CULTURE HAS BECOME quite controversial. If we allow our feelings or emotions to dictate our lives, things can become quite chaotic in that our emotions ebb and flow. Oftentimes I have asked myself the question, *Is this the truth of the situation or just how I'm feeling at the moment?* (**2 Corinthians 10:5**) As we prayerfully seek the truth in a situation, God will reveal it. We can rest in the reality that we are not in control and much of what we worry about is not even up to us. So often feelings of anxiety can lessen by simply inviting God's perspective (**Philippians 4:6**). We have the tendency to either ignore our feelings, sweeping them under a rug, or live by them, giving them too much power. How then, can we navigate our feelings in a way that is healthy and honoring to God? As strong feelings approach, *pause and invite God in* (**Psalm 62:8**). Humbly seeking God to help you reorient your mind to what is true can move irrational thinking aside and begin listening to His spirit, as opposed to your flesh. Navigating feelings and handling emotional highs and lows can be complicated; whereas, God's peace brings stability to our chaos.

> *You will keep in perfect peace those whose minds are steadfast, because they trust in you.* — Isaiah 26:3 (NIV)

> *We destroy every proud obstacle that keeps people from knowing God. We capture their rebellious thoughts and teach them to obey Christ.* — 2 Corinthians 10:5

> *Don't worry about anything; instead, pray about everything. Tell God what you need, and thank him for all he has done.* — Philippians 4:6

> *O my people, trust in him at all times. Pour out your heart to him, for God is our refuge.* — Psalm 62:8

November 28

No matter how many holidays go by, when we have loved ones who have moved on from this earth we can experience the weight of missing them (**1 Corinthians 15:55-57**). This morning I was really missing my mama, and my husband came to hug me, and I immediately said *it's okay*, almost like a reflex. He said, "You don't have to say it's okay. I know you miss your mama." Immediately I thought of how God doesn't need us to make excuses or minimize our grief. He wants us to experience those emotions and let Him hold us through them (**2 Corinthians 1:3-4**).

As the day progressed, I reflected on the thankfulness in my heart for my God who always sees me and of course the eternal hope of Heaven. We were not created for complete satisfaction on this earth, and we will all experience suffering and loss. We can *embrace our Heavenly Father's comfort* and encouragement with the eagerness of knowing His everlasting arms never grow tired of holding us, not here on this earth, not in Heaven, not ever. What a beautiful assurance.

> *For I am the Lord, your God, who takes hold of your right hand and says to you, Do not fear; I will help you. — Isaiah 41:13 (NIV)*

> *O death, where is your victory? O death, where is your sting? For sin is the sting that results in death, and the law gives sin its power. But thank God! He gives us victory over sin and death through our Lord Jesus Christ.*
> *— 1 Corinthians 15:55-57*

> *All praise to God, the Father of our Lord Jesus Christ. God is our merciful Father and the source of all comfort. He comforts us in all our troubles so that we can comfort others. When they are troubled, we will be able to give them the same comfort God has given us. — 2 Corinthians 1:3-4*

November 29

TODAY AT A FAMILY THANKSGIVING CELEBRATION my Jesus-loving mother-in-law chose to read **Psalm 103** out loud before we said the blessing for the meal. She reflected on how we all have so much to be thankful for, none of which holds a candle to how thankful we should be for the opportunity for salvation (**Psalm 103:1-4**). The day moved along to be your typical chaotic family holiday gathering, full of games, debates, and photos, but driving home my mind reflected on how powerful the strong words from the scriptures were. God's Word overshadows everything when we cultivate a love for it—allowing it to marinate in our hearts—renewing our mind and thoughts (**Romans 12:2**). The holidays bring with them stress and heightened emotions—both positive and negative. We have to be extremely intentional to keep our focus on what truly matters, remaining rooted in the Word of God daily. The more we keep a continual conversation going with God, the more we can sense His presence, which is and will always be—the most important thing, even during the holidays.

> *Call to me and I will answer you and tell you great and unsearchable things you do not know.*
> — *Jeremiah 33:3 (NIV)*

> *Let all that I am praise the Lord; with my whole heart, I will praise his holy name. Let all that I am praise the Lord; may I never forget the good things he does for me. He forgives all my sins and heals all my diseases. He redeems me from death and crowns me with love and tender mercies.*
> — *Psalm 103:1-4*

> *Don't copy the behavior and customs of this world, but let God transform you into a new person by changing the way you think. Then you will learn to know God's will for you, which is good and pleasing and perfect.*
> — *Romans 12:2*

November 30

There are some Christian catchphrases that we have all heard over the years that are, in all actuality, not Biblical at all. For example, "God helps those who help themselves." There are times when the brokenness and woundedness is so deep, asking for help is unrealistic (**Leviticus 19:9-10**). As followers and image bearers of Christ, *we should pray that our eyes be open* to see those in desperate need of Jesus around us. Oftentimes people are unaware of the freedom and healing God can provide given the opportunity. It is true God's desire is that we would choose Him, but He certainly uses His children as ambassadors (**2 Corinthians 5:20**).

Our spiritual enemy does a good job in our culture of keeping us distracted with social media, television, and other self-interests. What could it look like to take even half of that time seeking God's guidance in offering His hope to someone in need? (**Matthew 25:40**). How pleasing to God is a prayer saying, "Open the eyes of my heart to see those around me in need of your healing touch."

> Jesus went through all the towns and villages, teaching in their synagogues, preaching the good news of the kingdom and healing every disease and sickness. When he saw the crowds, he had compassion on them, because they were harassed and helpless, like sheep without a shepherd.
> — Matthew 9:35-36 (NIV)

> When you harvest the crops of your land, do not harvest the grain along the edges of your fields, and do not pick up what the harvesters drop. It is the same with your grape crop—do not strip every last bunch of grapes from the vines, and do not pick up the grapes that fall to the ground. Leave them for the poor and the foreigners living among you. I am the Lord your God.
> — Leviticus 19:9-10

> So we are Christ's ambassadors; God is making his appeal through us. We speak for Christ when we plead, "Come back to God!" — 2 Corinthians 5:20

> And the King will say, 'I tell you the truth, when you did it to one of the least of these my brothers and sisters, you were doing it to me!' — Matthew 25:40

December 1

NOT ONLY IS TODAY THE BEGINNING OF A NEW MONTH, it is also the beginning of the Advent season (**Isaiah 9:2-6**). This season bears the reminder of the hope we have all because of Christ. For me personally, in my life there was a dramatic shift from darkness to light. Although I made the choice to turn from my darkness and move towards God, Christ shining His light in my life is all about what He has done, not my doing.

Oftentimes during the Christmas season I reflect on the grand exchange between God's children and Himself. He brings light, eternal hope, and peace (**Romans 15:13**). What type of changes can we make this season—physically, spiritually, and emotionally—to continue growing and moving towards wholeness? We could choose to remind ourselves every day what this season is really about, telling someone new of the hope of Christ. We could *be specifically prayerful* about that relative we will see that annoys us, and attempt to find common ground for connection. Physically we could choose treats in moderation, staying away from stress eating or using food for comfort. Most importantly may we remember what this season is really about, reflecting on and being thankful for Jesus!

> *Every good and perfect gift is from above, coming down from the Father of the heavenly lights, who does not change like shifting shadows. — James 1:17 (NIV)*

> *The people who walk in darkness will see a great light. For those who live in a land of deep darkness, a light will shine. You will enlarge the nation of Israel, and its people will rejoice. They will rejoice before you as people rejoice at the harvest and like warriors dividing the plunder. For you will break the yoke of their slavery and lift the heavy burden from their shoulders. You will break the oppressor's rod, just as you did when you destroyed the army of Midian. The boots of the warrior and the uniforms bloodstained by war will all be burned. They will be fuel for the fire. For a child is born to us, a son is given to us. The government will rest on his shoulders. And he will be called: Wonderful Counselor, Mighty God, Everlasting Father, Prince of Peace.*
> *—Isaiah 9:2-6*

> *I pray that God, the source of hope, will fill you completely with joy and peace because you trust in him. Then you will overflow with confident hope through the power of the Holy Spirit. — Romans 15:13*

December 2

TODAY I HAD THE OPPORTUNITY TO BE PART OF A DISCUSSION regarding the victory we can experience through faith in Christ (**1 John 5:4**). When we choose to navigate life with all its trials through the lens of imminent victory, it changes things. Although we will experience suffering and pain this side of heaven, we can know that one day all will be well (**Romans 8:28**). Ultimately we are not citizens of this world, which means we are not held captive to the chaos occurring here. God's desire and design is that we be *in* the world, not *of* it (**John 17:17**). To be "not of the world" looks like not conforming to the culture's morals and ideologies. This also means learning to *stand strong on Biblical principles* even when that's not popular. On the other hand, this does not involve pride, hate, or combativeness (**Proverbs 15:4**). Walking in the victory Christ has provided should motivate us to be both confident and compassionate, modeling our sincere love for all people after the One who has done everything for us. A great way to thank Him for the victory is to embrace it.

But thanks be to God! He gives us the victory through our Lord Jesus Christ.
— 1 Corinthians 15:57 (NIV)

For every child of God defeats this evil world, and we achieve this victory through our faith. — 1 John 5:4

And we know that God causes everything to work together for the good of those who love God and are called according to his purpose for them.
— Romans 8:28

Make them holy by your truth; teach them your word, which is truth.
— John 17:17

Gentle words are a tree of life; a deceitful tongue crushes the spirit.
— Proverbs 15:4

December 3

I CANNOT EMPHASIZE ENOUGH THE NUMBER OF TIMES I UTTER THE WORDS, "God, I can't, but You can." There is a strange sense of peace in my human frailty realizing I don't have the power to control scenarios or outcomes (**Psalm 46:1**). As we grow in our reliance and relationship with the Lord, the realization of how capable He is becomes more clear. Finding peace and comfort within uncertainty provides supernatural strength in the weakest of moments (**2 Corinthians 12:9**). What does it look like to arrive at this heart posture? It certainly involves the removal of pride, arrogance, and self-suffering, maybe *prayerfully seeking where in our life lies unconfessed sin and unforgiveness.* We can stand confident before God knowing there is nothing He will point out to us that He will not help us navigate through (**Romans 8:31**). We can stand firm in the reality God is for us, and as messy or complicated things may seem in the here and now, God's got it. He is over it and He will carry us through it.

> *"Is anything too hard for the Lord? I will return to you at the appointed time next year and Sarah will have a son."* — Genesis 18:14

> God is our refuge and strength, always ready to help in times of trouble.
> — Psalm 46:1

> Each time he said, "My grace is all you need. My power works best in weakness." So now I am glad to boast about my weaknesses, so that the power of Christ can work through me. — 2 Corinthians 12:9

> What shall we say about such wonderful things as these? If God is for us, who can ever be against us?
> — Romans 8:31

December 4

THE SCRIPTURES CONTAIN SO MANY RAW EXAMPLES OF HUMAN EMOTION. Throughout thousands of years and changing cultures, it's remarkable how we can relate to those who have gone before us in this way (**Psalm 42:1-2, Psalm 13:1-2**). So many of the Psalms embody the longing for more of God and the deep felt need of His mercy and care. The strong coexistence of lament and gratitude are prevalent in these passages. **Psalm 13** begins with lament, questioning where is God, but ends in gratitude, praising the gift of salvation. Human emotions are fascinating, beautifully complex, and God-given (**Psalm 139:13-14**). We should *find magnificent comfort in that God welcomes those emotions*, desiring us to pour out authentically and regularly. Personally, I find as I am transparent with God, sharing my heart freely, He gives me greater insight into why I am the way I am and why certain things impact my heart greatly, both positive and negative. We are all beautifully complex, and what a gift to serve a creator who longs to hear our heart cries and provide shelter, hope, and comfort like only He can.

> And the peace of God, which transcends all understanding, will guard your hearts and your minds in Christ Jesus. — Philippians 4:7 (NIV)

> As the deer longs for streams of water, so I long for you, O God. I thirst for God, the living God. When can I go and stand before him? — Psalm 42:1-2

> O Lord, how long will you forget me? Forever? How long will you look the other way? How long must I struggle with anguish in my soul, with sorrow in my heart every day? How long will my enemy have the upper hand? — Psalm 13:1-2

> You made all the delicate, inner parts of my body and knit me together in my mother's womb. Thank you for making me so wonderfully complex! Your workmanship is marvelous—how well I know it. — Psalm 139:13-14

December 5

I AM ALWAYS IN AWE OF THE WAY GOD SENDS ENCOURAGEMENT into our lives, whether it be by a person, nature, or simply a gentle whisper in our spirit (**1 Kings 19:11-12**). The Holy Spirit's intimate connection to our inner being is an invaluable gift and true reflection of God's heart for us (**Romans 8:16**). Whenever and wherever these subtle signatures of God show up they bring with them the opportunity to praise Him for His nearness and attention to detail, highlighting the reality of acknowledging He knows exactly where I am right now, what I'm going through, and what I need (**Psalm 139:8**). Knowing the God of the Universe sees me lessens my desperation to be understood by others. *We can trust God* to put those people in place at just the right time in just the right way. How comforting to know we are always seen, heard, and understood completely. This is one of the most sought after desires of any human heart and is always and only available through Christ.

> And may you have the power to understand, as all God's people should, how wide, how long, how high, and how deep his love is. May you experience the love of Christ, though it is too great to understand fully. Then you will be made complete with all the fullness of life and power that comes from God. — Ephesians 3:18-19

> "Go out and stand before me on the mountain," the Lord told him. And as Elijah stood there, the Lord passed by, and a mighty windstorm hit the mountain. It was such a terrible blast that the rocks were torn loose, but the Lord was not in the wind. After the wind there was an earthquake, but the Lord was not in the earthquake. And after the earthquake there was a fire, but the Lord was not in the fire. And after the fire there was the sound of a gentle whisper. — 1 Kings 19:11-12

> For his Spirit joins with our spirit to affirm that we are God's children. — Romans 8:16

> If I go up to heaven, you are there; if I go down to the grave, you are there. — Psalm 139:8

December 6

TODAY I HAD THE VALUABLE OPPORTUNITY TO PRAY OVER MY SON as he was leaving for a church retreat. My prayer for him, as well as others on the trip, was that God would continue to open their spiritual eyes, revealing more of Himself in new and different ways (**Hebrews 1:1**). *Spiritual sensitivity is vital in our experiences with God.* We as believers need to stay hungry and curious for more and not become complacent or ritualistic in our faith (**Matthew 5:6**). We have all heard cliches throughout our lives like "what you feed grows" or "you will find what you seek." And spiritually speaking, these actually apply to all of us, asking ourselves challenging questions like, "Am I really hungry for God? or, "How has my relationship with God grown since a year ago?" (**2 Corinthians 13:5**). These are areas worth exploring and nurturing. Our journey with God is ongoing and everlasting, which makes it more than worthy of examination. He meets us where we are and has more in store for us than we could ever imagine.

Now to him who is able to do immeasurably more than all we ask or imagine, according to his power that is at work within us.
— Ephesians 3:20 (NIV)

Long ago God spoke many times and in many ways to our ancestors through the prophets.
— Hebrews 1:1

God blesses those who hunger and thirst for justice, for they will be satisfied.
— Matthew 5:6

Examine yourselves to see if your faith is genuine. Test yourselves. Surely you know that Jesus Christ is among you; if not, you have failed the test of genuine faith. — 2 Corinthians 13:5

December 7

WE ALL REQUIRE PERIODIC EXAMINATION OF OUR OUTER AND INNER MAN. Oftentimes people will use the phrase, "they need to examine their heart." (**Psalm 139:23-24**). The scriptures encourage us to invite the Lord's illumination of areas we need to be made aware of that could be toxic to our heart and soul. Heart exams of this nature are not a solitary endeavor. We clearly need the wise counsel of God, but we also have need of the wisdom and accountability of others (**Hebrews 13:16-17**). None of us are immune to blind spots or pockets of sin that may be so deeply ingrained we fail to notice. However, God loves His children too much to leave us in the dark concerning changes that would benefit us and those around us (**Isaiah 43:19**). God's detection, conviction, and timing is perfect, so we are wise to respond to the work on our souls He lovingly points us to. We have all ignored His promptings only to be right back at the same spot. May we all display willingness and *allow Him to do the heart surgery only He can do.*

> Create in me a pure heart, O God, and renew a steadfast spirit within me.
> — Psalm 51:10 (NIV)

> Search me, O God, and know my heart; test me and know my anxious thoughts. Point out anything in me that offends you, and lead me along the path of everlasting life.
> — Psalm 139:23-24

> And don't forget to do good and to share with those in need. These are the sacrifices that please God. Obey your spiritual leaders, and do what they say. Their work is to watch over your souls, and they are accountable to God. Give them reason to do this with joy and not with sorrow. That would certainly not be for your benefit.
> — Hebrews: 13:16-17

> For I am about to do something new. See, I have already begun! Do you not see it? I will make a pathway through the wilderness. I will create rivers in the dry wasteland. — Isaiah 43:19

December 8

During a conversation with a dear friend today she emphasized to me, "God's got you." I responded to her with tears in my eyes that God's love is actually overwhelming to me, as I tangibly felt held in His arms at that moment (**Deuteronomy 33:27**). As we allow our walls of self-sufficiency and self-protection to fall we give God room to show up in our lives to care for us in supernatural ways. The walls we build spiritually and emotionally can be the result of unbelief, hurt, or simply pride. God's desire is that we grow to trust and depend on Him in a way that reflects both vulnerability and confidence (**2 Corinthians 12:9**). Trusting God with the most delicate areas of our heart is a journey, but one well worth taking (**Proverbs 3:5-6**). Acknowledging and accepting our limited understanding is an integral piece of this process. God doesn't require understanding on our part, only dependence on His sovereignty. *Inviting God into a situation* is not about making Him aware, but allowing His Lordship to rule in our hearts. The day will come with no more pain, but until then He will hold us, love, guide and direct us for our good and His glory.

I can do all this through Him who gives me strength. — Philippians 4:13 (NIV)

The eternal God is your refuge, and his everlasting arms are under you. He drives out the enemy before you; he cries out, 'Destroy them!' — Deuteronomy 33:27

Each time he said, "My grace is all you need. My power works best in weakness." So now I am glad to boast about my weaknesses, so that the power of Christ can work through me. — 2 Corinthians 12:9

Trust in the Lord with all your heart; do not depend on your own understanding. Seek his will in all you do, and he will show you which path to take. — Proverbs 3:5-6

December 9

THE CRITICAL VALUE OF SURRENDER IS RADIATING IN MY HEART TODAY. Surrender is one of the most necessary components to our spiritual and emotional well-being. It is as difficult as it is freeing (**Mark 8:34-35**). Why is it so hard to lay down the issues that burden our souls? Ultimately, because although we can't manage life's obstacles on our own, it's overwhelming to entrust them to God. This tension requires us to completely trust God with the outcomes and uncertainties (**Psalm 56:3-4**). On the other hand, the freedom and peace that accompanies surrendering our struggles is unmatched. Oftentimes I will say out loud, "I do not have to orchestrate or manipulate anything because God's got this." I cherish the security of knowing He knows my situation better than I do and He never leaves me on my own (**Deuteronomy 31:6**) Surrender is born in trust, giving up control, admitting we can't handle it, and yielding to God's overarching wisdom and power (**Proverbs 1:7**). The reality that we are continually challenged in our faith makes it alive and personal. His desire is we *stay fully devoted, fully surrendered, knowing we are completely and perfectly loved.*

> So do not fear, for I am with you; do not be dismayed, for I am your God. I will strengthen you and help you; I will uphold you with my righteous right hand. — Isaiah 41:10 (NIV)

> Then, calling the crowd to join his disciples, he said, "If any of you wants to be my follower, you must give up your own way, take up your cross, and follow me. If you try to hang on to your life, you will lose it. But if you give up your life for my sake and for the sake of the Good News, you will save it." — Mark 8:34-35

> But when I am afraid, I will put my trust in you. I praise God for what he has promised. I trust in God, so why should I be afraid? What can mere mortals do to me? — Psalm 56:3-4

> So be strong and courageous! Do not be afraid and do not panic before them. For the Lord your God will personally go ahead of you. He will neither fail you nor abandon you. — Deuteronomy 31:6

> Fear of the Lord is the foundation of true knowledge, but fools despise wisdom and discipline. — Proverbs 1:7

December 10

As my sister and I exchanged Christmas gifts this morning, I was reminded of the countless ways she has been by my side through the years. Our sweet relationship is a gift from God I have forever cherished. Companionships are divinely orchestrated and we desperately need them (**Genesis 2:18**). *The Lord himself is our most intimate, faithful companion as we move toward Him in relationship and trust* (**Psalm 27:8**). We are wise to remember spiritual markers in our lives, ways God has shown up and seasons He has clearly navigated. The idea of keeping a journal of these milestones and answered prayers can bolster our faith and increase a posture of gratitude (**Colossians 2:7**). After meeting with my sister this morning, I sent her a message of how I cherish our memories and relationship, acknowledging her constant presence in my life. How much more should we all praise the God of the Universe for all He is and all He has done to make a way for our freedom, peace, and abundant life? (**Romans 8:2**). It is medicine for our souls to remember and acknowledge the goodness of God. We can't even imagine all He has in store for us.

> *Now to him who is able to do immeasurably more than all we ask or imagine, according to his power that is at work within us.* — Ephesians 3:20 (NIV)

> *Then the Lord God said, "It is not good for the man to be alone. I will make a helper who is just right for him."* — Genesis 2:18

> *My heart has heard you say, "Come and talk with me." And my heart responds, "Lord, I am coming."* — Psalm 27:8

> *Let your roots grow down into him, and let your lives be built on him. Then your faith will grow strong in the truth you were taught, and you will overflow with thankfulness.* — Colossians 2:7

> *And because you belong to him, the power of the life-giving Spirit has freed you from the power of sin that leads to death.* — Romans 8:2

December 11

Have you ever talked to an elderly believer who says, "I just love being in the presence of the Lord"? Hopefully we can all say that, but there is a special quality in that seasoned believers have had years to practice His presence (**Psalm 16:8**). Maybe it's because they feel they are nearing their heavenly home, although their affection for being in the presence of God may simply be they realize that is where pure joy is found (**Psalm 16:11**). One of the beautiful benefits of aging is that we begin to know what is worthy of our time and what is not. We also create personal rhythms of practicing His presence that, as with most things, becomes habits that define who we are (**Psalm 23:4**). Those who have been walking with the Lord for decades seem to have a confident awareness of His nearness resulting from years of being comforted in His arms. Experiencing His provision during hard seasons builds confident expectation and a strong sense of trusting His timing. Learning to *enjoy solitude with the Lord*, whether it's worshiping, praying, or merely sitting at his feet in silent adoration, is both life giving and habit forming. Practicing His presence is essential and will not disappoint.

> When you pass through the waters, I will be with you; and when you pass through the rivers, they will not sweep over you.
> — Isaiah 43:2

> I know the Lord is always with me. I will not be shaken, for he is right beside me.
> — Psalm 16:8

> You will show me the way of life, granting me the joy of your presence and the pleasures of living with you forever.
> — Psalm 16:11

> Even when I walk through the darkest valley, I will not be afraid, for you are close beside me. Your rod and your staff protect and comfort me.
> — Psalm 23:4

December 12

One of my sweet friends had the opportunity to share at a local Celebrate Recovery meeting (**Mark 5:19**). We are encouraged throughout the scriptures to acknowledge and testify of God's goodness and restorative power in our lives. So often people think of recovery programs in conjunction with "obvious issues" such as alcohol, drugs, or other outwardly destructive issues, but the reality is we are all in need of a savior and there is heart work needed in every human soul (**Romans 3:23**). We may suffer from pride, self-righteousness, self-sufficiency, or all of the above. These are areas of struggle not so apparent to others at first glance, but glaringly apparent to those closer to us (**Romans 3:20**). The more we grow in our knowledge and love for the Lord (and allow the scriptures to teach us truth) the clearer our need for His redemptive power in our lives (**1 Peter 5:10**). *Cultivating a heart posture that is self-aware, humble, and recognizes* we all have blind spots is essential for continued growth in becoming who God created us to be.

> *Create in me a pure heart, O God, and renew a steadfast spirit within me.*
> *— Psalm 51:10 (NIV)*

> *For everyone has sinned; we all fall short of God's glorious standard.*
> *— Romans 3:23*

> *For no one can ever be made right with God by doing what the law commands. The law simply shows us how sinful we are.*
> *— Romans 3:20*

> *In his kindness God called you to share in his eternal glory by means of Christ Jesus. So after you have suffered a little while, he will restore, support, and strengthen you, and he will place you on a firm foundation. — 1 Peter 5:10*

December 13

OFTENTIMES WHEN WE FIND OURSELVES IN CRISIS MODE OVER disappointments, discouraging news, or things simply not going our way, we have an important decision of who we choose to "vent" to (**Ephesians 4:22-24**). During these times, if we follow our flesh, we will most likely seek out the people we know will affirm our frustration and focus on the unfair situation we find ourselves in. This route is typically unhealthy and leads to prolonged conversations focused on grumbling and self-pity (**Philippians 4:6-7**). If we make a better choice to be guided by our spirit, we will find ourselves seeking wise counsel and going to the Lord first with our authentic frustrations. So often these interactions result in us being challenged to change our focus, leading us into a completely different perspective (**Isaiah 55:8-9**). The trials we may experience in this life are important but maybe not as important as we think. Reorienting our hearts and minds back to God, and focusing only on the next step He is navigating, will calm the angst and unclutter the noise of anxiety. *Inviting the Holy Spirit* to walk us back to the path of peace is always the wisest move to make.

> *I will instruct you and teach you in the way you should go; I will counsel you and watch over you. — Psalm 32:8*

> *Throw off your old sinful nature and your former way of life, which is corrupted by lust and deception. Instead, let the Spirit renew your thoughts and attitudes. Put on your new nature, created to be like God—truly righteous and holy. — Ephesians 4:22-24*

December 14

Social media can be a very controversial topic these days to say the least, but, as with most things, it has *pros* and *cons*. This morning I witnessed a strong *pro* when I saw an eight-year-old young man using his You-Tube channel to spread God's truth with his peers (**Romans 1:5**). His courage and boldness to take a stand for Jesus filled my heart with gratitude in that the Lord had captivated this young man's heart in such a powerful way at such a young age (**Ephesians 3:17**). When Christ comes and takes hold of our hearts, we can't help but want to share this joy and victory with those around us. His presence in our lives is simply too powerful to hide or take for granted. Although we all have different gifts and personalities, God has placed in us some type of platform to share His love and goodness with others (**John 15:12**). That shows in the way we love, the way we serve our community or maybe like this brave young man preaching the Word with his creative skills on social media. As we truly *connect with Jesus* in our lives we want to share the one and only life source that provides freedom, joy, and peace forever.

> "'Peace I leave with you; my peace I give you. I do not give to you as the world gives. Do not let your hearts be troubled and do not be afraid.'"
> — John 14:27 (NIV)

> Through Christ, God has given us the privilege and authority as apostles to tell Gentiles everywhere what God has done for them, so that they will believe and obey him, bringing glory to his name. — Romans 1:5

> Then Christ will make his home in your hearts as you trust in him. Your roots will grow down into God's love and keep you strong. — Ephesians 3:17

> This is my commandment: Love each other in the same way I have loved you. — John 15:12

December 15

I SAW A YOUNG MAN WITH A T-SHIRT THAT READ, "There is Power in the Potential," and the background was the image of a cross (**1 Corinthians 1:18**). How true it is that nothing in this world is beyond repair simply because of the cross and the redemptive power it represents. As God himself observes His children He sees us and loves us knowing the potential we have in Christ. Realizing that as we *surrender every area of our lives to His Lordship* is what enables us to walk in victory, and is critical to our faith (**James 4:7**). The cross represents many benefits, including sacrificial love, eternal hope, and unmatched power providing the ultimate antidote for any type of suffering we may experience here on earth. The mere existence of the cross is a permanent refuge for believers and is available for anyone who asks Jesus into their heart to be Lord of their life (**Psalm 91:2**). We should ask ourselves if the cross and all it represents stirs up emotion in our hearts. If we find ourselves unmoved by its greatness, that would be an invitation to allow the Holy Spirit to awaken that recognition and adoration. Every day presents a new opportunity to deepen our connection to the perfect lover of our souls.

> *For God so loved the world that he gave his one and only Son, that whoever believes in Him shall not perish but have eternal life.* — John 3:16

> *The message of the cross is foolish to those who are headed for destruction! But we who are being saved know it is the very power of God.* — 1 Corinthians 1:18

> *So humble yourselves before God. Resist the devil, and he will flee from you.* — James 4:7

> *This I declare about the Lord. He alone is my refuge, my place of safety; he is my God, and I trust him.* — Psalm 91:2

December 16

ONE OF THE MOST BEAUTIFUL OVERARCHING BENEFITS OF BEING A CHRIST follower is the healing He brings into our lives (**Psalm 103:2-3**). Since He is concerned with spiritual, emotional, and even sometimes physical healing for us, this process takes time. He knows better than anyone what and how much we can handle when it comes to revisiting past hurt or trauma (**Ecclesiastes 8:6**). Oftentimes when a painful memory resurfaces, our immediate response is to brush it back under the rug, or use whatever means of escape to forget about it again. What if we shift our perspective to God, highlighting this area for healing? (**Psalm 147:3**) We can rest in the truth that God will equip, strengthen, and provide the resources or people essential for that process. Although the journey of restoration is complex and sometimes ongoing, He never leaves us on our own (**Hebrews 13:5-6**). Holidays can lead to both joy and pain, especially with complicated relationships or maybe loss. What if we move into this Christmas season with a willingness to *allow God to heal* areas He reveals are in need of His touch? May we be prayerful and sensitive to how the Holy Spirit is leading our interactions and love for those around us.

He will bring me glory by telling you whatever he receives from me.
— John 16:14

Above all, love each other deeply, because love covers over a multitude of sins.
— 1 Peter 4:8 (NIV)

For there is a time and a way for everything, even when a person is in trouble.
— Ecclesiastes 8:6

Let all that I am praise the Lord; may I never forget the good things he does for me. He forgives all my sins and heals all my diseases. — Psalm 103:2-3

He heals the brokenhearted and bandages their wounds. — Psalm 147:3

Don't love money; be satisfied with what you have. For God has said, "I will never fail you. I will never abandon you." So we can say with confidence, "The Lord is my helper, so I will have no fear. What can mere people do to me?"
— Hebrews 13:5-6

December 17

One of the most beautiful and fascinating attributes of God is how He is the "author of the unlikely." All throughout scripture we as believers are encouraged and oftentimes commanded to go against the grain of the culture. Phrases like "turn the other cheek" or "repay evil with good" are references supporting spiritual strength and Christlike love (**Matthew 5:39, Romans 12:21**). *Choosing to live a life marked by this type of behavior is a direct reflection of Christ's work in our hearts.* There is nothing more brave than asking the Holy Spirit to illuminate the fruits of the spirit in our lives, such as gentleness, humility, and self-control, not to mention the power of patience. These are all counter cultural characteristics, and oftentimes praying for them highlights where we are falling short (**Galatians 5:22-23**). Our culture is highly defensive due to a deep need to prove themselves, demanding respect and feeling valued. This ideology directly opposes the peace of resting in Christ, knowing we are valued and loved not because of our own doing but because of Him (**Ephesians 2:8**). There is immense freedom in receiving and reflecting His love and heart. God's children are intended to be set apart, including our lifestyles, our focus in life, and our reactions to the world around us. Only He can equip us to live this out.

> "...equip you with everything good for doing His will, and may He work in us what is pleasing to Him, through Jesus Christ, to whom be glory forever and ever. Amen." — Hebrews 13:21 (NIV)

> But I say, do not resist an evil person! If someone slaps you on the right cheek, offer the other cheek also. — Matthew 5:39

> Don't let evil conquer you, but conquer evil by doing good. — Romans 12:21

> But the Holy Spirit produces this kind of fruit in our lives: love, joy, peace, patience, kindness, goodness, faithfulness, gentleness, and self-control. There is no law against these things! — Galatians 5:22-23

> God saved you by his grace when you believed. And you can't take credit for this; it is a gift from God. — Ephesians 2:8

December 18

Losing a loved one at what seems to be a premature time is arguably one of the more painful experiences we have on earth. Although there is nothing that can erase the pain of such losses, if we can allow our mind and heart to be open to God's comfort, as well as some perspective shifts, we can have more peaceful grief (**Psalm 139:16**). First of all, we can remind ourselves that in God's hands there are no premature passings, in that He knows the day we enter this world as well as the day we go home to be with Him. The Lord is all-wise and merciful in His perfect timing, and I have often thought of His divine timing as protection (**Psalm 31:15**). *Our curiosities need to be more pricked for heaven.* It is amazing how setting our gaze on eternity is like healing medicine for our grief (**Revelation 21:4**). Building anticipation and excitement for our heavenly home can deepen our faith, providing healing and encouragement for ourselves and others. Remembering that this life, as we know it, is fleeting and fragile prepares our hearts for what is to come. Inviting God to fill the empty spaces and hold us tight throughout our healing process is the vital ingredient for peaceful grief.

Blessed are those who mourn, for they will be comforted. — Matthew 5:4

You saw me before I was born. Every day of my life was recorded in your book. Every moment was laid out before a single day had passed. — Psalm 139:16

My future is in your hands. Rescue me from those who hunt me down relentlessly. — Psalm 31:15

He will wipe every tear from their eyes, and there will be no more death or sorrow or crying or pain. All these things are gone forever. — Revelations 21:4

December 19

WE ALL FIND OURSELVES NAVIGATING THROUGH MANY DISTINCT SEASONS during our time on earth. Some seem to last forever, yet radically change in the blink of an eye (**Ecclesiastes 3:1**). The transitioning from one season to the next has the potential to stretch and challenge us. Two people close to me are experiencing different life adjustments in the way of retirement and a child leaving for college. Although these are times to be celebrated, they also bring grief for what has ended (**Isaiah 43:19**). We need to make room to miss the past while anticipating the new things God has in store for the future. If God is creating more margin in our lives, He may open up new opportunities to serve or spend extra time nurturing different relationships (**Psalm 90:12**). When we *prayerfully seek God's wisdom* and direction as to the best investment of our time, He will respond. God may encourage a time of rejuvenation and rest which could be preparation for what's to come. As we only know where we've been, God knows where we're going. So we are wise to follow His lead, enjoying the journey. We can have confidence knowing He will bring new mercies, joy, and blessings in every season in new and creative ways. He is a God of new beginnings.

> *But those who hope in the Lord will renew their strength. They will soar on wings like eagles; they will run and not grow weary; they will walk and not be faint.* — Isaiah 40:31

> *For everything there is a season, a time for every activity under heaven.* — Ecclesiastes 3:1

> *For I am about to do something new. See, I have already begun! Do you not see it? I will make a pathway through the wilderness. I will create rivers in the dry wasteland.* — Isaiah 43:19

> *Teach us to realize the brevity of life, so that we may grow in wisdom.* — Psalm 90:12

December 20

THE JOY-FILLED HUSTLE AND BUSTLE OF THE HOLIDAYS CAN QUICKLY TURN INTO anxiety and stress. Oftentimes if we can stop anxiety before it sets in by allowing God to reorient our thoughts, victory over our emotions comes (**Isaiah 26:3**). Anytime the feelings of being overwhelmed surface I hear the Lord say, "remember," meaning remember what is true, remember what is real, and remember what is important. The Word of God is absolute truth, and there is no subject that in some way it does not address. This allows us to always ask ourselves, "What does scripture say about this?" (**2 Timothy 3:16-17**). What is real is what is actually happening, not some imagined scenario we're worried about. Think on what the true reality of a situation is as opposed to fear-based thinking (**Nehemiah 6:8**). Finally, what is really important is not running around getting tasks accomplished, but taking the time to *sit at the feet of Jesus*, allowing Him to set the pace for the day, allowing Him to align your priorities (**Matthew 6:33**). Remembering who this season is about can quiet your mind and allow you to enjoy what really matters, celebrating our Savior's birth, spending time with loved ones, and shining His light every chance we get.

In the same way, let your light shine before men, that they may see your good deeds and praise your Father in heaven. — Matthews 5:16

You will keep in perfect peace all who trust in you, all whose thoughts are fixed on you! — Isaiah 26:3

All Scripture is inspired by God and is useful to teach us what is true and to make us realize what is wrong in our lives. It corrects us when we are wrong and teaches us to do what is right. God uses it to prepare and equip his people to do every good work. — 2 Timothy 3:16-17

I replied, "There is no truth in any part of your story. You are making up the whole thing." — Nehemiah 6:8

Seek the Kingdom of God above all else, and live righteously, and he will give you everything you need. — Matthew 6:33

December 21

A SPECIAL FRIEND OF MINE, WHO IS A STRONG SISTER IN CHRIST, reached out inviting me into a prayer challenge for the coming year. A rich vibrant prayer life is a sweet gift available to us all (**Luke 11:1**). Prayer radically changes things in that it moves our hearts to be aligned with God and increases our intimate connection to our heavenly Father. God's power is on display when we are alert and intentionally seeking the way He is responding to our prayers (**Mark 11:24**). Adding the extra layer of accountability—partnering with someone regarding specific prayers—holds the potential to not only share confessions, burdens, and praises, but also have a front row seat to each other's revelations. Experiencing God in these tangible ways ignites our passion for God and His Kingdom activity (**1 Corinthians 16:13**). Intentionally keeping record of how God is moving as we seek His wisdom, guidance, and revelation creates an atmosphere for growth and spiritual maturity. All too often we become comfortable where we are, and we need to remember we were made for more. *Continually inviting God* to stretch us in creative ways keeps us humble, hungry for more and empowered to be ambassadors, living on purpose for our good and His glory.

> *We are therefore Christ's ambassadors, as though God were making His appeal through us. We implore you on Christ's behalf: Be reconciled to God.*
> *— 2 Corinthians 5:20 (NIV)*

> *Once Jesus was in a certain place praying. As he finished, one of his disciples came to him and said, "Lord, teach us to pray, just as John taught his disciples."*
> *— Luke 11:1*

> *I tell you, you can pray for anything, and if you believe that you've received it, it will be yours. — Mark 11:24*

> *Be on guard. Stand firm in the faith. Be courageous. Be strong. — 1 Corinthians 16:13*

December 22

THE CHRISTMAS SEASON IS A PERFECT TIME TO REFLECT ON THE ATTRIBUTES OF CHRIST. Reflecting on all He is and has done is a great catalyst for a heart posture fueled by humility and gratitude (**Psalm 51:10**). The foundation of our faith is not transactional in that our salvation is not based on what we do, but only what He has done at Calvary (**Ephesians 2:8**). What can we offer to celebrate His very existence and sacrificial faithfulness? He desires our hearts, so... what steps can we take toward surrender every day? We can *begin in all humility to seek His plan and purpose* for every day being aware we can create our own agendas, but His plans will prevail (**Proverbs 19:21**). We can turn our devotion towards Him by considering His holiness in all we do, especially how we love, serve, and react to others (**John 13:35**). Thirdly, we can rest confidently in His arms knowing He always has our best interests in mind, and even when a season seems particularly stressful, He is still on the throne and Lord over all (**Psalm 103:19**). In light of all the blessings He showers on His children, we can worship and honor Him best by devotion, obedience, and gratitude displayed by our love for him and those around us.

> *Create in me a clean heart, O God. Renew a loyal spirit within me.* — Psalm 51:10

> *God saved you by his grace when you believed. And you can't take credit for this; it is a gift from God.* — Ephesians 2:8

> *You can make many plans, but the Lord's purpose will prevail.* — Proverbs 19:21

> *Your love for one another will prove to the world that you are my disciples.* — John 13:35

> *The Lord has made the heavens his throne; from there he rules over everything.* — Psalm 103:19

December 23

THROUGHOUT THE SCRIPTURES ARE REFERENCES TO THE REALITY THAT GOD dwells among His people (**Revelation 21:3, John 1:14**). The idea of the Lord being a dwelling place for His people is also emphasized (**Psalm 91:9-10, Psalm 27:4**). There are several ways in which we experience the supernatural gift of this exchange. The confident realization that He is actually among us and present is powerful. This is one of those affirming prayers to say, "God, I thank you that You are in our midst and I am not alone." This type of verbal reminder strengthens our faith and increases our awareness of His presence. *Acknowledging that Christ lives in our hearts* when we accept Him as Lord of our life is essential to the Holy Spirit confidence that strengthens us from the inside out. To say we desire to dwell in the house of the Lord produces the imagery of basking in His presence, taking time to soak in His presence, allowing the fullness of simply who He is to surround our being like a soft blanket. The idea of Him being our dwelling place is also related to Him being our place of protection, security, and perfect love. Our sacred gift is having a Heavenly Father who still dwells among His people and deserves our full adoration.

> *How lovely is your dwelling place, O Lord Almighty! My soul yearns, even faints, for the courts of the Lord; my heart and my flesh cry out for the living God. — Psalm 84:1-2*

> *I heard a loud shout from the throne, saying, "Look, God's home is now among his people! He will live with them, and they will be his people. God himself will be with them." — Revelation 21:3*

> *So the Word became human and made his home among us. He was full of unfailing love and faithfulness. And we have seen his glory, the glory of the Father's one and only Son. — John 1:14*

> *If you make the Lord your refuge, if you make the Most High your shelter, no evil will conquer you; no plague will come near your home. — Psalm 91:9-10*

> *The one thing I ask of the Lord— the thing I seek most— is to live in the house of the Lord all the days of my life, delighting in the Lord's perfections and meditating in his Temple. — Psalm 27:4*

December 24

TODAY IS CHRISTMAS EVE, AND THERE WAS AN AMAZING INTERACTIVE celebratory service at church. There is a child-like energy to Christmas Eve that seems to never grow old, and joining together in corporate worship surrounding the birth of Jesus is powerful (**Isaiah 7:14**). The highlight of the service was a beautiful solo sung by an angelic voice focusing on the birth, life, and resurrection of our Savior. I have often said when we truly fall in love with the person of Jesus, real life transformation takes place (**2 Corinthians 5:17**). To fall in love means we have to "get to know" Him. God's deepest desire has always been the personal relationship available to us if we will only pursue that connection. The utter idea of what Christ has done and continues to do should move us to emotion. The magnitude of His love and compassion is matchless yet within our reach as we cry out to Him (**Romans 8:38-39**). Moving into the celebration of Christmas tomorrow, I would challenge you to spend the first moments of awakening acknowledging all He is and enables us to be even before allowing our feet to hit the floor. *Praise Him* for His powerful sacrificial love that pours over our chaotic world and anticipate His return in a spirit of hope, knowing the best is most surely yet to come.

> *You make known to me the path of life, you will fill me with joy in your presence, with eternal pleasures at your right hand.* — Psalm 16:11 (NIV)

> *All right then, the Lord himself will give you the sign. Look! The virgin will conceive a child! She will give birth to a son and will call him Immanuel (which means 'God is with us').* — Isaiah 7:14

> *This means that anyone who belongs to Christ has become a new person. The old life is gone; a new life has begun!* — 2 Corinthians 5:17

> *And I am convinced that nothing can ever separate us from God's love. Neither death nor life, neither angels nor demons, neither our fears for today nor our worries about tomorrow—not even the powers of hell can separate us from God's love. No power in the sky above or in the earth below—indeed, nothing in all creation will ever be able to separate us from the love of God that is revealed in Christ Jesus our Lord.* — Romans 8:38-39

December 25

Spending reflective moments today focusing on Jesus helps remind all of us what today is actually about (**John 3:16**). Taking time during festivities with family to discuss how we have seen Jesus move this year in and around us is a beautiful reminder of His presence and activity. The Holy Spirit moved in my heart illuminating how through Christ I have been rescued, restored, and continually regenerated. Since I have quite the colorful past, I never lose my awe of how God pursued and rescued me out of darkness into His light, radically changing my life for my good and His glory (**Ephesians 5:8**). God has the ability to restore the worst of situations, using the painful pockets of our past as breeding grounds for His healing, freedom, and victory (**Isaiah 53:4-5**). The reality that new life with Christ is constantly growing richer as we become more spiritually mature and aware is refreshing. *We are continually being regenerated to a closer version and clearer reflection of His image* (**Titus 3:5**). God's desire is that we never become stagnant or satisfied to exist in mediocre Christianity. We were meant to thrive and experience a vibrant personal connection with Jesus celebrating the truth that as we delight in Him our lives will be full, rich in love and eternally satisfied.

> For this is how God loved the world: He gave his one and only Son, so that everyone who believes in him will not perish but have eternal life.
> — John 3:16

> For once you were full of darkness, but now you have light from the Lord. So live as people of light! — Ephesians 5:8

> Yet it was our weaknesses he carried; it was our sorrows that weighed him down. And we thought his troubles were a punishment from God, a punishment for his own sins! But he was pierced for our rebellion, crushed for our sins. He was beaten so we could be whole. He was whipped so we could be healed. — Isaiah 53:4-5

> He saved us, not because of the righteous things we had done, but because of his mercy. He washed away our sins, giving us a new birth and new life through the Holy Spirit. — Titus 3:5

December 26

ONE OF THE MOST HEARTFELT PRAYERS WE CAN PRAY FOR ANYONE is that they would fall in love with Jesus. No matter who you are, He is the answer we seek whether we realize it or not (**Ephesians 3:17-19**). The richest version of intercessory prayer is asking that a heart be awakened to the joy, peace, and freedom found in Christ. I have often said people will walk away from a religion but not from a relationship. Oftentimes when we hear of people abandoning their faith it's because they never truly encountered the heart of Christ in a personal way. We can go through the motions, checking the boxes of Bible studies and church attendance, maybe even memorizing scripture, but if it's not transforming who we are, it's empty (**Matthew 15:8**). Head knowledge is never ultimately satisfying. Heart knowledge looks like encounters with Jesus, healing from brokenness and a longing to be in His presence where we know our hope and security are found (**Psalm 63:8**). We can ask ourselves the question, *Am I merely going through the motions, or am I experiencing God in a real and personal way?* He is ready and willing to carry us as we move toward him.

> "'Here I am! I stand at the door and knock. If anyone hears my voice and opens the door, I will come in and eat with him, and he with me.'" — Revelations 3:20 (NIV)

> Then Christ will make his home in your hearts as you trust in him. Your roots will grow down into God's love and keep you strong. And may you have the power to understand, as all God's people should, how wide, how long, how high, and how deep his love is. May you experience the love of Christ, though it is too great to understand fully. Then you will be made complete with all the fullness of life and power that comes from God. — Ephesians 3:17-19

> These people honor me with their lips, but their hearts are far from me. — Matthew 15:8

> I cling to you; your strong right hand holds me securely. — Psalm 63:8

December 27

THERE IS AN OLDER WORSHIP SONG THAT SAYS, "Better is one day in your courts than a thousand elsewhere." These lyrics present a beautiful reality (**Psalm 84:10**). The absolute truth in this song and scripture is we are better off in the worst situation we could imagine with Jesus than we would be in an amazing situation without Him. Explaining the reasons for this actuality to an unbeliever is challenging but simple. With Jesus, no matter what kind of mess we find ourselves in we know we are not alone. He makes a way when there seems to be no way (**Isaiah 43:18-19**) We also know that any trial, pain, or suffering is temporal. The only reality that lasts forever is eternity where the pain of this world will no longer be relevant. Cultivating a Kingdom mindset strips the weight from what feels overwhelming (**Philippians 4:13**). Embracing and truly believing the outcome of everything is up to God, and not ourselves, is enough to alleviate unwanted anxiety and the need to control. Without God we function from fear and desperation because we think we have more power than we actually do (**Romans 12:3**). We can thankfully *completely rest in the wisdom and provision of the Mighty God of the Universe* as we continue moving towards Him with all our heart, mind, and soul.

> *But if from there you seek the Lord your God, you will find Him if you look for Him with all your heart and with all your soul. — Deuteronomy 4:29*

> *A single day in your courts is better than a thousand anywhere else! I would rather be a gatekeeper in the house of my God than live the good life in the homes of the wicked. — Psalm 84:10*

> *For I can do everything through Christ, who gives me strength. — Philippians 4:13*

> *Because of the privilege and authority God has given me, I give each of you this warning: Don't think you are better than you really are. Be honest in your evaluation of yourselves, measuring yourselves by the faith God has given us. — Romans 12:3*

December 28

How often have we heard the phrase "my heart is not prepared for this" or "I need to prepare my heart"? The only way our hearts can handle anything difficult successfully is through Christ (**John 14:17**). We know that Christ can pour His peace over the hardest of situations making them bearable. When we sense the need to prepare our heart, what we really need is to bring our heart more in alignment with God (**Romans 8:29**). The peace we experience in this broken world is less about circumstances and more about how we handle and react to them. *We are all in the process of becoming more like Jesus*, and God is constantly refining us in creative ways (**Psalm 66:10**). Some of us are certainly more stubborn learners than others; whereas, we need to be shown the same lesson many times in different ways to get the point. Our loving Heavenly Father does not tire of helping us grow. His goal is for our hearts to be as aligned with His as much as possible for our good and to benefit those around us. He is the only one that can successfully prepare our heart for what He knows is to come.

> However, as it is written: No eye has seen, no ear has heard, no mind has conceived what God has prepared for those who love him. — 1 Corinthians 2:9

> He is the Holy Spirit, who leads into all truth. The world cannot receive him, because it isn't looking for him and doesn't recognize him. But you know him, because he lives with you now and later will be in you. — John 14:17

> For God knew his people in advance, and he chose them to become like his Son, so that his Son would be the firstborn among many brothers and sisters. — Romans 8:29

> You have tested us, O God; you have purified us like silver. — Psalm 66:10

December 29

I HAVE OFTEN REFERRED TO JESUS AS BEING A LIVING HEDGE OF PROTECTION around my heart (**Job 1:10**). The idea illustrates He is a barrier or safeguard in that we, as believers, possess a supernatural protection from any harm that would try to destroy or hurt us. This reality is two-fold; whereas, whatever could emotionally harm us cannot penetrate the truth we stand on in Christ. Obviously we will feel the sting of pain and suffering in this life, but only temporarily (**2 Corinthians 4:17**). Followers of Christ's identity, security, and approval is found in Jesus who will never leave or forsake us, so we can know with all confidence our needs are always taken care of (**Philippians 4:19**). We also know that any trial or circumstance is allowed by God, which means *we can trust Him* to carry us through the worst of situations. He will never waste any momentary suffering, even producing maturity and growth in its wake (**Romans 5:3-5**). We eternally and completely have the armor of Christ to ultimately shield us from anything that comes against us. We are victorious through Him.

For our present troubles are small and won't last very long. Yet they produce for us a glory that vastly outweighs them and will last forever! — 2 Corinthians 4:17

We can rejoice, too, when we run into problems and trials, for we know that they help us develop endurance. And endurance develops strength of character, and character strengthens our confident hope of salvation. And this hope will not lead to disappointment. For we know how dearly God loves us, because he has given us the Holy Spirit to fill our hearts with his love. — Romans 5:3-5

And this same God who takes care of me will supply all your needs from his glorious riches, which have been given to us in Christ Jesus. — Philippians 4:19

December 30

I HAD THE GIFT OF BECOMING A MAMA FOR THE THIRD TIME 16 YEARS AGO TODAY. One of the greatest blessings of my lifetime has been the opportunity to be a mother, especially since the doctors said it was impossible for me because of some irregularities with my reproductive system, but God said otherwise (**Mark 10:27**). My favorite tradition to do for my husband and children is to prepare a celebration table on their birthdays with photos, memories, and things I know will make them smile. Decorating the table brings me great joy and adds a little extra touch to their special day (**Psalm 139:1**). Reflecting on this tradition brought to mind God's heart for us, and all He has prepared for His children in advance. He knows each of us so personally and orchestrates blessings and reminders of His presence all around (**Psalm 139:5**). *He knows what will make us smile, or what will turn our heart and attention to think of Him.* His everlasting love for us is sacrificial, active, and permanent. Our human minds will never comprehend His care and provision for us any more than our earthly children will understand our love for them; until maybe they have the opportunity to one day have their own. We can be expectant for Him to demonstrate His love in creative ways only we will understand.

> *O Lord, you have examined my heart and know everything about me.*
> *— Psalm 139:1*

> *You go before me and follow me. You place your hand of blessing on my head. — Psalm 139:5*

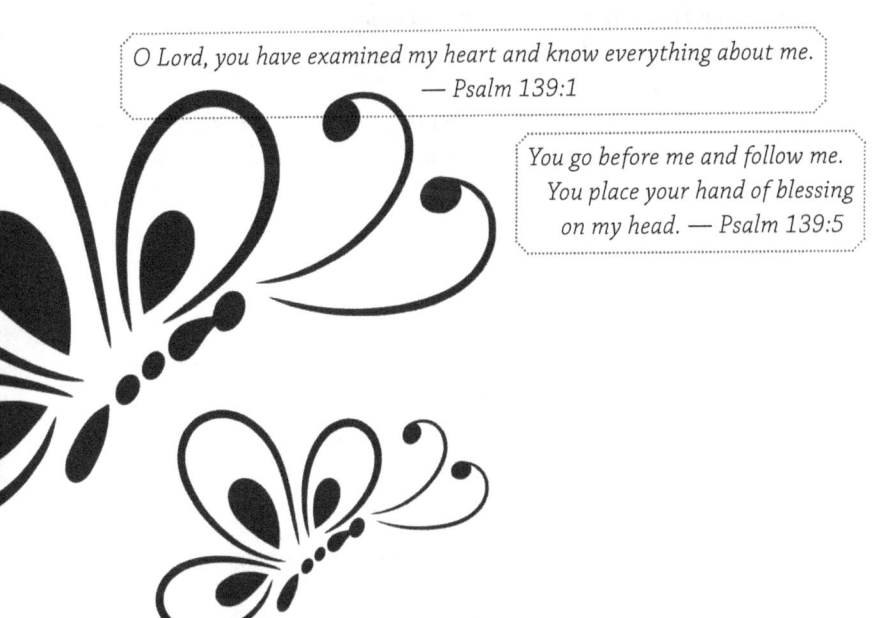

December 31

IN LIGHT OF THE NEW YEAR BEGINNING TOMORROW there are millions of resolutions being thought of and proclaimed. We would be wise to *pray and seek what God may have* in store for us this coming year (**1 Corinthians 2:9**). God desires for us to thrive spiritually, emotionally, and physically. Ask God to awaken any part of your spirit that may be lying dormant. Seek to deepen your intimacy with Him in the coming year by carving out more time with Him and less busyness (**Matthew 11:28-29**). Embrace more gratitude, focusing on truth and less on feelings for healthy emotions. Commit to talk to the Lord first thing in the morning before emails, texts, or the latest news. Pray for a revitalized hunger for His word and presence (**Matthew 5:6**). Plan to create one new healthy habit a month and experiment with what works well for your body and stage of life. We need to be nurtured from the inside out. God has assignments for all of us that He uses our gifts, experiences, and willingness to accomplish. Each and every one of us has the ability through Christ to make a difference in this lifetime. May we be people surrendered to God, allowing Him to have His way in our lives to accomplish what He created us to do.

> *For we are God's masterpiece. He has created us anew in Christ Jesus, so we can do the good things he planned for us long ago.* — Ephesians 2:10

> *That is what the Scriptures mean when they say, "No eye has seen, no ear has heard, and no mind has imagined what God has prepared for those who love him."* — 1 Corinthians 2:9

> *God blesses those who hunger and thirst for justice, for they will be satisfied.* — Matthew 5:6

> *Then Jesus said, "Come to me, all of you who are weary and carry heavy burdens, and I will give you rest. Take my yoke upon you. Let me teach you, because I am humble and gentle at heart, and you will find rest for your souls."* — Matthew 11:28-29

About

KATHRYN IS A DEVOTED WIFE AND MOTHER OF THREE beautiful children, and a passionate lover and follower of Jesus. God rescued her from herself during her twenties, captivating her heart with His transforming grace and love. Serving and worshiping God through loving others and encouraging their faith, is Kathryn's life mission. Kathryn has devoted her life as a volunteer—mentoring and discipling women for Miracle Hill's recovery program and at her home church.

She is grateful for the opportunity to share a glimpse of the truths that God has revealed to her this season.

Thank you for reading

Transformed by Design Our Willingness GOD'S WORK

by *Kathryn Alverson*

If this devotional has encouraged you to grow closer to God, please consider leaving a review on the listing of purchase.
This small gesture helps immensely to share the Word of God.
Thank you so much!
Be sure to follow **Take Heart Books** on FB to find more Christian authors sharing *the Good News.*

To contact Kathryn Alverson
send an email to: kathryn.alverson@yahoo.com

www.ingramcontent.com/pod-product-compliance
Lightning Source LLC
Chambersburg PA
CBHW071657170426
43195CB00039B/2217